Recent titles in
CASEBOOKS IN CRITICISM

Vladimir Nabokov's *Lolita*: A Casebook
Edited by Ellen Pifer

James Joyce's *A Portrait of the Artist as a Young Man*: A Casebook
Edited by Mark A. Wollaeger

Toni Morrison's *Song of Solomon*: A Casebook
Edited by Jan Furman

Chinua Achebe's *Things Fall Apart*: A Casebook
Edited by Isidore Okpewho

Richard Wright's *Black Boy (American Hunger)*: A Casebook
Edited by William L. Andrews and Douglas Taylor

William Faulkner's *Absalom, Absalom!*: A Casebook
Edited by Fred Hobson

Edith Wharton's *The House of Mirth*: A Casebook
Edited by Carol J. Singley

James Joyce's *Ulysses*: A Casebook
Edited by Derek Attridge

Joseph Conrad's *Heart of Darkness*: A Casebook
Edited by Gene M. Moore

RALPH ELLISON'S
Invisible Man

◆ ◆ ◆

A CASEBOOK

Edited by
John F. Callahan

OXFORD
UNIVERSITY PRESS
2004

OXFORD
UNIVERSITY PRESS

Oxford   New York

Auckland   Bangkok   Buenos Aires   Cape Town   Chennai
Dar es Salaam   Delhi   Hong Kong   Istanbul   Karachi   Kolkata
Kuala Lumpur   Madrid   Melbourne   Mexico City   Mumbai
Nairobi   São Paulo   Shanghai   Taipei   Tokyo   Toronto

Copyright © 2004 by Oxford University Press, Inc.

Published by Oxford University Press, Inc.
198 Madison Avenue, New York, New York 10016

www.oup.com

Oxford is a registered trademark of Oxford University Press

Library of Congress Cataloging-in-Publication Data
Ralph Ellison's Invisible man : a casebook / edited by John F. Callahan.
p. cm.—(Casebooks in criticism)
Includes bibliographical references.
ISBN 978-0-19-514536-6 (pbk.)
1. Ellison, Ralph. Invisible man. 2. African American men in literature.
3. African Americans in literature. I. Callahan, John F., 1940–
II. Series.
PS3555.L62515365 2004
813'.54—dc21
2003049890

3 5 7 9 8 6 4 2

Printed in the United States of America
on acid-free paper

To my daughters, Eve and Sasha,
dear friends of Ralph, and of his
book, and to my granddaughter,
Ava Callahan Taylor.

Credits

Burke, Kenneth. "Ralph Ellison's Trueblooded *Bildungsroman*." In *Speaking for You: The Vision of Ralph Ellison*, edited by Kimberly Benston. Washington, D.C. Howard University Press, 1987. Reprinted by permission of the Kenneth Burke Literary Trust.

Callahan, John F. "Ellison's *Invisible Man*." A Bradley Lecture Series Publication, Library of Congress, Washington, D.C., 2001. Reprinted by permission of the author.

Dickstein, Morris. "Ralph Ellison, Race, and American Culture." *Raritan: A Quarterly Review* 18, no. 4 (Spring 1999). Reprinted by permission of the author.

Ellison, Ralph. Excerpts from letters to Albert Murray, from *Trading Twelves: The Selected Letters of Ralph Ellison and Albert Murray*. New York: Random House, 2000. Reprinted by permission of Mrs. Fanny Ellison and the Estate of Ralph Ellison.

by Kimberly Benston. Washington, D.C.: Howard University Press, 1987. Reprinted by permission of the author.

Scott, Nathan A., Jr. "Ellison's Vision of *Communitas.*" *Carleton Miscellany: A Review of Literature and the Liberal Arts.* Carleton College, 1980. Reprinted by permission of author.

Smith, Valerie. "The Meaning of Narration in *Invisible Man.*" In *New Essays on Invisible Man,* edited by Robert O'Meally, 25–53. New York: Cambridge University Press, 1988. Reprinted with the permission of Cambridge University Press.

Tate, Claudia. "Notes on the Invisible Women in Ralph Ellison's *Invisible Man.*" In *Speaking for You: The Vision of Ralph Ellison,* edited by Kimberly Benston. Washington, D.C.: Howard University Press, 1987. Reprinted by permission of the Estate of Claudia Tate.

Wright, John S. "The Conscious Hero and the Rites of Man: Ellison's War." In *New Essays on Invisible Man,* edited by Robert O'Meally, 157–86. New York: Cambridge University Press, 1988. Reprinted with the permission of Cambridge University Press.

Acknowledgments

I AM INDEBTED TO William Andrews, general editor of this series, for inviting me to edit the casebook on *Invisible Man*, and for his patient, generous advice about matters of form and substance. I owe an even greater debt to my assistant, Angie McGinnis, without whose technical expertise and savvy detective work this volume might not have come to fruition. I also wish to acknowledge Lewis and Clark College, both in the person of former President Michael Mooney, who supported my work by giving me the time to do it, and the many students, who have read *Invisible Man* in my classes these last thirty-five years, and from whom I have learned a thing or two about the novel. Finally, once again I am pleased to thank Mrs. Fanny Ellison for the inspiration she gave Ralph as he wrote *Invisible Man*, and for the permission she gave me to quote abundantly from his published and unpublished work.

Contents

Introduction   3
JOHN F. CALLAHAN

Part I   Prologue: Ralph Ellison on *Invisible Man*

Before Publication   23

After Publication   35

Part II   Critical Essays on *Invisible Man*

Ralph Ellison's Trueblooded *Bildungsroman*   65
KENNETH BURKE

Ellison's Zoot Suit   81
LARRY NEAL

Ellison's Vision of *Communitas*   109
NATHAN A. SCOTT, JR.

Ralph Ellison, Race, and American Culture   125
MORRIS DICKSTEIN

The Rules of Magic: Hemingway as Ellison's "Ancestor"   149
ROBERT G. O'MEALLY

The Meaning of Narration in *Invisible Man*   189
VALERIE SMITH

The Conscious Hero and the Rites of Man: Ellison's War   221
JOHN S. WRIGHT

Notes on the Invisible Women in Ralph Ellison's
Invisible Man   253
CLAUDIA TATE

Luminosity from the Lower Frequencies   267
LEON FORREST

Ellison's *Invisible Man*   287
JOHN F. CALLAHAN

Part III   Epilogue

On Initiation Rites and Power: A Lecture at West Point   323
RALPH ELLISON

Selected Bibliography   345

Ralph Ellison's
Invisible Man

A CASEBOOK

Introduction

JOHN F. CALLAHAN

◆　◆　◆

WRITING FROM ROME IN 1956 when *Invisible Man* had been in the world a mere five summers, Ralph Ellison told Albert Murray that he had "picked up a book of criticism published in England under the title, *Catastrophe and the Imagination*." The book "gives *Invisible* lots of space," Ellison wrote, even "picks it for a short list of novels which that wild stud thinks will be of interest a century from now." Obviously pleased, Ellison concluded with a witty line of disbelief: "Surely the man must be on the weed."[1] Given Ellison's biochemical hunch, one is tempted to say the "weed" allowed the critic to "slip into the breaks and look around," as Invisible Man did, when, himself under the influence of a reefer, he became aware of "those points where time stands still or from which it leaps ahead."[2] At fifty, *Invisible Man* is going so strong that, despite its narrator's cautionary tale about the prizefighter and the yokel in which "the smart money hit the canvas," and "[t]he long shot got the nod," the novel must be considered an overwhelming favorite to enjoy an undiminished, robust longevity worldwide, in its centennial fifty years from now.

Invisible Man is one of those rare novels whose commercial and critical success coincide in a continually accelerating, rising curve. Translated into more than twenty languages, the various editions of the novel have sold more than a million copies since Ellison's death in 1994, alone. Moreover, critics who gave the book fulsome accolades upon publication return to it decades later only to up the ante of their praise. The late R. W. B. Lewis, for example, ended his 1952 review by saying, "No novel since *Light in August* has given so much, or holds itself so well." Almost thirty years later Lewis wrote: "I think, today, if anything, I would make that statement stronger, yet. The novel continues to grow and to swell in my mind."[3] The foregoing is not meant to suggest that *Invisible Man*, whose eponymous narrator's hibernation makes him a re-incarnation of Jack the Bear, has enjoyed an uninterrupted bull market. Immediately upon the novel's appearance in 1952, the ideological bears were out; in America they wore the shaggy win-ter coats of Marxism and Black Nationalism, both of whose world views, as projected by Ellison's characters, come in for intense, bitingly satiric treatment in the novel. Elsewhere there were other, far-flung objections. As if to vindicate the self-proclaimed exile of James Joyce, one of the literary ancestors to whom Ellison looked as he composed the novel, the Republic of Ireland banned *Invisible Man* on grounds that the book was morally offensive.

Ellison's view of his accomplishment had, in the years imme-diately after publication, a degree of ambivalence. On the one hand he had devoted almost seven years to the writing and re-vision, relying on his wife, Fanny, for continuous emotional and financial support. He endured skepticism and even ridicule from some in Harlem's intellectual circles who thought he would not finish the novel, and told him so publicly. His frank letters to Albert Murray in the two years before publication reveal a con-fidence, even bravado, that he had struck it literally rich, side by side with a nervousness, even anxiety, that he had merely dis-covered fool's gold. There were public signs of ambivalence as well. His address upon receiving the National Book Award (re-printed here), while showing traces of modesty, essentially makes a tactful, early case for *Invisible Man*'s place in the line of classic

American novels. Two years later, in what is perhaps his fullest and most important interview about *Invisible Man*, a long discussion with editors from the *Paris Review*, Ellison tenaciously defends and explains his choice of theme and plot as if *Invisible Man* is literary scripture. Then in almost the same breath he volunteers the opinion that his book is "not an important novel. I failed of eloquence," he begins, then tentatively qualifies his judgment. "If it does last, it will be simply because there are things going on in its depths that are of more permanent interest than on its surface. I hope so anyway."[4]

Ellison's mention of "depths" conjures up Invisible Man's closing metaphor of "the lower frequencies," and recalls a vital critical pronouncement he made in 1946 affirming what he and his inchoate narrator considered the collaborative relationship necessarily entered into by any conscientious writer and reader. "Once introduced into society," he wrote in "Twentieth-Century Fiction and the Black Mask of Humanity," "the work of art begins to pulsate with those meanings, emotions, ideas brought to it by its audience, and over which the artist has but limited control" (*Essays*, 94). If Ellison's many comments about the novel, both of a general and a highly specific nature (sometimes his detailed exegesis qualifies as *explication de texte*), are any indication, he coveted his role as reader as well as author of *Invisible Man*. Many of his responses to questions about his novel have about them the double-conscious sensibility of one simultaneously a writer and a reader.

Perhaps it was Ellison's dual identity as artist and audience which prompted John Hersey to declare that "[o]ne of the most significant views of the work of Ralph Ellison happens to be his own" (*Essays*, 785). For this reason, despite the enormous volume of criticism on *Invisible Man* over the past fifty years, I have included between the covers of this volume a fair sampler of Ellison's commentary, both on the totality and on specific key passages and scenes from his novel. As a critic and novelist, Ellison is scrupulously faithful to the feel of American and African-American society under the values and regime of segregation as the country hovered on the cusp of the great changes soon to be set in motion by the *Brown v. Board of Education* Supreme Court decision of 1954, and the Civil Rights Movement fired by the Montgomery bus boycott of 1955.[5] In the second place, Ellison is so schooled in American culture and history, both vernacular and classical, that he is often the most learned and reliable scholarly source for many of the eclectic allusions in the text of *Invisible Man*. For another thing, unlike some writers, Ellison is forthcoming, almost to a fault, about his novel's relationship to other novels. "Don't forget," he took pains to remind Steve Cannon, Ishmael Reed, and Quincy Troupe in 1977, "the main source of any novel is other *novels*." Ellison was a connoisseur of novels and *the* novel, always in pursuit of what he called the "culture of the form."[6] As a guardian of the novel's brier patch, Ellison steered criticism of *his* novel away from sociology toward the challenges and requirements of literary art, literary form.

What, then, are the sources of *Invisible Man*'s remarkable staying power? The answers are complex and multifaceted. In the first place, there is the fortunate convergence of form with language, without which no novel crosses the threshold of a classic. In the case of *Invisible Man*, Ellison propels his character's story forward with the velocity of jazz and the unsparing, anguished, joyful lyricism of the blues. Invisible Man, narrator and protagonist, acts as Ellison's Ellington; he is both conductor and featured performer of the novel. His voice is the novel's bass line; like a good jazz bandleader he knows when to yield to his soloists and sidemen. Some blow solos, which are memorable departures from the straight line of the narrative. But more frequent and cumulatively perhaps even more telling than Jim Trueblood's tale of race relations, incest, and blues-inspired transcendence, and the Reverend Homer Barbee's *faux* mythic Founder's Day sermon are the short takes—the riffs and speeches, the brief solos—of many other characters, such as the slave woman of the prologue, Invisible Man's grandfather, the vet at the Golden Day, Mr. Norton, President Bledsoe, Peter Wheatstraw, Mary Rambo, Brother Tarp, Tod Clifton, Ras the Exhorter, and the multifarious, walk-on cameo characters like the two half-looped black studs who describe Ras the Destroyer's wild ride on horseback during the Harlem riot, with reference not to the Africa of tribal princes but to the Lone Ranger of Hollywood and the comic book.

Ellison's (and his narrator's) form complements the "wild star burst" (xxiii) metamorphosis of idiomatic jazz styles, which drives the novel's language. Invisible Man's picaresque memoir is "one long, loud, rant, howl and laugh"—what R. W. B. Lewis calls "the all-hell-breaks-loose element."[7] Lewis refers to that stream of American literary tradition he associates closely with Ellison—the vernacular tradition of southwestern humor picked up and extended by Mark Twain and William Faulkner. To this uproarious, episodic form of the picaro, Ellison adds a prologue and epilogue meant to frame the adventures of Invisible Man and signify his conscientious, self-conscious transformation from rabble-rousing orator into literary artist.

The form of *Invisible Man* reinforces its theme of identity. Ellison's complex metaphor of invisibility leads him and his narrator to embrace all the glories of the American language, especially the signifying rhetoric and blues imagery of African-American speech. Then, too, the novel recapitulates abiding patterns of experience, which cross the color line and other lines of arbitrary demarcation in American life. The novel's world is a labyrinth Invisible Man finds his way through only after numerous starts and stops. In this sense Ellison imaginatively recapitulates his own life. Born in Oklahoma in 1914[8] to parents who had migrated there a few years after statehood (1907) hoping the new state would embrace the values of frontier possibility more than those of the Jim Crow South, young Ellison experienced both worlds. To the end of his life he wrote and spoke of the lasting, positive influence of his father's wide acquaintance among whites and Indians as well as black friends and associates. After Lewis Ellison's death, when his son was two or three, young Ralph lived in straitened circumstances with his mother, Ida, and younger brother, Herbert, whom he often minded while his mother worked as a domestic to support her two young sons.

Although Ida Ellison worked as a domestic, she was never domesticated. She canvassed for the Socialist Party when Eugene Debs was its presidential candidate, and later, in the early 1930s, when Ellison was away at Tuskegee, she participated in protests against the restricted housing covenants in Oklahoma City masterminded and led by Roscoe Dungee, editor and publisher of the *Black Dispatch*. In his essay "On Being the Target of Discrimination" (1989), Ellison proudly recalls his mother taking him and Herbert to the Oklahoma City Zoo in violation of Jim Crow ordinances, and all but sassing the white guard who apprehended them *after* they had seen the animals. His mother regularly brought books and magazines home from the white houses she cleaned; she was determined that her son become acquainted with the widest possible world of culture, music, and politics. Clearly, as a boy Ellison felt his mother was carrying on the aspirations expressed by Lewis Ellison in the act of naming his son for Ralph Waldo Emerson in the hope that he might become a poet and man of letters.

Growing up in Oklahoma City, Ellison lived with music— classical in school under the tutelage of Mrs. Zelia N. Breaux; jazz and the blues from Slaughter's dance hall down on Second Street in "Deep Deuce" within earshot of home. When he was eight, his mother sacrificed to buy him a used cornet. In addition to Mrs. Breaux, he later received encouragement and instruction in classical music from Ludwig Hebestreit, "a conductor who formed the nucleus of what became the Oklahoma Symphony— a German for whom I used to cut the grass in exchange for trumpet lessons" (*Essays*, 71). And it was Mrs. Breaux who recommended him for a scholarship to Tuskegee, where he matriculated in 1933 seeking to become a symphonic composer as well as a professional trumpeter.

At Tuskegee Ellison received an education in the ways of the world as well as in music and literature. Later on he was right when he insisted that the Negro college in *Invisible Man* was not Tuskegee, and stressed that his novel was an autobiography of his imagination. All the same, Ellison repeatedly acknowledged that, like his own Tuskegee, Invisible Man's college was located in the country of aspiration. Ellison lacked his character's ambition to become a political leader and orator, but he shared his narrator's belief that "the possibility existed. I had only to work and learn and survive in order to go to the top" (355). Only for Ellison the "top" did not mean ascending the greasy pole of politics; it meant making a mark in the arts. At first, as he left Tuskegee in the fateful summer of 1936, ostensibly to earn money for his senior year, Ellison's aspirations were in music; perhaps he would be able to bide his time as a trumpet player with one or another jazz group while adding fresh coals to the embers of his dream to compose symphonies. Ironically reminiscent of the cynical, fool's-errand letters Invisible Man carried to New York over the signature of the ruthless President Bledsoe, which told trustees, in polite, euphemistic, unmistakable terms, to "keep this nigger boy running," Ellison arrived in New York armed with letters of introduction from famed Tuskegee choir director and composer William Dawson. (Although his relationship with the proud, prickly Dawson had become ambivalent as Ellison devoted more and more of his time and energy to reading T. S. Eliot and other moderns in the library, and less on the technical fundamentals of his musical education, Dawson's letters were genuine.) Another letter was from his art teacher, Eva Hamlin, to the sculptress Augusta Savage, but a chance encounter with Langston Hughes redirected young Ellison to Roland Barthe, a young sculptor, whom Hughes considered more avant-garde and modern than Savage.

Hughes's interest in his welfare notwithstanding, Ellison remained something of a greenhorn in New York. Down and out, fitfully employed at best, occasionally sleeping on Harlem park benches, he failed to earn the money necessary to fund his senior year at Tuskegee. Yet one senses from his fragmentary accounts of his first summer in New York that Ellison chose the fluidity and possibility he glimpsed in New York, however transitory and insubstantial, over the predictability of a return to Tuskegee. At this same time Ellison "had been devoting as much time and energy to reading and writing as to music and was passionately engaged, night and noon, in acquiring the basic knowledge and skills of the novelist" (*Essays*, 49). Thus, it is not surprising that a meeting with Richard Wright, arranged by the ever-generous and helpful Hughes, shortly after Wright's arrival in New York from Chicago in early June 1937 proved fateful to Ellison's artistic am-

bitions, nor that the medium of choice turned out to be literature. At Wright's suggestion, Ellison wrote a review of Waters
Edward Turpin's novel *These Low Grounds* for *New Challenge*, a magazine of the Left under Wright's editorship. Wright then urged
Ellison to turn his hand to fiction, which he did in the form of
a short story called "Hymie's Bull," which was set in galleys but
not published because the *New Challenge* became defunct after a
single issue.

It was during a painful sojourn in Dayton, Ohio, in the months
following his mother's unexpected, heart-wrenching, probably
preventable death in Cincinnati in October 1937 that Ellison
"started trying seriously to write and *that was the breaking point*" (*Essays*, 73). Returning to New York, where he had landed a job on
the New York Federal Writers Project of the Works Progress Administration (WPA), with a cache of short fiction, over the next
seven years Ellison wrote reviews for the *New Masses* and published
short fiction in its pages and in other like-minded journals on
the Left. After a stint as managing editor of the *Negro Quarterly*
during 1942 and 1943, he joined the U.S. Merchant Marine and
continued to write fiction as he ferried munitions and other military supplies to Swansea in Wales and Murmansk at the north-
western edge of the Soviet Union.

In 1944, seeking to end his apprenticeship and launch himself
as a novelist, Ellison won a Rosenfeld fellowship, and set about
to write a novel "focused upon the experiences of a captured
American pilot who found himself in a Nazi prisoner-of-war camp
in which he was the officer of higher rank and thus by a convention of war the designated spokesman for his fellow prisoners"
despite his identity as an African American. Curiously, the
paragraph-long account of this projected novel in Ellison's introduction to the thirtieth anniversary edition of *Invisible Man* is
richer than the scant several pages of outline and text left behind
in his papers. Richer still—and more candid—are his remarks in
his 1969 "Lecture at West Point" (reprinted in this volume). Of
particular salience is Ellison's retrospective comment that his early
fragment "turned out to have been a blundering step toward the
present novel" (xi). Careful readers will recognize his idea for the

prison camp novel and its downed-pilot protagonist as a sequel to the short story "Flying Home," even as the inchoate idea fore-shadows the theme and metaphor of invisibility soon to emerge in *Invisible Man*.

Ellison's 1981 introduction also tells much of the story of his circumstances and preoccupations as he composed *Invisible Man* from 1945 to 1951. Here and elsewhere he pays homage to his wife, Fanny, citing her "faith in my talent" and her dedication through toil and love to "the desperate gamble involved in my becoming a novelist" (xi). What he does not say but one gleans from his letters to Murray is the possibility that if the book had failed critically or commercially, the toll on its thirty-eight-year-old author's emotional and material resources would have been considerable, perhaps even devastating. But *Invisible Man* did not fail. On the contrary, as Ellison struggled to write and finish a second novel, his first continued to grow in popularity and critical reputation. Almost perversely, *Invisible Man*'s ascent to the literary pantheon during Ellison's lifetime increased critical expectations for the novel in progress (*"very* long in progress," he noted dryly when he published the "Night-Talk" episode in 1969), and may have inhibited his drive to finish the second.

"If you're lucky," Ellison told John Hersey, "if you splice into one of the deeper currents of life, then you have a chance of having your work last a little bit longer" (*Essays*, 806). Little did he know in 1974 that by the millennium *Invisible Man* would grace almost every short list of great American novels of the twentieth century and that the novel's story and theme of identity and its inspired metaphor of invisibility would provide a narrative template, in different ways, for every succeeding generation of Americans.

Not surprisingly, in the fifty years since *Invisible Man*'s publication scholarly work on the novel has accelerated, leaving an ever-increasing critical mass, much of it work of distinction. Now that posthumous volumes of Ellison's essays and short stories have appeared in print, as well as *Juneteenth*, a reader's edition of the central narrative from his unfinished second novel, reconsideration of Ellison's work is under way. It is to be expected that in the next decade new studies of *Invisible Man* will focus, more extensively than previous work, on the novel's relation to the essays and short stories. Criticism of *Invisible Man* should also profit from the fact that all of Ellison's manuscripts and notes concerning his masterpiece are archived and now open without restriction in the Ralph Ellison Papers at the Library of Congress.

That said, it is impossible to represent adequately the enormous, existing body of critical work on *Invisible Man* between the covers of a single volume. In lieu of attempting anything remotely like a representative selection, I have chosen ten essays which speak to each other, to Ellison's own commentaries, and to the central issues which have preoccupied readers of the novel over the five decades since publication. Inevitably, there are lacunae in my selections. I have not chosen, for example, essays which focus primarily on a single episode in the novel, nor chapters from books, whether about Ellison; Ellison and another writer such as Joyce or Melville, or Morrison; or books about American, African-American, or modern literature more generally. Nor have essays been selected with a view to constituting a decade-by-decade survey of the criticism.

The ten essays included are framed by a prologue composed of selections by Ellison from his considerable commentary on *Invisible Man* before the novel's publication in 1952 up to the month before his eightieth birthday in 1994, and an epilogue consisting of the talk he gave at West Point in 1969, together with the transcript of his question-and-answer session with students on the same occasion. It seems fitting to give the last words in the volume to the writer and to his colloquy with some of the thousands of undergraduates who have read and studied *Invisible Man* in the generations since its emergence fifty years ago.

The first essay in the sequence of ten is Kenneth Burke's "Ralph Ellison's Trueblooded *Bildungsroman.*" Burke met and corresponded with Ellison in the late 1940s while he was at Bennington College, where Ellison, not long embarked on *Invisible Man*, would visit, occasionally lecture, and participate in long bull sessions with Burke, Shirley Jackson, Stanley Edgar Hyman, Dick Lewis, and other lively, original minds then in residence. Begun as a letter to Ellison, the piece was expanded by Burke for Kimberly Benston's 1987 collection, *Speaking for You: The Vision of Ralph Ellison*. Burke takes flight from "comments in my *Rhetoric of Motives* (1950) with reference to the 'Negro intellectual, Ralph Ellison,' who said that Booker T. Washington 'described the Negro community as a basket of crabs, wherein should one attempt to climb out, the others immediately pull him back.' "

Thirty-five years after his first take on Ellison's "literary situation" as an African American, Burke defines *Invisible Man* as a *Bildungsroman*. For Burke, "the greatest prototype" of the genre is "Goethe's *Wilhelm Meister*, which details the character's progressive education from 'apprenticeship' through 'journeymanship' toward the ideal of 'mastery' that shows up in his name." Burke traces Invisible Man's progression toward mastery in ways compatible with his own pattern of "purpose, passion, and perception," words Ellison scribbled on the typescripts of *Invisible Man* to denote the novel's movement and structure. Burke shrewdly identifies Ellison's use of technology as a contemporary form of "symbolic action" testing man's ability to master his own inventions. The letter/essay concludes with the assertion that *Invisible Man* is an "epoch-making book" that now, decades after its invention, "both reconstructs its time and takes on a universal poignancy."

In "Ellison's Zoot Suit," Larry Neal, one of the principal founding figures of the Black Arts Movement, recapitulates the "fuming" of the "literary Left, both white and Negro," "over Ellison's rejection of white-controlled left-wing politics." Citing an unsigned 1943 Ellison editorial from the *Negro Quarterly*, Neal reveals Ellison sounding themes that would become central in *Invisible Man*. "Much in Negro life remains a *mystery*," Ellison wrote. "Perhaps the *zoot* suit conceals profound political meaning; perhaps the symmetrical frenzy of the Lindy-hop conceals clues to great potential power—if only Negro leaders would solve this *riddle*" (italics Neal's). He proposes that "rather than locating the mechanisms for organizing political power totally in an analysis of the black man's class structure, Ellison turns Marxism on its head, and makes the manipulation of cultural mechanisms the basis for black liberation." Neal's is a powerful analysis of how Ellison roots history and culture in the black folk tradition. No longer the antagonist he was in the early days of the Black Arts Movement, Neal discerns the "black aesthetic at its best" permeating *Invisible Man.*

The next essay in the volume is "Ellison's Vision of *Communitas*" by Nathan A. Scott, Jr. Scott locates *Invisible Man* in a line of twentieth-century modernist fictions "organized toward the end of envisaging new forms of life for the soul." His essay draws on Victor Turner's theory of culture, and in ways complementary to Burke, Scott suggests that "amidst the troubling ambiguities" of Invisible Man's liminality, "there is born in him a profound hunger for *communitas.*" Scott notes the "prophetic discernment" of *Invisible Man,* exemplified by the narrator's last words to the reader in which he "is speaking about a condition that embraces not just his ancestral kinsmen but the human generality of his age." Writing in the late 1970s, Scott argues, as critics have done in every decade since the novel's publication, for *Invisible Man's* "special relevance to the American situation of our own immediate present"; in particular he finds the novel's painfully arrived at "sense of common purpose and of common destiny" a welcome antidote to the country's condition of "pluralism gone mad." (In a suggestive coda written especially for this volume Scott proposes an aesthetic and critical mutuality between Ellison's later essays and *Invisible Man.*)

At the end of the twentieth century, Morris Dickstein in "Ralph Ellison, Race, and American Culture" explores *Invisible Man's* relation to the immediate moment of the late 1940s and early 1950s and speculates on the novel's power to foreshadow the fluid situation of American culture from the 1960s to a still-raging "end-of-century debate over pluralism and multiculturalism." In Dickstein's view, "Of all African-American writers and intellectuals, Ellison stakes the greatest claims—not for a separate black culture or literary tradition, but for an inestimably great role within *American* culture." Perhaps most intriguingly, he suggests that with the passage of time, "[w]hat once looked tame or apolitical in Ellison's work—his emphasis on identity, freedom, and the vast potential for diversity in American life—has come to seem more radical than the political criticism that rejected it." Dickstein, like Scott, grounds his consideration of *Invisible Man* in Ellison's essays; for him the "novel is even more impressive, a veritable *Ulysses* of the black experience, rich with folklore, verbal improvisation, mythic resonance, and personal history." In the end *Invisible Man* strikes Dickstein as "a great ideological novel." In an ironic reversal, reminiscent of Ellison's metaphor of the boomerang, he sees the book as "the triumph of the center, the victory of moderation."

Robert G. O'Meally's "The Rules of Magic: Hemingway as Ellison's 'Ancestor' " is an extended meditation on Ellison's famous pronouncement that while a writer cannot choose his relatives, he can, indeed must, choose his ancestors. Taking as his starting point Ellison's comments to Irving Howe about his (Ellison's) relation to (and use of) the work of Richard Wright and Ernest Hemingway, O'Meally describes Ellison using Hemingway's techniques in his early stories and his attempts to get on paper the speech patterns and stories of the Harlem residents he interviewed between 1938 and 1941 in his work for the Federal Writers Project of the WPA. O'Meally recapitulates Ellison reworking Hemingway's themes of courage and stoicism in the face of violence and war, death and defeat. He also links Hemingway's stance of "grace under pressure" to Ellison's use of the blues in *Invisible Man*. And he proposes connections between Hemingway's portrait of the matador as artist and Invisible Man's journey from rabble-rouser to writer. Perhaps most important, O'Meally contends that as an influence Hemingway was exactly that—an ancestor, freely chosen, from whom the younger writer learned and with whom he then parted company on his journey "to tell his story truer than the facts."

The next essay, Valerie Smith's "The Meaning of Narration in *Invisible Man*," holds that the "character of the artist in Ellison's nonfiction corresponds to the portrait of the protagonist of *Invisible Man*." Smith explores Invisible Man's "double consciousness of reliving one's story as both narrator and protagonist." She suggests that "on the lower frequencies" Ellison's narrator gains ironic self-knowledge from sharecropper Jim Trueblood's careful self-presentation and performance in his oft-told tall tale of grievous incestuous sin and redemption through the transcendent healing life force of the blues. Moreover, she contends that Invisible Man deliberately calls the reader's attention to his (Invisible Man's) shortcoming—what Ellison named as his "refusal to run the risk of his own humanity" (*Essays*, 221). Finally, Smith contends that in the hiatus of his epilogue Invisible Man "loads the dice in his own favor" in ways that might not have worked to persuade the reader had he gone on to tell of his reemergence into the world. Thus, Smith's Invisible Man is a version of the artist as trickster who steps inside his readers' sense of time, and leaves the world of possibility in need of reinterpretation.

John S. Wright, in "The Conscious Hero and the Rites of Man," discusses the pertinence of Lord Raglan's *The Hero* as a source for Ellison's musing on the nature of Negro leadership in the United States. Ellison, Wright notes, liked to quote Clausewitz's dictum that politics is often war by other means; Invisible Man's grandfather issues such a call when on his deathbed, as he tells his son and grandchildren that he has been carrying on the fight for freedom and equality through a trickster's adaptation of the minstrel mask of subservience. Alert to Ellison's reliance on folk traditions and the blues, Wright argues that "Ellison's awareness of the suppressed psychic and symbolic 'power of blackness' attuned him more than Raglan had been to the dark side of the heroic myth." More keenly than other critics who have explored *Invisible Man* as Ellison's "portrait of the artist as rabble-rouser," Wright links vernacular style to the riddles of identity, history, and leadership. He concludes that in *Invisible Man* Ellison makes "artistic transcendence the one insuppressible means through which human freedom is imagined and achieved and human beings made whole."

In "Notes on the Invisible Women in Ralph Ellison's *Invisible Man*," Claudia Tate challenges the critical complaint that women characters in the novel are either nonexistent or thinly realized stereotypes. In her essay Tate looks "for the concealed truth which lies beneath the stereotyped exteriors of his [Ellison's] female characters." She contends that through his contact with black and white women Invisible Man becomes sharply aware of the limitations and possibilities bound up with his complex condition of invisibility. Tate's vantage point leads her to reread certain ambiguous scenes in the novel, such as the battle royal, the narrator's sexual encounters with the woman in red and Sybil, and his abortive impulse toward Mary Rambo before he descends into the underground. In the end however, Tate holds that Invisible Man's "efforts to leave the underground, though valiant, will be aborted time and time again, since he has no mother to give him birth."

In "Luminosity from the Lower Frequencies," novelist Leon Forrest rehearses the influences of Kenneth Burke, Lord Raglan, Dostoevski, and Faulkner on *Invisible Man*. Unlike Tate, Forrest is convinced that "at the end of the novel, our hero, reborn, is about to emerge from his womb of safety in the underground." Forrest's essay is especially original and perceptive about the vernacular theme and processes of *Invisible Man* as well as the complexity of the novel's jazz style and theme exemplified by the narrator's determination to embrace, in his rebirth, "the liberating bad air that riffs through the chamber of the good-bad horn of plenty (which also resembles the chamber from whence all life emerges)."

The last critical essay in the volume is "Ellison's *Invisible Man*." A revised and expanded version of the Bradley Lecture which I delivered at the Library of Congress in 1999, the essay pursues Ellison's movement from apprentice to journeyman and, finally, to master during the years before and during his composition of *Invisible Man*. Concerned with Ellison's "experimental attitude" toward time, form, and identity, the essay ties the narrator's ambiguous quest for eloquence to Ellison's complementary novelistic persona as a "moral historian" of American and African-American experience. It concludes with exemplary references to the drafts housed in the Ellison papers at the Library of Congress. These manuscripts offer scholars and readers firm ground from which to assess the novel's painstaking evolution from a promising, first novel in progress into a masterpiece. Comparing penultimate and final versions of the novel's last paragraphs, I attempt to show the inspired revisions behind the open-ended, questioning form of the epilogue, especially Invisible Man's last concluding question (and challenge), which is addressed to everyone who reads the novel, whatever that individual's time, place, or identity.

THE LAST WORDS in the volume belong to Ellison and the cadets who asked him questions after he delivered "On Initiation Rites and Power: A Lecture at West Point" in 1969. For one thing Ellison appears less guarded and more genuinely at ease conversing with these students than he does when he speaks about *Invisible Man* in many of his interviews. In the essay he provides frank details of the cultural autobiography that lies behind *Invisible Man*, and he is unusually forthcoming about the relevance of his personal experiences to his novel. Perhaps because he is talking informally to students, who, as West Point cadets, were about to put their lives dangerously into society's keeping, Ellison stresses "our fate as Americans to achieve that sense of self-consciousness through our own efforts." In this connection Ellison implies that "our traditions and national ideals" are kin to "the lower frequencies" of his narrator's voice. Both, he tells the students, "move and function like a firm ground bass, like the deep tones of your marvelous organ there in the chapel, repeating themselves continually while new melodies and obbligatos sound high above." This lecture and conversation between the writer and his student readers is a model for what I hope may occur in the classrooms where this volume is read and discussed as a companion to *Invisible Man*.

Notes

1. Ralph Ellison, *Trading Twelves: The Selected Letters of Ralph Ellison and Albert Murray*, ed. Albert Murray and John F. Callahan (New York: Random House, 2000), 157–58.

2. Ralph Ellison, *Invisible Man* (New York: Random House, 1952), 8. Subsequent quotations from *Invisible Man* will be to the second Vintage international edition, 1995, and will be cited in the text in parentheses.

3. R. W. B. Lewis, "The Ceremonial Imagination of Ralph Ellison," *Carleton Miscellany* 18, no. 3 (Winter 1980): 35.

4. Ralph Ellison, *The Collected Essays of Ralph Ellison*, ed. John F. Callahan (New York: Random House, 1995), 217. Subsequent quotations from the *Collected Essays* will be cited in the text in parentheses as *Essays*.

5. For the case on behalf of *Invisible Man* as the exemplary "novel of segregation," see the documents in Eric J. Sundquist's *Cultural Contexts for Ralph Ellison's Invisible Man* (St. Martin's Press, 1995), as well as Sundquist's excellent introduction.

6. Ralph Ellison, *Conversations with Ralph Ellison*, ed. Maryemma Graham and Amritjit Singh (Jackson: University Press of Mississippi, 1995), 373.

7. Lewis, "Ceremonial Imagination," 38.

8. Although Ellison gave March 1, 1914, as his date of birth, there is no official birth certificate. There are also some documents which cite his birth date as March 1, 1913. I acknowledge the discrepancy and ambiguity but, on the basis of an early photograph of Ellison on the back of which was written, likely in his mother's hand, the words "Ralph, age 4 mos., July 1914," I am sticking with the March 1, 1914, date cited consistently by Ellison. For evidence favoring March 1, 1913, see Lawrence Jackson's *Ralph Ellison: The Emergence of Genius* (New York: Wiley, 2002), 447 n.3.

Part 1

◆ ◆ ◆

PROLOGUE: ELLISON ON *INVISIBLE MAN*

Before Publication

SOMETIME NOT TOO LONG AFTER beginning *Invisible Man* in the summer of 1945, Ellison composed his "Working Notes for Invisible Man." He began the document by meditating on American Negro personality and the factors that led to the condition of invisibility. He then situates "our character" in the South for what will evolve into the early chapters of Invisible Man. Section II is a discursive outline of Ellison's early plan for the episodes and action of the novel to be set in New York. Read alongside the published text of *Invisible Man*, the "Working Notes" provide rich clues to the evolution of Ellison's protagonist and story, and his developing craft as a novelist.

I have also included excerpts from four of Ellison's letters to Albert Murray, first published in *Trading Twelves: The Selected Letters of Ralph Ellison and Albert Murray*. Written over the two years prior to *Invisible Man*'s publication on April 19, 1952, the letters show Ellison running a self-revealing gamut of emotions. By turns confident, uncertain, anxious, proud, playful, wary, and eager, his words have the self-deprecating and self-absorbed quality of someone at a crossroads in his life letting his hair down to a trusted friend.

Working Notes for Invisible Man

First a couple of underlying assumptions: "Invisibility," as our rather strange character comes in the end to conceive it, springs from two basic facts of American life. From the racial conditioning which often makes the white American interpret cultural, physical, or psychological differences as signs of racial inferiority; and, on the other hand, it springs from great formlessness of Negro life wherein all values are in flux, and where those institutions and patterns of life which mold the white American's personality are missing or not so immediate in their effect. Except for its upper levels, where it tends to merge with the American whole, Negro life is a world psychologically apart. Its tempo of development from the feudal-folk forms of the South to the industrial urban forms of the North is so rapid that it throws up personalities as fluid and changeable as molten metal rendered irridescent from the effect of cooling air. Its class lines are fluid, its values unstable, and it is in conflict with the white world to which it is bound. Out of this conflict personalities of extreme complexity emerge; personalities which in a short span of years move from the level of the folk to that of the sophisticate, who combine enough potential forms of western personality to fill many lives, and who are "broad" in the sense of which Ivan Karamazov spoke. Sometimes in responding to the conflict between their place in life as Negroes and the opportunities of America which are denied them, these personalities act out their wildest fantasies, they assume many guises without too much social opposition (Father Divine becomes God) first because within the Negro world the necessities of existence, those compromises men must make in order to survive, are such that they do not allow for a too rigid defining of value or personality (only the lower-class Negroes create their own values, the middle class seeks to live up to those of the whites); second, because whites tend to regard Negroes in the spirit of the old song "All Coons Look Alike to Me," seldom looking past the abstraction "Negro" to the specific "man." Thus a Negro is rendered invisible—and to an extent invincible when he, as our hero comes to do, attempts to take advantage of the white man's psychological blind spot. And even this involves a sacrifice of personality and manhood on the Negro's part, and many of his actions are motivated by spite and an effort to revenge himself against this scheme of things.

The other thing to be said about our character specifically is that he is a man born into a tragic, irrational situation, who attempts to respond to it as though it were completely logical. He has accepted the definition of himself as handed down by the white South and the paternalism of northern philanthropy. He sets out with the purpose of succeeding within the tight framework granted him by Jim Crow and he blinds himself to all those factors of reality which reveal the essential inadequacy of such a scheme for the full development of personality.

Ironically, he also represents the Negro individualist, the personality that breaks away from the pre-individual community of southern Negro life to win its way in the Jimcrow world by guile, uncletomming or ruthlessness. In order to do this he must act within the absurd predicament in which Negroes find themselves, upon the assumption that all is completely logical. Against the tragic-comic attitude adopted by folk Negroes (best expressed by the blues and in our scheme by Trueblood) he is strictly, during the first phase of his life, of the Nineteenth Century. Thus neither he nor Mr. Norton, whose abolitionist father's creation he is, can respond to Trueblood's stoicism, or to the Vet's need to get close to the naked essence of the world as he has come to see it. Life is either tragic or absurd, but Norton and the boy have no capacity to deal with such ambivalence. The boy would appease the gods; it costs him much pain to discover that he can satisfy the gods only by rebelling against them. The Invisible Man has dedicated himself to a false dream but one that has been presented couched in the form of the great rituals of human hope, such as Barbee with a semi-folk evocation of the Founder—mocked by time and reality in the very process—attempts to manipulate in his address to the student body. It is this hope which gives the Invisible Man's quest any semblance of dignity.

Section II Outline

I. When the boy attempts to contact the gentlemen to whom his letters are addressed he is given the run-around by each. They remain mysterious and powerful figures who control his destiny but whose desires, though he is willing to do anything to fulfill them, he can never discern. Finally, it is the secretary of the seventh trustee who out of some vague impulse of pity reveals to him the contents of one of the letters signed by Bledsoe; the message states in pious terms the equivalent of "Keep this nigger moving."

His action is one of disbelief. He accuses the secretary of plotting to prevent his getting the job. Returning to his room he suffers the first real doubts of his life. After waiting for several weeks he finally accepts the truth that the secretary has revealed.

II. The experience is such that combined with the tempo of the city life and the inadequacy of the heavy southern foods which he has continued to eat, he suffers a severe attack of nervous indigestion. His stomach goes completely dead. Rushed to the hospital he is seized by a group of medical pragmatists and thrown into a mysterious experimental machine which achieves its cure by giving its victim rhythmical electrical shocks and flashing strobe lights in his eyes. At the expense of much pain he is cured and leaves with only a mild case of photo-phobia which leaves him within a few days. The hospital experience is really a form of rebirth and the trauma comes with the physical effect very much like that he experienced on the charged carpet after the Battle Royal. After this he selects a diet more in keeping with the tensions of the city and begins to note within himself the psychosomatic changes undergone by southern Negroes when they adapt to the life of the city. His sensibilities quicken, his emotions expand and deepen, his curiosity grows, he discovers that he has been afraid and thus loses some of his fear. Having given up hope of succeeding along the lines laid out at the college he is deep in despair. He searches for work. In the swirling life around him he feels his personality slipping away.

III. He lives for a while with a family that has only recently moved to the North which is having a difficult time adjusting but going about it courageously. Under the blasting pressures of the city he sees members of the family involved in matters as tragic as those he discovered in Trueblood yet he is still unable to appreciate what is involved.

IV. He has his second affair with a girl. (Omitted from the first section is an affair which ends in failure when he approaches a folkish girl with a version of romantic love which he has gleaned from his reading. She is amused at his antics and rejects him.)

V. He becomes aware of the depression and the agitation for relief. Still desiring to become a leader and still compelled to make speeches, he stops one afternoon to watch an eviction and gives way to an impulse, makes an impassioned speech which incites the spectators to replace the evicted furniture in defiance of the police and to join in a march which threatens to become a riot. Though completely shocked by the force that he has unleashed he courageously accepts the results of his act and moves along in its sway. Suddenly he finds himself acclaimed a hero and taken up by a group of left wingers. They ask him to join them and he does; not because he believes, but because they ask him during his moment of deepest despair.

He now finds that he has been given an identity, a salary, and a great deal of prestige. He is spoken of as a leader, which he takes quite seriously, and he sets out in all sincerity to lead; reading, talking with people, working out ways to win their support. He is convinced that he has found a real democracy, and though somewhat suspicious of whites with whom he has to work he is willing to try. After a while, however, he finds that very few of his suggestions receive consideration and that he is a leader in name but not in fact.

VI. It is here that his sense of invisibility descends full upon him. He decides to resign and make a scandal. Then he begins to think of the whites as the all-powerful figures he regarded them in the South and gives in to his passive drives. Once more he looks for a sphere of action in which his own self-assertion is unnecessary, and self-definition uncalled for. He fails to see that he is dealing with well-meaning but blundering human beings, most of whom have misunderstood him because of the unconscious assumption that they knew what was best. His sense that he is losing a grip on himself grows. He phones his office several times a day to ask for himself, disguising his voice and finding reassurance in hearing the girl use this title when explaining that he isn't in.

He feels resentment against his colleagues which he expresses by making as many conquests with the women as he can. This is no solution however since he cannot allow husbands to know. He is disappointed when one discovers him and decides in the interest of politics to ignore it. The effect is humiliating for the Invisible Man who would have regarded divorce proceedings as evidence of his visibility. He becomes so insecure that he is never at peace unless he is treated as an inferior. Thus in a democratic organization he feels at peace only when the patterns of American race etiquette are suddenly observed. Yet, he is aware of his own sensitivity and intelligence and resents the power of his white colleagues over him.

VII. In this state he meets Louise, a young woman of great charm. Louise is the one person in the organization whom he can believe accepts him as a human being. He regards her as a symbol of democracy, of freedom and fertility which he can win only by accepting the task of defining himself against the opposition of the world. However, he is not sure whether he is attracted to Louise for herself or for her whiteness. Her whiteness is quite a problem. He is proud of it and he hates it. He receives pleasure from the resentment of those who object when they walk down the street. He is also afraid of the danger which he feels this involves and insists that she spend long hours beneath the sunlamp baking her complexion painfully close to that of a mulatto. Like Othello, whose situation he now parodies, he cannot accept himself nor believe that anyone like Louise could find him attractive. Finally, to end his conflict he drives her away.

VIII. Seeking a substitute for Louise and a milieu in which his self-doubts would not be so pressing he begins to travel in sophisticated Harlem circles in which he is accepted as a leader. Ironically, his leadership is now almost entirely on paper; since all those actions which might have allowed him to build a real following have been vetoed downtown. He tells himself that he travels in this crowd in order to influence it politically, actually he is drawn to its values and to its forms of disintegration. On the other hand, he ruthlessly expels a group of Negroes critical of some of the organization's policies. He closes his mind to the real shortcomings. Then an admirer presents him with a primitive African fertility god, an ugly little figure which he imagines argues with him concerning the aesthetics of democracy.

IX. Riot. A riot, which he has seen developing and sought to point out only to be ignored, occurs. He had been told that he should not attempt to make predictions. Then when the riot occurs he is ordered into the streets to use his prestige and following to persuade the rioters to return to their homes. Knowing full well that no one will listen to him, he ventures out and is attacked by some of the same people who had followed him at the beginning of his political career. He is badly beaten, escapes into a decaying building and finally gets away by running into the deepest level of the basement and hiding in the coal bin and emerges from the coal chute in the center of the sidewalk, covered with dirt and blackness, completely unrecognizable as the once suave politico. His political personality is dismembered.

X. He moves to another part of the city full of resentment. He decides to become a preacher, the leader of a cult. Has noticed the appeal which the redeemed criminal holds for folk Negroes announcing himself as such. He becomes the leader of

a small store-front church into which he introduces technological gadgets as a means of exploiting the congregation—
recording machines, P.A. systems, electric guitars, swing orchestras are all introduced. At this point he embraces his invisibility, adopting many personalities as he wanders up and
down the many social levels of the city. He feels deep resentment against society which fails to see him. But soon he is
forced to seek real understanding, compelled by his loneliness
to probe the forms of personality and experience developed
by urban Negroes and to relate them to more universal patterns. In the end he is defeated in his original purpose but has
achieved some perception of the nature of his life. He hopes
these, his memoirs, will, once they are read, allow him to
enter into the world of things known, will serve to define
himself. Characteristically, he doubts that they will be read.

From Ellison's Letters to Albert Murray

January 24, 1950

... And if I ever complete my endless you-know-what you'll get
a chance to see what different things we make of a common
reality. "You-know-what" indeed. Is it a rock around my neck; a
dream, a nasty compulsive dream which I no longer write but
now am acting out (in an early section the guy is obsessed by
gadgets and music, now I'm playing with cameras and have recently completed two high-fidelity amplifiers and installed a
sound system for a friend); a ritual of regression which makes
me dream of childhood every night (as a child I was a radio bug,
you know, and take it from me after getting around with the
camera bugs and the high-fi bugs and the model train bugs, you'll
have no doubts as to the regressive nature of this gadget minded
culture); or is it a kind of death, a dying? Certainly after it's all
over and done up in binders I will have passed through the god-
damnedest experience of my life and shall never be the same.
Perhaps that is why it's so difficult to finish. Nevertheless I'm near

the end and I'll be glad to get it over with. Perhaps as you say of my reviews there's a switchblade in it—if so, I'll be damned relieved to turn it against someone else for a while. Perhaps you've given me the subtitle: The Invisible Man: a Switchbladed Confession.

May 14, 1951

You are hereby warned that I have dropped the shuck.[1] About the middle of April, in fact; and strange to say I've been depressed ever since—starting with a high fever that developed during the evening we were clearing up the final typing. I suppose crazy things will continue to happen until that crowning craziness, publication.

June 6, 1951

Erskine[2] and I are reading it aloud, not cutting (I cut out 200 pages myself and got it down to 606) but editing, preparing it for the printer, who should have it July or August. I'm afraid that there'll be no publication until spring. For while most of the reader reactions were enthusiastic, there were some stupid ones and Erskine wants plenty of time to get advance copies into the hands of intelligent reviewers—whatever that means. I guess it's necessary, since the rough stuff; the writing on the belly, Rinehart (Rine-the-runner, Rine-the-rounder, Rine-the-gambler, rine-the-lover, rine-the-reverend, old rine and heart), yes, and Ras the exhorter who becomes Ras the *destroyer*, a West Indian stud who must have been created when I was drunk or slipped into the novel by someone else—it's all here. I've worked out a plan whereby I trade four-letter words for scenes. Hell, the reader can imagine the four-letter words but not the scenes. And as for MacArthur[3] and his corny—but effective—rhetoric, I'll put any three of my boys in the ring with him any time. Either Barbee, Ras, or Invisible, could teach that bastard something about signifying. He'd fade like a snort in a windstorm. . . . Anyway, just to put that many words down and then cut out two hundred pages, must stand for *something*. I'll get you an advance copy if possible. Erskine's having a time deciding what kind of novel it is, and I can't help him. For me it's just a big fat ole Negro lie, meant to be told during cotton picking time over a water bucket full of corn, with a dipper passing back and forth at a good fast clip so that no one, not even the narrator himself, will realize how utterly preposterous the lie actually is. I just hope someone points out that aspect of it. As you see I'm more obsessed with this thing now than I was all those five years.

January 8, 1952

... I completed the page proofs in December and expect bound copies sometime in Feb. Publication date is set for the day after Easter.[4] And the current issue of *Partisan Review* carries the prologue. Things are rolling, alright and I guess I'm now a slightly mammy-made novelist. There is quite a bit of excitement, with more calls for galleys than can be supplied, but who's puking and who's laughing I do not know. Keep your fingers crossed. I managed to keep in everything but that sour cream in the vagina that Ras the Exhorter talks about. It was too ripe for 'em, man. They called me and said, "Mr. E., that sour cream just naturally has to go." Maybe they know about "duck butter."[5] So I guess I sold out. I compromised; all the stuff that really counts is still there, and I didn't dodge before they drew back to strike.

February 4, 1952

As for the novel, I'm still sweating it out. Good things are being said and the publisher's hopes are high, but I'm playing it cool with my stomach pitching a bitch and my dream life most embarrassing. I keep dreaming about Tuskegee and high school, all the scenes of test and judgment. I'll be glad when it's over. The prologue has caused some comments, but I don't think Rahv[6] has decided what he thinks about the book as a whole. He does know that it isn't Kafka as others mistakenly believe. I tell them, I told Langston Hughes in fact, that it's the blues, but nobody seems to understand what I mean. But the thing is arousing interest.[7]

Editor's Notes

1. Ellison refers to the fact that he had finished the final typescript of *Invisible Man*.

2. Albert Erskine was Ellison's editor, first at Reynal and Hitchcock, which had tendered Ellison the original contract for his first novel, then from 1946 on at Random House until Erskine's death in 1993.

3. General Douglas MacArthur. After his dismissal for insubordination by President Harry S Truman, MacArthur electrified much of the nation and briefly dominated the headlines with a nostalgic speech to a joint session of Congress on April 20, 1951.

4. April 19, 1952.

5. See *Juneteenth*, 346, for a witty, ribald play on "duck butter."

6. Philip Rahv, editor of *Partisan Review* in the 1940s and 1950s, was a prominent critic on the Left, whose essay, "Palefaces and Redskins," Ellison read and respected.

7. In *The Omni-Americans* Murray was to call *Invisible Man* "*par excellence* the literary extension of the blues."

After Publication

IN THE PREFACE to his two-part interview with Ellison, begun in 1974, resumed and concluded in 1982, John Hersey remarked that "[o]ne of the most significant views of Ralph Ellison's work happens to be his own." Hersey understates the matter. Aware that his reputation rested largely on *Invisible Man*, Ellison wrote briefly and at length, over and over again, about any and every aspect of his novel in essays, interviews, and letters from the time of the novel's publication in 1952 until his death in 1994. Some of his comments, like those in "Brave Words for a Startling Occasion," his address on the occasion of accepting the National Book Award, place *Invisible Man* in the most ambitious, classic tradition of the American novel. Other remarks, like some of those made to interviewers from the *Paris Review*, sometimes downplay his novel's importance. But whether in his essays and interviews, or in letters written to students, scholars, readers, old friends, or all of the above, Ellison's words about *Invisible Man* reveal a learned, highly conscious artist as critic and an exacting critic as artist striving to write far more than a worthy first novel. The selections that follow are a sample of the best of the extensive theoretical and practical commentaries offered by Ellison in the four decades of his life after *Invisible Man* was published in 1952.

Brave Words for a Startling Occasion*

FIRST, as I express my gratitude for this honor which you have bestowed on me, let me say that I take it that you are rewarding my efforts rather than my not quite fully achieved attempt at a major novel. Indeed, if I were asked in all seriousness just what I considered to be the chief significance of *Invisible Man* as a fiction, I would reply: its experimental attitude, and its attempt to return to the mood of personal moral responsibility for democracy which typified the best of our nineteenth-century fiction. That my first novel should win this most coveted prize must certainly indicate that there is a crisis in the American novel. You as critics have told us so, and current fiction sales would indicate that the reading public agrees. Certainly the younger novelists concur. The explosive nature of events mocks our brightest efforts. And the very "facts" which the naturalists assumed would make us free have lost the power to protect us from despair. Controversy now rages over just what aspects of American experience are suitable for novelistic treatment. The prestige of the theorists of the so-called novel of manners has been challenged. Thus, after a long period of stability we find our assumptions concerning the novel being called into question. And though I was only vaguely aware of it, it was this growing crisis which shaped the writing of *Invisible Man*.

After the usual apprenticeship of imitation and seeking with delight to examine my experience through the discipline of the novel, I became gradually aware that the forms of so many of the works which impressed me were too restricted to contain the

*Address for presentation ceremony, National Book Award, January 27, 1953. From *The Collected Essays of Ralph Ellison*

experience which I knew. The diversity of American life with its extreme fluidity and openness seemed too vital and alive to be caught for more than the briefest instant in the tight, well-made Jamesian novel, which was, for all its artistic perfection, too concerned with "good taste" and stable areas. Nor could I safely use the forms of the "hard-boiled" novel, with its dedication to physical violence, social cynicism, and understatement. Understatement depends, after all, upon commonly held assumptions, and my minority status rendered all such assumptions questionable. There was also a problem of language, and even dialogue, which, with its hard-boiled stance and its monosyllabic utterance, is one of the shining achievements of twentieth-century American writing. For despite the notion that its rhythms were those of everyday speech, I found that when compared with the rich babel of idiomatic expression around me, a language full of imagery and gesture and rhetorical canniness, it was embarrassingly austere. Our speech I found resounding with an alive language swirling with over three hundred years of American living, a mixture of the folk, the Biblical, the scientific, and the political. Slangy in one stance, academic in another, loaded poetically with imagery at one moment, mathematically bare of imagery in the next. As for the rather rigid concepts of reality which informed a number of the works which impressed me and to which I owe a great deal, I was forced to conclude that reality was far more mysterious and uncertain, and more exciting, and still, despite its raw violence and capriciousness, more promising. To attempt to express that American experience which has carried one back and forth and up and down the land and across, and across again the great river, from freight train to Pullman car, from contact with slavery to contact with a world of advanced scholarship, art, and science, is simply to burst such neatly understated forms of the novel asunder.

A novel whose range was both broader and deeper was needed. And in my search I found myself turning to our classical nineteenth-century novelists. I felt that except for the work of William Faulkner something vital had gone out of American prose after Mark Twain. I came to believe that the writers of that period took a much greater responsibility for the condition of democracy and, indeed, their works were imaginative projections of the conflicts within the human heart which arose when the sacred principles of the Constitution and the Bill of Rights clashed with the practical exigencies of human greed and fear, hate and love. Naturally I was attracted to these writers as a Negro. Whatever they thought of my people per se, in their imaginative economy the Negro symbolized both the man lowest down and the mysterious, underground aspect of human personality. In a sense the Negro was the gauge of the human condition as it waxed and waned in our democracy. These writers were willing to confront the broad complexities of American life, and we are the richer for their having done so.

Thus to see America with an awareness of its rich diversity and its almost magical fluidity and freedom, I was forced to conceive of a novel unburdened by the narrow naturalism which has led, after so many triumphs, to the final and unrelieved despair which marks so much of our current fiction. I was to dream of a prose which was flexible, and swift as American change is swift, confronting the inequalities and brutalities of our society forthrightly, yet thrusting forth its images of hope, human fraternity, and individual self-realization. It would use the richness of our speech, the idiomatic expression and the rhetorical flourishes from past periods which are still alive among us. And despite my personal failures, there must be possible a fiction which, leaving sociology to the scientists, can arrive at the truth about the human condition, here and now, with all the bright magic of a fairy tale.

What has been missing from so much experimental writing has been the passionate will to dominate reality as well as the laws of art. This will is the true source of the experimental attitude. We who struggle with form and with America should remember Eidothea's advice to Menelaus when in the *Odyssey* he and his friends are seeking their way home. She tells him to seize her father, Proteus, and to hold him fast "however he may struggle and fight. He will turn into all sorts of shapes to try you," she says, "into all the creatures that live and move upon the earth, into water, into blazing fire; but you must hold him fast and press him all the harder. When he is himself, and questions you in the same shape that he was when you saw him in his bed, let the old man go; and then, sir, ask which god it is who is angry, and how you shall make your way homewards over the fish-giving sea."

For the novelist, Proteus stands for both America and the inheritance of illusion through which all men must fight to achieve reality; the offended god stands for our sins against those principles we all hold sacred. The way home we seek is that condition of man's being at home in the world, which is called love, and which we term democracy. Our task then is always to challenge the apparent forms of reality—that is, the fixed manners and values of the few—and to struggle with it until it reveals its mad, vari-implicated chaos, its false faces, and on until it surrenders its insight, its truth. We are fortunate as American writers in that with our variety of racial and national traditions, idioms and manners, we are yet one. On its profoundest level American experience is of a whole. Its truth lies in its diversity and swiftness of change. Through forging forms of the novel worthy of it, we achieve not only the promise of our lives, but we anticipate the resolution of those world problems of humanity which for a moment seem to those who are in awe of statistics completely insoluble.

Whenever we as Americans have faced serious crises we have returned to fundamentals; this, in brief, is what I have tried to do.

From "The Art of Fiction: An Interview"
(*Paris Review*, Spring 1955)

INTERVIEWERS: When did you begin *Invisible Man*?

ELLISON: In the summer of 1945. I had returned from the sea, ill, with advice to get some rest. Part of my illness was due, no doubt, to the fact that I had not been able to write a novel for which I'd received a Rosenwald fellowship the previous winter. So on a farm in Vermont where I was reading *The Hero* by Lord Raglan and speculating on the nature of Negro leadership in the United States, I wrote the first paragraph of *Invisible Man*, and was soon involved in the struggle of creating the novel.

INTERVIEWERS: How long did it take you to write it?

ELLISON: Five years, with one year out for a short novel which was unsatisfactory, ill-conceived, and never submitted for publication.

INTERVIEWERS: Did you have everything thought out before you began to write *Invisible Man*

ELLISON: The symbols and their connections were known to me. I began it with a chart of the three-part division. It was a conceptual frame with most of the ideas and some incidents indicated. The three parts represent the narrator's movement from, using Kenneth Burke's terms, purpose to passion to perception. These three major sections are built up of smaller units of three which mark the course of the action and which depend for their development upon what I hoped was a consistent and developing motivation. However, you'll note that the maximum insight on the hero's part isn't reached until the final section. After all, it's a novel about innocence and human error, a struggle through illusion to reality. Each section begins with a sheet of paper; each piece of paper is exchanged for another and contains a definition of his identity, or the social role he is to play as defined for him by others. But all say essentially the same thing: "Keep this nigger boy running." Before he could have some voice in his own destiny he had to discard these old identities and illusions; his enlightenment couldn't come until then. Once he recognizes the hole of darkness into which these papers put him, he has to burn them. That's the plan and the intention; whether I achieved this is something else. . . .

INTERVIEWERS: Can you give us an example of the use of folklore in your own novel?

ELLISON: Well, there are certain themes, symbols, and images which are based on folk material. For example, there is the old saying amongst Negroes: If you're black, stay back; if you're brown, stick around; if you're white, you're right. And there is the joke Negroes tell on themselves about their being so black they can't be seen in the dark. In my book this sort of thing was merged with the meanings which blackness and light have long had in Western mythology: evil and goodness, ignorance and knowledge, and so on. In my novel the narrator's development is one through blackness to light, that is, from ignorance to enlightenment, invisibility to visibility. He leaves the South and goes North; this, as you will notice in reading Negro folktales, is always the road to freedom, the movement upward. You have the same thing again when he leaves his underground cave for the open. . . .

INTERVIEWERS: Do you think a reader unacquainted with this folklore can properly understand your work?

ELLISON: Yes, I think so. It's like jazz; there's no inherent problem which prohibits understanding but the assumptions brought to it. We don't all dig Shakespeare uniformly, or even "Little Red Riding Hood." The understanding of art depends finally upon one's willingness to extend one's humanity and one's knowledge of human life. I noticed, incidentally, that the Germans, having no special caste assumptions concerning American Negroes, dealt with my work simply as a novel. I think the Americans will come to view it that way in twenty years— if it's around that long.

INTERVIEWERS: Don't you think it will be?

ELLISON: I doubt it. It's not an important novel. I failed of eloquence, and many of the immediate issues are rapidly fading away. If it does last, it will be simply because there are things going on in its depth that are of more permanent interest than on its surface. . . .

INTERVIEWERS: Would you say that the search for identity is primarily an American theme?

ELLISON: It is *the* American theme. The nature of our society is such that we are prevented from knowing who we are. It is still a young society, and this is an integral part of its development.

INTERVIEWERS: A common criticism of first novels is that the central incident is either omitted or weak. *Invisible Man* seems to suffer here; shouldn't we have been present at the scenes which are the dividing lines in the book—namely, when the Brotherhood organization moves the narrator downtown, then back uptown?

ELLISON: I think you missed the point. The major flaw in the hero's character is his unquestioning willingness to do what is required of him by others as a way to success, and this was the specific form of his "innocence." He goes where he is told to go; he does what he is told to do; he does not even choose his Brotherhood name. It is chosen for him and he accepts it. He has accepted party discipline and thus cannot be present at the scene since it is not the will of the Brotherhood leaders. What is important is not the scene but his failure to question their decision. There is also the fact that no single person can be everywhere at once, nor can a single consciousness be aware of all the nuances of a large social action. What happens uptown while he is downtown is part of his darkness, both symbolic and actual. No, I don't feel that any vital scenes have been left out.

INTERVIEWERS: Why did you find it necessary to shift styles throughout the book, particularly in the prologue and epilogue?

ELLISON: The prologue was written afterwards, really—in terms of a shift in the hero's point of view. I wanted to throw the reader off balance, to make him accept certain nonnaturalistic effects. It was really a memoir written underground, and I wanted a foreshadowing through which I hoped the reader would view the actions which took place in the main body of the book. For another thing, the styles of life presented are different. In the South, where he was trying to fit into a traditional pattern and where his sense of certainty had not yet been challenged, I felt a more naturalistic treatment was adequate. The college trustee's speech to the students is really an echo of a certain kind of southern rhetoric, and I enjoyed trying to re-create it. As the hero passes from the South to the North, from the relatively stable to the swiftly changing, his sense of certainty is lost and the style becomes expressionistic. Later on, during his fall from grace in the Brotherhood, it becomes somewhat surrealistic. The styles try to express both his state of consciousness and the state of society. The epilogue was necessary to complete the action begun when he set out to write his memoirs.

INTERVIEWERS: After four hundred pages you still felt the epilogue was necessary?

ELLISON: Yes. Look at it this way. The book is a series of reversals. It is the portrait of the artist as a rabble-rouser, thus the various mediums of expression. In the epilogue the hero discovers what he had not discovered throughout the book: you have to make your own decisions; you have to think for yourself. The hero comes up from underground because the act of writing and thinking necessitated it. He could not stay down there.

INTERVIEWERS: You say that the book is "a series of reversals." It seemed to us that this was a weakness, that it was built on a series of provocative situations which were canceled by the calling up of conventional emotions—

ELLISON: I don't quite see what you mean.

INTERVIEWERS: Well, for one thing, you begin with a provocative situation of the American Negro's status in society. The responsibility for this is that of the white American citizen; that's where the guilt lies. Then you cancel it by introducing the Communist Party, or the Brotherhood, so that the reader tends to say to himself: "Ah, they're the guilty ones. They're the ones who mistreat him, not us."

ELLISON: I think that's a case of misreading. And I didn't identify the Brotherhood as the C.P., but since you do I'll remind you that they, too, are white. The hero's invisibility is not a matter of being seen, but a refusal to run the risk of his own humanity, which involves guilt. This is not an attack upon white society. It is what the hero refuses to do in each section which leads to further action. He must assert and achieve his own humanity; he cannot run with the pack and do this, and this is the reason for all the reversals. The epilogue is the most final reversal of all; therefore it is a necessary statement.

INTERVIEWERS: And the love affairs—or almost love affairs?

ELLISON: (*Laughing*) I'm glad you put it that way. The point is that when thrown into a situation which he thinks he wants, the hero is sometimes thrown at a loss; he doesn't know how to act. After he had made this speech about the Place of the Woman in Our Society, for example, and was approached by one of the women in the audience, he thought she wanted to talk about the Brotherhood and found she wanted to talk about brother-*and-sisterhood*. Look, didn't you find the book at all *funny?* I felt that such a man as this character would have been incapable of a love affair; it would have been inconsistent with his personality.

INTERVIEWERS: Do you have any difficulty controlling your characters? E. M. Forster says that he sometimes finds a character running away with him.

ELLISON: No, because I find that a sense of the ritual understructure of the fiction helps to guide the creation of characters. Action is the thing. We are what we do and do not do. The problem for me is to get from A to B to C. My anxiety about transitions greatly prolonged the writing of my book. The naturalists stick to case histories and sociology and are willing to compete with the camera and the tape recorder. I despise concreteness in writing, but when reality is deranged in fiction, one must worry about the seams.

INTERVIEWERS: Do you have difficulty turning real characters into fiction?

ELLISON: Real characters are just a limitation. It's like turning your own life into fiction: you have to be hindered by chronology and fact. A number of the characters just jumped out, like Rinehart and Ras.

INTERVIEWERS: Isn't Ras based on Marcus Garvey?[1]

ELLISON: No. In 1950 my wife and I were staying at a vacation spot where we met some white liberals who thought the best way to be friendly was to tell us what it was like to be Negro. I got mad at hearing this from people who otherwise seemed very intelligent. I had already sketched Ras, but the passion of his statement came out after I went upstairs that night feeling that we needed to have this thing out once and for all and get it done with; then we could go on living like people and individuals. No conscious reference to Garvey is intended.

INTERVIEWERS: What about Rinehart? Is he related to Rinehart in the blues tradition, or Django Rheinhardt, the jazz musician?

ELLISON: There is a peculiar set of circumstances connected with my choice of that name. My old Oklahoma friend, Jimmy Rushing, the blues singer, used to sing one with a refrain that went:

> Rinehart, Rinehart,
> It's so lonesome up here
> On Beacon Hill . . .

which haunted me, and as I was thinking of a character who was a master of disguise, of coincidence, this name with its suggestion of inner and outer came to my mind. Later I learned that it was a call used by Harvard students when they prepared to riot, a call to chaos. Which is interesting, because it is not long after Rinehart appears in my novel that the riot breaks out in Harlem. Rinehart is my name for the personification of chaos. He is also intended to represent America and change. He has lived so long with chaos that he knows how to manipulate it. It is the old theme of *The Confidence Man*. He is a figure in a country with no solid past or stable class lines, therefore he is able to move about easily from one to the other.

You know, I'm still thinking of your question about the use of Negro experience as material for fiction. One function of serious literature is to deal with the moral core of a given society. Well, in the United States the Negro and his status have always stood for that moral concern. He symbolizes among other things the human and social possibility of equality. This is the moral question raised in our two great nineteenth-century novels, *Moby-Dick* and *Huckleberry Finn*. The very center of Twain's book revolves finally around the boy's relations with Nigger Jim and the question of what Huck should do about getting Jim free after the two scoundrels have sold him. There is a magic here worth conjuring, and that reaches to the very nerve of the American consciousness, so why should I abandon it? Our so-called race problem has now lined up with the world problems of colonialism and the struggle of the West to gain the allegiance of the remaining nonwhite people who have thus far remained outside the Communist sphere; thus its possibilities for art have increased rather than lessened. Looking at the novelist as manipulator and depictor of moral problems. I ask myself how much of the achievement of democratic ideals in the United States has been affected by the steady pressure of Negroes and those whites who were sensitive to the implications of our condition, and I know that without that pressure the position of our country before the world would be much more serious even than it is now. Here is part of the social dynamics of a great society. Perhaps the discomfort about protest in books by Negro authors comes because since the nineteenth century American literature has avoided profound moral searching. It was too painful, and besides, there were specific problems of language and form to which the writers could address themselves. They did wonderful things, but perhaps they left the real problems untouched. There are exceptions, of course, like Faulkner, who has been working the great moral theme all along, taking it up where Mark Twain put it down. I feel that with my decision to devote myself to the novel I took on one of the responsibilities inherited by those who practice the craft in the United States: that of describing for all that fragment of the huge diverse American experience which I know best, and which offers me the possibility of contributing not only to the growth of the literature but to the shaping of the culture as I should like it to be. The American novel is in this sense a conquest of the frontier; as it describes our experience, it creates it.— *The Collected Essays of Ralph Ellison*, 218–219, 215–216, 217, 219–224.

From "Change the Joke and Slip the Yoke"
(1958)

... So intense is Hyman's[2] search for archetypical forms that he doesn't see that the narrator's grandfather in *Invisible Man* is no more involved in a "darky" act than was Ulysses in Polyphemus's cave.[3] Nor is he so much a "smart-man-playing-dumb" as a weak man who knows the nature of his oppressor's weakness. There is a good deal of spite in the old man, as there comes to be in his grandson, and the strategy he advises is a kind of jujitsu of the spirit, a denial and rejection through agreement. Samson, eyeless in Gaza, pulls the building down when his strength returns; politically weak, the grandfather has learned that conformity leads to a similar end, and so advises his children. Thus his mask of meekness conceals the wisdom of one who has learned the secret of saying the "yes" which accomplishes the expressive "no." Here, too, is a rejection of a current code and a denial become metaphysical. More important to the novel is the fact that he represents the ambiguity of the past for the hero, for whom his sphinx-like deathbed advice poses a riddle which points the plot in the dual directions which the hero will follow throughout the novel.

Certainly B. P. Rhinehart (the P. is for "Proteus," the B. for "Bliss")[4] would seem the perfect example of Hyman's trickster figure. He is a cunning man who wins the admiration of those who admire skullduggery and know-how, an American virtuoso of identity who thrives on chaos and swift change; he is greedy, in that his masquerade is motivated by money as well as by the sheer bliss of impersonation; he is godlike, in that he brings new techniques—electric guitars, etc.—to the service of God, and in that there are many men in his image while he is himself unseen; he is phallic in his role of "lover"; as a numbers runner he is a bringer of manna and a worker of miracles, in that he transforms (for winners, of course) pennies into dollars, and thus he feeds (and feeds on) the poor. Indeed, one could extend this list in the manner of much myth-mongering criticism until the fiction dissolved into anthropology, but Rhinehart's role in the formal structure of the narrative is to suggest to the hero a mode of escape from Ras, and a means of applying, in yet another form, his grandfather's cryptic advice to his own situation. One could throw Rhinehart among his literary betters and link him with Mann's Felix Krull, the Baron Clappique of Malraux's *Man's Fate*, and many others, but that would be to make a game of criticism and really say nothing.

The identity of fictional characters is determined by the implicit realism of the form, not by their relation to tradition; they are what they do or do not do. Archetypes are timeless; novels are time haunted. Novels achieve timelessness through time. If the symbols appearing in a novel link up with those of universal myth they do so by virtue of their emergence from the specific texture of a specific form of social reality. The final act of *Invisible Man* is not that of a concealment in darkness in the Anglo-Saxon connotation of the word, but that of a voice issuing its little wisdom out of the substance of its own inwardness—after having undergone a transformation from ranter to writer. If, by the way, the hero is pulling a "darky act" in this, he certainly is not a smart man playing dumb. For the novel, his memoir, is one long, loud rant, howl, and laugh. Confession, not concealment, is his mode. His mobility is dual: geographical, as Hyman points out, but, more important, it is intellectual. And in keeping with the reverse English of the plot, and with the Negro American conception of blackness, his movement vertically downward (not into a "sewer," Freud notwithstanding, but into a coal cellar, a source of heat, light, power, and, through association with the character's motivation, self-perception) is a process of *rising* to an understanding of his human condition. He gets his restless mobility not so much from the blues or from sociology but because he appears in a literary form which has time and social change as its special province. Besides, restlessness of the spirit is an American condition that transcends geography, sociology, and past condition of servitude.—*The Collected Essays of Ralph Ellison*, 109–111.

From "An Interview with Allen Geller" (1963)

ELLISON: ... *Invisible Man* is a memoir of a man who has gone through that experience and now comes back and brings his message to the world. It's a social act; it is not a resignation from society but an attempt to come back and to be useful. There is an implied change of role from that of a would-be politician and rabble-rouser and orator to that of writer. No, there's no reason for him to lose his sense of a social role. But I think the memoir, which is titled *Invisible Man*, his memoir, is an attempt to describe reality as it really exists rather than in terms of what he had assumed it to be. Because it was the clash between his assumptions, his illusions about reality, and its actual shape which made for his agony.——*Conversations with Ralph Ellison*, 76.

From "The World and the Jug" (1964)

... If *Invisible Man* is even "apparently" free from "the ideological and emotional penalties suffered by Negroes in this country,"[5] it is because I tried to the best of my ability to transform these elements into art. My goal was not to escape or hold back, but to work through; to transcend, as the blues transcend the painful conditions with which they deal. The protest is there not because I was helpless before my racial condition, but because I *put* it there. If there is anything "miraculous" about the book it is the result of hard work undertaken in the belief that the work of art is important in itself, that it is a social action in itself.——*Collected Essays of Ralph Ellison*, 183.

From "An Interview with Richard Kostelanetz" (1965)

RE: ... There is a kind of ideal reader and that ideal reader would be a Negro who was in full possession of all the subtleties of literature and art and politics. You see what I mean? Not out of racist motives do I imagine this ideal reader, but to give my own experience, both acquired and that which I was born with, its broadest possibilities. . . . The best reader of course is the person who has the imagination, regardless of what his color is. Some readers, I suspect, bring more imagination to a work than the author has put into it. And when you get that kind of reader you're very fortunate because he gives you a stature, let's say, that you haven't really earned. . . . Well, I wasn't writing about *the* Negro. I was writing about a specific character, in specific circumstances, at a specific time. The invisibility, there is a joke about that which is tied up with the sociological dictum that Negroes in the United States have a rough time because we have *high* visibility.—*Conversations with Ralph Ellison*, 94–95.

From Letter to John Lucas, July 29, 1969

. . . As I recall it, [Tod] Clifton's smile is a complex emblem signifying among other things his recognition that the Brotherhood had sold out both Harlem and himself, and that he, in his naïve idealism and eagerness to lead, had himself been an accomplice as well as a dupe in that sell-out; and (2) that there was little possibility of his ever explaining his position to the protagonist, since he saw in the Invisible Man a reflection of his former (and now rejected) role of naïve, figurehead leader, and one too full of illusions to face up to the Machiavellian nature of political reality.

Clifton's selling of the dolls was a consciously symbolic action through which he expressed his rejection of his former dedication to the Brotherhood. By selling them he acts out a decision to punish himself by embracing the negative stereotypes as a means of cleansing himself of any shreds of hope in the promises of Brotherhoodism. Clifton is, in effect, washing his hands; and is indicating that he knows that more was involved in his experience than the simple black & white matter of selling out or being sold out. He had, in other words, learned irony, a bitter, masochistic irony, and a cynicism that sent him into midtown New York to manipulate the false, racist values, which he had once sought to destroy.

Perhaps there is also embodied here an acceptance of Ras's rhetoric of the night of the street fight—in the smile, that is. I'd better stop right here before I make the damned smile far more ambiguous than it could possibly have been—But have you noticed, by the way, the resemblance between Clifton's dolls and the gollywog appearance of our current crop of instant-Afro militants? I have, man, and it amuses the hell out of me!

My answer to your next question is yes. I do believe that the protagonist does in fact lock Ras's jaws with Ras's spear. Since the spear was thrown in an attack it becomes a "free-floating" weapon, and the protagonist's use of it symbolized a turning of violence upon a violent attacker—who up to that moment in the action had confined most of his violence to angry rhetoric. Since the protagonist was yearning for a reconciliation both with reality and with Ras, it seemed right that he wouldn't wish to kill him but would try somehow to stop him from exhorting the group to hang him. That he struck Ras in the jaws was a lucky accident and shouldn't be taken too symbolically.

I suppose some few actions in the novel should be viewed simply as acts in themselves and without symbolic extension. I should confess however that I was not above throwing in such an episode as the conjunction between the spear and the jaws as a means of laying a false trail for my friend Stanley Edgar Hyman, who has a great enthusiasm for Freudian speculation. During the time the book was being composed ole Stanley regarded all fighting taking place in literature as a form of fucking! Seriously however, there seems to have been a striving for symmetry here. Both are rabble-rousers and both have reached the end of a phase in their respective careers, thus it would seem fitting that the protagonist should strike Ras in the area where he was most to be feared; for in his capacity for achieving a physical transformation of society Ras was far less effective than such a character as Dupre, the building burner.

As you probably know or suspect, the name "Dupre" was fairly common in the Southwest where there were many families from Louisiana. I used the name not because of any desire to make a direct allusion to the blues but because it sounded right for the character, his scene, and his act.

The same goes for the name "Maceo" which, during my childhood, was also quite common; doubtlessly because of the southern Negroes' fascination with the countries to the south of us. That fascination, going back to slavery, was intensified with the Cuban declaration of independence during 1895 and reached a peak with the Spanish-American War of 1898. Therefore I suppose that a number of the "Maceos" whom I knew were named in honor of the Cuban general Antonio Maceo, a revolutionary leader who was ambushed by government troops in 1896 and killed. So I guess all those Maceo Browns, Greens, Thompsons, etc., had been dedicated to some kind of heroic action. I knew an A. Maceo Smith who is a widely known civil rights and insurance figure out in Oklahoma. And Texas, and Maceo Pinkard, the old-time theatrical agent (who is still operating in Harlem) was known to me long before I was conscious of the blues-involved Maceos.

Concerning Buddy Bolden's blues you've come close to the mark. I've owned Jelly Roll's recording for many years, but I am also aware that it is a cleaned-up, jelly-rolled version of an older, scatological jingle titled "Funky-butt," which went, "Oh, I thought I heard somebody say/Funky-butt, funky-butt, take him away."

From "An Interview with John O'Brien" (1972)

ELLISON: Vico, whom Joyce used in his great novels, described history as circling. I described it as a boomerang because a boomerang moves in a parabola. It goes and it comes. It is never the same thing. There is implicit in the image the old idea that those who do not learn from history are doomed to repeat its mistakes. History comes back and hits you. But you

really cannot break down a symbol rationally. It allows you to say things that cannot really be said . . . Bledsoe is cynical, but Bledsoe never lied to this guy. And Bledsoe's acceptance was based upon rebellion too. He bawled out the Invisible Man because he had allowed Norton to get a glimpse of the chaos of reality and the tragic nature of life. Bledsoe expected him to be a man who could equivocate because Bledsoe looked upon equivocation as, what we now call [*laughing*], the "credibility gap." Bledsoe lived within and manipulated the credibility gap. But this young man is an idealist. He went through the agony of the "battle royal" because he wanted to go on following an ideal, wanted to become a leader; and this experience is an initiation into the difficulties of a heroic role, especially given his background and place in society. Finally, if there's any lesson for him to learn, it's that he has to make sense of the past before he can move toward the future.—
Conversations with Ralph Ellison, 231.

From "An Interview with Arlene Crewdson and Rita Thomson" (1974)

ELLISON: Oh, I started out by writing a phrase, "I'm an invisible man." I spent the next five years discovering what I meant by it. I did make an outline, a conceptual outline; I knew certain incidents, but as I put it together I discovered that certain things began to happen which seemed to have no direct connection with the concept which lay behind me . . .

CREWDSON: . . . Why did you choose to write the novel as a first-person "I" narration and perhaps limited its view?

ELLISON: Well, for a number of reasons. I felt that I had to test my own abilities, and I wanted to test certain theories of a writer whom I admire very much and that was Henry James, who felt that Dostoevski was not much of a novelist because he wrote in the first person, and novels in the first person tend to be great baggy monsters, and I also admired Ernest Hemingway, and he had written two very wonderful, moving, and,

I think, great novels in the first person, and so had Scott Fitzgerald and so had Melville in *Moby-Dick*. So I wanted to see if I could do that. Now that's one part of it. I also felt that I could achieve certain types of intensity and vividness if I wrote in the first person, and I also wanted to challenge myself to see if I could create a dramatic action while being narrated in the first person and at the same time make that an integral part of the experience because you notice that the man moves from someone who talks all the time (the exact reversal of what has happened to me, I now talk all the time) but he started out as an orator in school, and he really ends up, though he doesn't say so, by writing a book.

THOMSON: I imagine, too, that writing the book in the first person has led so many people to ask if it is autobiographical, and I know in "The Art of Fiction" that you say, no, it is not autobiographical. What do you tell people when they ask about that?

ELLISON: Well, I say that if they will grant me that I'm all the men and all the women and all the children and animals and the black people and the white people, yes, it's all me. But it has very little to do with the factual biography of Ralph Ellison. It does have a lot to do with the shape of his imagination . . .

THOMSON: I wonder too about Trueblood. What significance does he have? Does he tend to sort of be symbolic, too, in the story?

ELLISON: Well, Trueblood involved himself in incest, which is always a tragic action, and the point was, involving himself, he accepted the consequences of his act and tried to act manly about it, but his tragedy became a kind of entertainment for Mr. Norton and an embarrassment for the narrator. I put it up to the reader to take his own choice as to the quality of Trueblood's action, and I am hoping that more and more readers will understand there was a little bit of the hero in this fellow, who was right in the center of the context of irony in which the whole action of that part of the book unfolded.—
Conversations with Ralph Ellison, 260, 263–264, 270–271.

From "An Interview with Ishmael Reed,
Quincy Troupe, and Steve Cannon" (1977)

Sc: . . . I was looking at *Invisible Man* while thinking about a few
things that happened in nineteenth-century American literature, and the whole narrative sequence of events updated to
the turn of the century. It reads very much like a slave narrative, doesn't it? Would you say you've borrowed the techniques?

Re: No, that's coincidental. And frankly, I think too much has
been made of the slave narrative as an influence on contemporary writing. Experience tends to mold itself into certain
repetitive patterns, and one of the reasons we exchange experiences is in order to discover the repetitions and coinci-
dences which amount to a common group experience. We tell
ourselves our individual stories so as to become aware of our
general story. I wouldn't have had to read a single slave narrative
in order to create the narrative pattern of *Invisible Man*. It
emerges from experience and from my own sense of literary
form, out of my sense of experience as shaped by history and
my familiarity with literature. However, one's sense of group
experience comes first because one communicates with the
reader in terms of what he identifies as a viable description of
experience. You project our vision of what *can* happen in terms
of what he accepts as the way things *have happened* in the past,
his sense of "the way things are." Historically, we were trying
to escape from slavery in a scene consisting of geographical
space. First, to the North and then to the West, going to the
Nation (meaning the Indian Nation and later the Oklahoma
Territory), just as Huckleberry Finn decided to do, and as Bessie
Smith states in one of her blues. Of course, some of us escaped
south and joined the Seminoles and fought with them against
the U.S. Geography forms the scene in which we and our
forefathers acted and continue to act out the drama of Afro-
American freedom. This movement from region to region in-

volved all of the motives, political, sociological, and personal, that come to focus in the struggle. So, the movement from the South to the North became a basic pattern for my novel. The pattern of movement and the obstacles encountered are so basic to Afro-American experience (and to my own, since my mother took me north briefly during the twenties, and I came north again in '36), that I had no need of slave narratives to grasp either its significance or its potential for organizing a fictional narrative. I would have used the same device if I had been writing an autobiography.

Then, there is the imagery and the incidents of conflict. These come from all kinds of sources. From literature, from the spirituals and the blues, from other novels, and from poetry, as well as from my observations of socio-psychological conflicts and processes. It comes from mythology, fool's errands, children's games, sermons, the dozens, and the Bible. All this is not to put down the slave narrative, but to say that it did not influence my novel as a conscious functional form. And, don't forget, the main source of any novel is other *novels*; these constitute the culture of the form, and my loyalty to our group does nothing to change that; it's a cultural, literary reality.—*Conversations with Ralph Ellison*, 372–373.

From Letter to Alan Nadel,[6] January 27, 1984

. . . . For you, in a sense, have blown my cover—think of the mixed emotions which Henry James might have felt if someone had solved upon first reading the still elusive mystery of *A Turn of the Screw*! But instead of being displeased with your exposure of my corny pranks and coney tricks I find myself delighted. You point to aspects of my work about which I had to remain silent lest I appear to claim for it subtleties that might exist less in the text than in my mind—Oh, Hermes! Where were you when I needed you?

"Ellison," the critics would have said, "you talk a good game, but you sure haven't written one!" And I would have had no answer. Henry James, fine critic and theorist that he was, knew when to talk and when to play it mum, when to wear the critic's top hat, and when to don the turban which marked him as a thirty-second-degree magician. His trick (and challenge) was to keep his dual roles dissociated; thus where his own work was concerned he spoke to enhance the technical magic of his craft while being careful not to invade his fellow critics' territory. And a good thing too, considering what he did to Hawthorne!

But for hundreds of years writers and critics have been engaged in a game of hare and hounds, and until recently both have observed certain unwritten rules of the game. Hence with no Bloom-Hartman & Company waiting to defenestrate me I felt fairly secure in my amusement over critics who had no nose for the sources and objects of my manipulations. Sometimes it was as though I'd written an invisible text. Or as though they assumed that my work couldn't possibly have any connection whatsoever with what others had written. And it wasn't that I hadn't cued them with Captain Delano and Eliot's Harry and laid down a trail of other signs and clues:

> THROW ME INTO THE BRIER PATCH!
> THIS HEAHS A BLACK GUINEA BANK!
> HEY! TOD CLIF' IS ONA CLIFF
> HE'S FATED TO FALL!

But I refer mainly to my many debts to Joyce and Melville, Mark Twain and Eliot—not to mention the violence I've done them. But also ignored was my preoccupation with what I consider the distortions and omissions which characterize much of what passes for American history, literary criticism, and sociology. Talk about voodoo economics! Hell, the present gurus of the GNP learned it from historians!

Seriously though, I am especially grateful for your analysis of the "Golden Day" section of my novel. For some thirty years I'd waited for somebody to remark the extent to which Mumford's work was being attacked and argued with. For as you point out in fine detail *The Golden Day* is indeed the countertext (a term that had little meaning for me at the time I was writing) to all that wildness that erupts in mine, and I feared that I was being so embarrassingly obvious that Mumford's supporters would be after me cheek and thigh. But much to my chagrin I was wrong. Thus as far as I am aware you're the first critic to point out the outrageous extent that I was out to dynamite the illustrious gent's conception of American history and culture . . .

And yet it wasn't that I didn't admire Mumford. I have owned a copy of the sixth Liveright printing of *The Golden Day* since 1937 and own, and have learned from, most of his books. I was simply upset by his implying that the war which freed my grandparents from slavery was of no real consequence to the broader issues of American society and its culture. What else, other than sheer demonic, masochistic hell-raising, was that bloody war all about if not slavery and the contentions which flowed therefrom?

As a self-instructed student I was quite willing for Mumford to play Aeschylus, Jeremiah, or even God, but not at the price of his converting the most tragic incident in American history into bombastic farce. For in doing so he denied my people the sacrificial role which they had played in the drama. I can't thank you enough for pointing to my little attempt at undermining such "accepted" ways of "deconstructing" our common historical experience.

I must confess, however, that at the time of writing I was by no means prepared to go after Ralph Waldo Emerson in the manner that I went after Mumford. After all, I do have my pieties, and sharing his first names was inhibiting in more ways than one. Ralph-the-Exhorter was my father's favorite author—perhaps because being from post-Reconstruction South Carolina my dad found solace in Emerson's encouragement of self-reliance. So rather than going after Emerson's oracular stance, I went after some of the bombast that had been made of his pronouncements. This you make quite clear but I'd suggest, if I may, that it might help if you pointed up the distinction you make between my trustee "Emerson" and ole Waldo, who strikes me, incidentally, as being as difficult to pin down as the narrator's grandfather.

At any rate it might amuse you to hear that on one of my

book shelves there are two small bronze medallions and a small wooden plaque. The medallions are inscribed with images of Emerson and Lincoln, respectively, and the plaque with an image of Janus. Janus sits between Emerson and Lincoln so that he can give them his divided yet unified attention. They appear to be communing, but although I've tried for years to grasp the drift of their deliberations thus far I've been unsuccessful. So for consolation I have a small photograph of Mark Twain, who hangs above my typewriter smoking a cigar and dressed in the academic regalia which he donned to accept his degree from Oxford. Being a word-man of southern background, he encourages me sometimes by singing a spiritual, or by recounting a Negro folktale. And once when interrupted by a yell of "Make it new!" from Ezra Pound across the room, Mark yelled back, "Hell, if you get some of this stuff in it it can't help but be new! Didn't you hear Tom Eliot say that he speaks with a nigger accent?" Well, dammit, to anyone who knows how to listen, he does!

From Letter to Cheryl Muldrow, April 10, 1985

And yes, you failed to encounter a name for the narrator because it is his intent to keep his identity secret; perhaps in hope that the reader will use his or her own experience in bringing the action alive. But I refused to give him a name out of respect for his desire for privacy, and out of my writer's need to project his story as an account of "Everyman." Thus the title of the novel is *Invisible Man* rather than "The" *Invisible Man.*

From Letter to John Callahan,[7] May 12, 1985

... You write that my Iowa statement[8] led you to examine TMWLU [Richard Wright's 1944 novella, "The Man Who Lived Underground"] "both as an ancestor and a relative of IM (because) although their fates diverge. . . . Fred Daniels and . . . IM share a common passion to speak to people about the kinship between the official world and the unacknowledged underground reality of both self and society." And you go on to speculate that "Surely, Ellison acknowledged and built upon Wright's parable of the unshrewd, oblivious, fatally undouble-conscious voice of Fred Daniels." And it is here that I must disagree, not only because this is all too deterministic, but because by focusing on my relationship with Wright you overlook the debt which both Wright and I owe to other novelists and forms of fiction. What's more, it's like assuming that because a goose and a swan happen to occupy the same barnyard, swim in the same pond, and are friends it guarantees that the goose will follow the swan's example and instead of laying eggs that produce goslings it will bring forth cygnets. But while there's no question that both goose and swan will lay eggs (!) their respective offspring will be determined not by their proximity but by their genetics. A bee pollinates great varieties of plants (here let Dostoevski be the bee) but each will produce its own flowers and fruit in kind. True, a critic might decide to slip a swan's egg under the goose's butt, but while this might stir up arguments as to whether the hatchling which comes forth is a goose, a swan, Daffy Duck in drag, or some kind of Frank Perdue fuckup that has too little black meat or too much white to be a proper "oven-stuffer" the egg will produce a cygnet that was signed and sealed—if not incubated—by swans. But all joking aside, I know, John, that you're not that kind of critic, therefore I suggest in all seriousness that you take a fresh look at *Notes*.

If you do and then look at the prologue to IM you'll see that the opening rhythm (or riff) alludes to *Notes*:

> "I am a sick man . . . I am a spiteful man. No, I am not a pleasant man at all. I believe there is something wrong with my liver. . . ."—*Notes from Underground*

> "I am an invisible man. No, I am not a spook like those who haunted Edgar Allan Poe; nor am I one of your Hollywood-movie ectoplasms. . . ."—*Invisible Man*

And what the hell is *Poe* doing here? Forget it! But if you'll list the characteristics shared by my narrator and the "author" of *Notes* you'll see that both are talkers who employ irony and that both address the reader as *writers*. You'll also note that just as Fred Daniels is far from effective as a speaker, he has absolutely *no* identity as a writer. It wasn't at all necessary that he be so lacking in eloquence—the vernacular is rich with such possibilities—but instead of allowing him an eloquence fitting of his background Wright looped a rope around his neck and tried to animate him in the manner that Tod Clifton animated his dancing dolls. Had Daniels been a swan or a goose the poor guy would have been incapable either of dive or flight, no matter the ability and passion of his creator. Thus he'd have done no better against predators of sky and water than he does against the cops.

"Visible Man" by David Remnick[9]
(*New Yorker*, March 14, 1994)

. . . . Letting go of the book[10] is difficult, because I'm so uncertain. I want it to be of quality. With *Invisible Man*, I wasn't all that certain, but I had friends like Stanley Edgar Hyman, who worked on the *New Yorker*, and who was invaluable to me. There's a photograph of Stanley reading *Invisible Man* in Francis Steegmuller's office. I'll always remember: he looked up at me and said, "Say, this thing is funny!" When you are younger, you are so eager to be published, I am eager to publish this book. That's why I stay here, and not in the country. I'm eager to finish it and see how it turns out.—*Conversations with Ralph Ellison*, 395.

Editor's Notes

1. Marcus Garvey, Negro nationalist and founder of a Back to Africa Movement in the United States during the early 1900s.
2. Stanley Edgar Hyman was a critic and scholar whom Ellison de-

scribed as his "friend and intellectual sparring partner." "Change the Joke and Slip the Yoke" began as a letter Ellison wrote to Hyman in response to his comments about *Invisible Man*. A subsequent version became Ellison's part of "The Negro Writer in America: An Exchange," which originally appeared in Partisan Review, Spring 1958.

3. Ellison playfully signifies on Ulysses and Polyphemus in *Juneteenth*, 324.

4. There is one reference to Rinehart as Bliss in *Invisible Man*; mistaking him for her lover, Rinehart, a young woman murmurs, "Bliss daddy." Significantly, about the time Ellison responded to Hyman in 1957 from Rome he was creating the protean character Bliss in his novel in progress, this time a "little boy of indefinite race," who, though he talks and acts black, leaves the church folk who raised him, and, passing for white, eventually becomes Adam Sunraider, a race-baiting U.S. senator from a New England state.

5. The words in quotation marks are Irving Howe's in "Black Boys and Native Sons," an essay which led to a rejoinder by Ellison, to which Howe responded, and Ellison in turn replied. Ellison's contributions to the lengthy exchange became his famous essay "The World and the Jug."

6. Alan Nadel is the author of *Invisible Criticism*, a study which explores Ellison's allusions to (and signifying on) modern literature, especially nineteenth- and twentieth-century American literature.

7. The letter is Ellison's response to an early draft of a chapter of *In the African-American Grain* in which the editor of the present casebook argued that "The Man Who Lived Underground" was an important catalyst for *Invisible Man*.

8. "Remembering Richard Wright," an address given at the University of Iowa on July 18, 1971, published in *Going to the Territory* (1986) and *The Collected Essays of Ralph Ellison* (1995).

9. Remnick's article is largely based on an interview with Ellison two weeks before the writer's eightieth birthday in 1994.

10. Ellison's unfinished second novel.

Part II

◆　◆　◆

CRITICAL ESSAYS ON
INVISIBLE MAN

Ralph Ellison's Trueblooded *Bildungsroman*

KENNETH BURKE

◆ ◆ ◆

Dear Ralph:

The several pages I wrote you by way of first draft have vanished. One usually feels either desolate or furious about such a slip, depending upon one's inclination to think of the notes as either lost or pilfered. But in this case I am neither. For I had already decided on a new start, and my first effort hadn't seemed quite right, anyhow.

I had taken off from comments in my *Rhetoric of Motives* (1950) with reference to "the Negro intellectual, Ralph Ellison," who said that Booker T. Washington "described the Negro community as a basket of crabs, wherein should one attempt to climb out, the others immediately pull him back." I sized up the black man's quandary thus: "Striving for freedom as a human being generically, he must do so as a Negro specifically. But to do so as a Negro is, by the same token, to prevent oneself from doing so in the generic sense; for a Negro could not be free generically except in a situation where the color of the skin had no more social meaning than the color of the eyes."

I moved on from there to a related "racist" problem, sans the accident of pigment, as dramatized in the role of Shakespeare's Shylock; and then on to promises of being purely and simply a person (and visibly so) "thereby attaining the kind of transcendence at which all men aim, and at which the Negro spiritual had aimed, though there the aim was at the spiritual transcending of a predestined material slavery, whereas the Marxist ultimates allow for a material transcending of inferior status."

My job in that book was to feature the persuasiveness of such designs, be they true or false; and I went on accordingly, with variations on the theme of the special cultural (sociopolitical) problems that the inheritance from slavery imposed upon the Negro "intellectual" who would carve a "supply side" career under conditions of "freedom and equality," as ambiguously developed since the explicit constitutional proclaiming of emancipation, a few years after the czar had abolished serfdom in Russia. (It sometimes seems as though the inheritance from serfdom has also left its ambiguities.)

Those paragraphs I wrote in connection with your literary situation then were done, of course, when I had not the slightest idea of what you were to unfold in your (literally) "epoch-making" novel[1] ("epoch-making" in the strict sense, as a work that, by its range of stories and corresponding attitudes, sums up an era). I had heard you read a portion of the early section on the battle royal, and had vaguely sensed the introductory nature of your narrator's fumbling acquiescence to the indignities implied in the encounter. But the actuality of your inventions was wholly beyond any but your imagining.

Recently, on rereading the book, I began to see it differently. As I see it now, "retrospectively," and in the light of your own development since it was first published, despite its (we might say "resonant") involvement with the cultural problems of the Negro in the United States, its "fixation" on that theme, I would propose to class it primarily as an example of what the Germans would call a *Bildungsroman*.

I guess the greatest prototype of such fiction is Goethe's *Wilhelm Meister*, which details the character's progressive education from "apprenticeship" through "journeymanship" toward the ideal of "mastery" that shows up in his name. Also, its brand of fact and fiction shows up in its fluctuations, like yours, between "realistic detail and poetic allegory" (I quote verbatim from the resources most available to me now, namely, my copy of the *Encyclopedia Brittanica*, eleventh edition). Yes, you have written the story of your Education. And the details of your life since then, with that most charming helpmeet-helpmate of yours in attitudinal collaboration, testify clearly enough to your kind of mastery, in these mussy times when who knows where to turn next?

With regard to your book and its ingenious ways of dealing with the black-white issue, my notes didn't seem to be getting anywhere. Then I gradually came to realize: Your narrator doesn't "solve" that problem. For it's not quite the issue as implicitly presented in that opening "traumatic" incident out of which your plot develops. The whites were superciliously condescending to reward your "apprentice" for being able to be educated (and never forget that the literal, but obsolete meaning of "docile" is "teachable"). And they were right. According to the book itself, your boy was teachable. It tells step by step how he got taught, in the most astute of realistic terms, plus the sometimes even fun-loving twists of what the encyclopedia article would call "poetical allegory."

At least half a century has passed since I read Goethe's novel which, by its subtitles, likens the acquiring of an education in the art of living to the stages of development among the members of such craftsmanship as was exemplified in the kinds of sodality operant among the masons that build the cathedrals (as per the etymological interchangeability of "edifice" and "edification"). So my memory of Goethe's book is much on the fuzzy side—and I don't have the time or opportunity now to hurry back and verify my notions. In any case, even if my recollections happen to be a bit wrong, my observations will serve accurately for present purposes with regard to your, in its way, superb enterprise, if it is viewed as such a story. Viewed thus, your book shows us, page by page, the author in the very act of using as "spokesman" a fictive narrator and putting him through the transformations needed to present the entire inventory of the "ambiguities" the author had to confront in the process of growing up when that author was your comprehensive kind of black man.

First, we should note, the character's step from apprenticeship to journeymanship is as clear as could be. His apprenticeship (his emergence out of childhood) concerns the stage of life when a black man at that time in our history was confronting strong remembrances from the days of the plantation from which "your kind of humans" had not long ago by constitutional amendment been "emancipated." And your narrator's "grandfather" (who remembered being a slave) introduces the whole unfolding, with admonitions that will figure to the end. As your spokesman-narrator puts it: "The mind that has conceived a plan of living must never lose sight of the chaos against which that pattern was conceived" (*IM*, 438). He says this when he's about to "emerge" from his "hibernation." And his author's book did help its author to do precisely that, superbly.

Obviously, the step from apprenticeship to journeymanship takes place when your narrator comes north. Goethe's word for that stage in one's career is *Wanderjahre*, from the root of which we get our word "wander" in the sense of "travel," the second half of the word meaning "years." Your story takes an ironically "perfect" twist here. At the end of the first chapter your narrator tells of a dream involving his grandfather (who figures the very essence of the book's subsequent motivational quandaries):

> He told me to open my brief case and read what was inside and I did, finding an official envelope stamped with the state seal; and inside the envelope I found another and another, endlessly, and I thought I would fall of weariness. "Them's years," he said. "Now open that one." And I did and in it I found an engraved document containing a short message in letters of gold. "Read it," my grandfather said, "Out loud!"
>
> "To Whom It May Concern," I intoned. "Keep This Nigger-Boy Running."
>
> I awoke with the old man's laughter ringing in my ears. (*IM*, 26)

Any time the book gets to terms like that for the withinness-of-withinness-of-withinness, and they are words by a black man's grandfather from out of the days of slavery, and it's a dream with all the prophetic quality of such, it's at the very heart of motivation. And what a "grandfather clause" that was!

Whoever knows your story will realize how well the incident foretells the end of chapter 9 introducing the critical step from apprenticeship in the South to his journeymanship in the North, when your spokesman finds that the supposed letters of recommendation he had brought with him were of the "Bellerophontic" sort. Bulfinch tells us that "the expression 'Bellerophontic letters' arose to describe any species of communication which a person is made the bearer of, containing matter prejudicial to himself'; and your Invisible Man sizes up the letters as designed to give him the runaround, as though they were phrased exactly, "Please hope him to death, and keep him running" (*IM*, 147).

In any case, chapter 10 begins the turn from southern apprenticeship to northern journeymanship in a big way, we might even say allegorically. For in going to apply for his first job after being dismissed from a southern college (and via fantastic twists indeed!), when going to the plant in Long Island, he "crossed a bridge in the fog to get there and came down in a stream of workers" (*IM*, 149). Morbidities of the black-white issue had all been of a quite realistic presentation. But here the whole next phase was to be in terms of "a huge electric sign" proposing to KEEP AMERICA PURE WITH LIBERAL PAINTS that were pure white! Forty pages later, he says:

> I found the bridge by which I had come, but the stairs leading back to the car that crossed the top were too dizzily steep to climb, swim or fly, and I found a subway instead. . . .
>
> We, he, him—my mind and I—were no longer getting around in the same circles. Nor my body either. Across the aisle a young platinum blonde nibbled at a red Delicious apple as station lights rippled past her. The train plunged. I dropped through the roar, giddy and vacuum-minded, sucked under and out in late afternoon Harlem. (*IM*, 189–90)

Those chapters (10, 11, and 12) vigorously trace a series of such transformations as epitomize, within the conditions of the fiction, a "myth-and-ritual" of "being born again." (Incidentally, that new start comes close to the center of the book.) They are simultaneously one author's personal way of intuiting such a psychic process while doing so in ways such that, despite their localization in terms of this particular fiction, are addressed to a *general* responsiveness on the part of readers. There is a sense in which the whole book is a continual process of transformation. But here occurs the initiation of the narrator's turn from apprentice to journeyman. Henceforth his ways of being "teachable" will be correspondingly modified. Yet as I interpret the story in its entirety, despite the ideological sharpness of the black-white issue, there was not to be a resolution of a total Saul/Paul sort. Here is the tangle, when the salient details are brought together, and viewed in imagery that reflects the actions, passions, and attitudes of the narrator.

After he learns that the president of the college had given him those supposed letters of recommendation which were nothing of the sort, he starts the next phase by getting a job in a factory that was hiring black workers (suspected by the white workers as being finks) to produce white paint, with the slogan "If It's Optic White, It's the Right White." He works in a cellar that has boilers, with gauges controlled by valves. Everything comes to a focus when he gets into a furious fight with his black boss while telling himself, *"you were trained"* to accept what the whites did, however foolish, angry, spiteful, drunk with power, and so on (*IM*, 171). At the height of his rage he insults the elderly man with rebukes that his grandfather taught him. The machine blows up because the quarreling had caused him to neglect the gauges. Suddenly the situation becomes clear. The boss shouts for him to turn the valve. "Which?" he yelled. Answer: "The white one, fool, the white one!" Too late. He tries to escape. Then he "seemed to run swiftly up an incline and shot forward with sudden acceleration into a wet blast of black emptiness that was somehow a bath of whiteness" (*IM*, 173–74). The gradual regaining of consciousness in a hospital after the explosion is marked by various distinguish-

ings and confusings of white and black. And in the midst of trying
to define his identity (I would make much of this sentence) he
says, "But we are all human, I thought, wondering what I meant"
(*IM*, 182). Two pages later we read:

> I felt a tug at my belly and looked down to see one of the
> physicians pull the cord which was attached to the stomach
> node, jerking me forward.
> "What is this?" I said.
> "Get the shears," he said.
> "Sure," the other said. "Let's not waste time."
> I recoiled inwardly as though the cord were part of me.
> (*IM*, 184)

Obviously, as part of a rebirth ritual, this detail figures the
severing of the umbilical cord. With that expression "part of" in
mind, turn to this passage in the epilogue, five pages from the
end of the book:

> "Agree 'em to death and destruction," grandfather had ad-
> vised. Hell, weren't they their own death and their own de-
> struction except as the principle ["the principle on which the
> country was built and not the men"] lived in them and in us?
> And here's the cream of the joke: Weren't we *part of them* as
> well as apart from them and subject to die when they died?
> (*IM*, 433–34)

And in this connection recall that the Saul/Paul reversal, as a
paradigm of rebirth, was referred to by the grandfather thus:

> When you're a youngun, you Saul, but let life whup your
> head a bit and you starts to trying to be Paul—though you
> still Sauls around on the side. (*IM*, 288)

All told, I take it that the motivational design of the book is
in its essence thus: Though "ideological" prejudices (and I would
call the black-white issue a branch of such) make humans be

"apart from" one another, we are all, for better or worse, "part
of" one humankind—and, at least on paper, an amended U.S.
Constitution holds out that same promise to us all.

I want to discuss an episode in your book which bears upon
the complications implicit in all that follows. It involves the generically human (as distinguished from the ideologically divisive).
For it's the story of Jim Trueblood's incest. Obviously in itself the
"critical occasion" about which the anecdote is built is by sheer
definition wholly black-white. But the book's ways of adapting it
to your narrator's circumstantially goaded development toward
graduation as a "master" can deflect attention from what I consider a major aspect of its "rightness" as a motive.

Incest is a familial motive, involving problems of identity that
are variously confronted as the individual, under the incentives
of sexual maturation, develops from infantile narcissism (the primary "autistic" stage) to a kind of divisiveness that comes to
fruition in the taboos ("incest awe") that are featured in psycho-
analysis. The whole range of perversions, neuroses, sublimations
could be classed under the one head of responses to the need of
modifying the sense of identity out of which human infants variously "emerge." Sibling incest was even institutionalized in the
legal fictions of ancient Egyptian rule, as the pharaoh was expected to cohabit with his sister, both of the offspring being "part
of" the same dynastic identity. Incest taboos, viewed from the
standpoint of family identity, are seen to reflect a breach that
implicitly transforms what was "a part of" into the "apart from."
Trueblood (perfect name) symbolizes the all-blackness of the
identity that either the narrator or his author in childhood
started from by way of experiences with the sense of family identity—and the pattern gets fittingly ("perfectly") rounded out by
his role as a singer of the all-black Negro spirituals (even when
performance before whites introduces the black-white ideology as
a motivational dimension having to do with the overall plot, a
dimension also lithely exploited by references to the special attention he gets from white sociological-anthropological research-
ers, whose interviews with him give them data for their studies).

And all told, here is the place to sum up what I think can be gained if, when considering your book's way of carving out a career, we discuss it not just in itself, but by comparison and contrast with the Goethean pattern. Both were dealing with periods of pronounced social mobility, in Germany the kind of transitions that would come to a crisis in the French Revolution, in the United States in the aftermath of a war designed to decide whether all the states would remain part of the same Union or whether some would form a Confederacy apart from the uneasy national identity that had been bequeathed us by *our* revolution.

There was the critical difference between Wilhelm Meister as white and your narrator as black. Whereas Goethe's father was quite well-to-do, you began with the vexations that were vestiges of life as experienced by slaves on the southern plantations. The second stage of Wilhelm's apprenticeship (the first had been a kind of Bohemianism, among people of the theater) centered in friendly relations to the landed gentry. And the theme of his *Wanderjahre* is "resignation," an attitude that is denied you so long as so many blacks are still so underprivileged. And though your book's championship is dignified by the fact that it fights not just the author's battle but the battle of your "people," its ways of doing so are not the ways of other doughty "spokesmen" for your cause, whose poetical or rhetorical methods vow them to different rules (some so different that anything a white man might say in your favor might be cited as, on its face, a charge against you).

Not long before you entered the world's unending dialogue, our amended Constitution had promised blacks and whites equal opportunities so far as color is concerned. You have clearly stated your ironic stand on that matter. You are thoroughly aware of how flagrantly it was flouted, even by condescension on the part of white philanthropists for whom your narrator presents Bledsoe as designing the "teachable-docile" kind of education he takes them to be paying for. In his *Critique of Practical Reason*, Kant says that, although we cannot scientifically prove the grounds of a belief in God, freedom, and immortality, we should harbor such beliefs and frame our conduct on such a basis. You did a Kantian "as if" by acting as if the constitutional promise has the markings of reality—and within feasible limits, it worked! And I think it worked in part because, within the ideological conflict forced upon you by the conditions local to the vestiges of black slavery in that stage of our history, there was also the more general sense of "growing up" in general. I interpret that kind of motivation as implicit in the Trueblood episode, which is formally there as a necessary stage—a process of maturing, a transition from the simplicity of a black identity in a black child's "pre-ideological" view of familial relationships.

But I should do a bit more about my ironic "matching" of Wilhelm Meister's all-white involvements and your narrator's black-white tension. A character with a name having the overtones of "Will-Helm-(Helmit)-Master" starts out under good auspices of which your narrator has no share. Also it turns out that, unbeknown to him, he had been being watched by some fellows of goodwill whose benign spying ended in his welcoming them to their sodality (a slant quite different from the conspiratorial Brotherhood that marked your protagonist's mode of socialization). Some years back, Goethe had gotten a resounding start by a contribution to the *storm-and-stress* wave of that time. Troubled by a love affair that drove him to the edge of suicide, he "creatively" solved his problem by writing *The Sorrows of Young Werther*, the story of a similarly unhappy lover who does commit suicide—and it was a success enough to launch him, to cause a rash of suicides, and to set a pattern . . . for such writers as Kleist to be self-victimized by. The first syllable of the name is English "worth." So it would seem to be indicated that the victim chosen to be Goethe's surrogate was, prima facie, admirably endowed.

And as for Goethe's Faust, the adjective *faustus* in Latin, from the root *fav*, from which we get "favorable," has such predestinating meanings as "bringing good luck or good fortune, fortunate, lucky, auspicious." Faustulus was the mythic herdsman who saved and brought up Romulus and Remus, whose brotherhood became a fratricide, with Romulus surviving to become the eponymous founder of Rome. In its purely Germanic line, *Faust* means "fist," "hand," an implicit pun of which I was always conscious.

I don't know whether readers whose native language-consciousness is *echt deutsch* ever hear such connotations in the term. And I tend to suspect that I am much more responsive to such accidental connotations in English than the average user and abuser of our idiom is (this side of Joyce, of course!). But here's how it turned out. The author's hand wrote of how Faust sealed a contract with the devil, selling his soul to eternal damnation in hell. Thanks to this deal, Faust was able to seduce a naive girl who loved him almost reverently and would have married him without the slightest hesitation; he killed her brother; his impregnating of her led her to kill her child in madness; but innocence incarnate, she was all set for heaven. Then the same hand wrote a sequel—and in *Faust II* things got to so turn out that the benignly predestinating connotations of the Latin adjective and the happy side of the diminutive noun for the mythic herdsman ultimately prevailed. The Faust story traditionally ends in Faust's damnation. Recall Christopher Marlowe's play, for instance, with Faust on his way to eternal hell as the clock strikes twelve. But Goethe's Faust, against all tradition, ends up among the saved. You put your boy through the mill and brought him out the other side, but you couldn't contrive a transformation like that. But Meister-Master didn't either; for neither he nor your protagonist began from a contract with the Devil.

And Goethe's initiate had a "Nordic" nostalgia for the South with which your man's going north could not be quite in tune. Mignon's *Heimweh* song, the very thought of which makes me want to cry (knowest thou the land where bloom the lemon trees? *Kennst du das Land wo die Citronen blühen?*) is an example of your perceptive notions about the psychology of geography. Yet by the same token you and your narrator began their apprenticeship under unforgettably traumatic conditions. (Dr. Bledsoe, the black head of the black college, called your man a "Nigger.")

Incidentally, the nostalgic theme of Mignon's song is there, though with appropriately quite different appurtenances. I refer to your narrator's avowals that gravitate about the lines: "I'd like to hear five recordings of Louis Armstrong playing and singing 'What Did I Do to Be so Black and Blue'—all at the same time" (*IM*, 6).

But I have a hunch of this sort: I think of your Mary Rambo in the spirit of the article on her by Melvin Dixon in the *Carleton Miscellany*. He would "suggest that Mary Rambo, more than any other character, is the pivotal guide in the hero's effort to discover and to articulate the form of his identity and experience. He learns that this form is housed in a vernacular consciousness, not in the alien ideology of the Brotherhood or of industrial capitalism, or in racial absorption." I have not seen the text in which you wrote of her elsewhere. But I should agree with Dixon's observation, remembering my Goethe "workmanship" analogy (which, in the *Faust* plays, becomes striving, *Streben*): "Rambo's full character as depicted in this episode encapsulates the major drama of self-realization at the heart of *Invisible Man*." (R. W. B. Lewis's article in the *Carleton Miscellany* refers to this overall development as "the myth of initiation.")[2]

She is in principle what I think you might be willing to call a "vernacular" Virgin Mary, in her wholly feminine role as nurse and mother. Like a mother, she doesn't ask for pay. She nurses the newborn journeyman. And her "fromness" from the South is just naturally part of her. And here comes the final twist. Our hero says:

There are many things about people like Mary that I dislike. For one thing, they seldom know where their personalities end and yours begins; they usually think in terms of "we" while I have always tended to think in terms of "me"—and that has caused some friction, even with my own family. Brother Jack and the others talked in terms of "we," but it was a different, bigger "we." [Maybe that's why conspiratorial brother Hambro has a name that sounds so much like hers.]

Well, I had a new name and new problems. I had best leave the old behind. Perhaps it would be best not to see Mary at all, just place the money in an envelope and leave it on the kitchen table where she'd be sure to find it. (*IM*, 240)

Yes, he was ready for the Next Phase. So he had outgrown his new adolescence and had to hurry on, in effect, growing up and

"leaving home." Dixon quotes you as saying, "Mary Rambo de-
served more space in the novel and would, I think, have made
it a better book." Yet there's something to be gained by her role
being left less pointedly so.

There's only one thing left for this time. It has to do with my
salute to your book as "epoch-making." It is remarkable how
much your book brings together, in its two methods of book-
keeping, accounting both what it is to be growing up and what
it is to be a black man growing up in one particular stage of U.S.
history. At the end of your epilogue we read:

> In going underground, I whipped it all except the mind,
> the *mind*. And the mind that has conceived a plan of living
> must never lose sight of the chaos against which that pattern
> was conceived. That goes for societies as well as for individuals.
> (*IM*, 438)

And it goes for an epoch-making book, too. There was the
chaos of its unfinishedness while you hung on during the writing
with what Augustine would call your *donum perseverandi*, your gift
of persevering. Then, when your book constitutes the culmination of all those entanglements, the chaos out of which it
emerged is there the other way around, in the memory. The
epoch-making function of the book's emerging "mind" ends for
the reader as a retrospective "mind." And I take the frame of
your prologue and epilogue to be, in effect, saying so.

But an epoch-making book rules out a sequel. As I see it,
technology got developed to a stage when the South could be
developed by the importation of Negroes for slave labor on plantations in the South. At the same time in other parts of the
country conflicting ways of using technological resources led to
the abolition of slavery. That led to political conditions such that
the ways of distributing the profits made by the use of technological resources brought about the epoch in which, through
which, and out of which the descendants of black slaves in this
country experienced such cultural developments as you have so
comprehensively summed up.

But technology has moved on. "What *is* the next phase?" your man says in his epilogue (*IM*, 435). Technology transcends race, not in the sense that it solves the problem of racial discrimination, but in the sense that technology itself *is* the problem. In that connection my compulsory (and damnably boring) *idée fixe* is along these lines: In various ways people incline to keep asking, "What is the meaning of life? What is its purpose? And is there some attitude that offers us an overall purpose?"

There is one that makes wholly rational sense. It has been given to us by the fact that the human animal's great prowess with the resources of symbolic action has carried us so extensively far in the astoundingly ingenious inventions of technology. Now, owing to technology's side effects (not only in the hellish possibilities it now contributes to the disastrousness of war but also to the kinds of pollution and desiccation that result from its gruesomely efficient resourcefulness in the expansion of purely peaceful enterprises) the whole of humankind has now one questionable purpose. We are all part of the same threat to our destiny. So all must join together in seeking for ways and means (with correspondingly global attitudes) of undoing the damage being done by the human animal's failure to control the powers developed by that same organism's own genius. With the current terrific flowering of technology the problem of self-control takes on a possibly fatal, and certainly ironic,. dimension. We must all conspire together, in a truly universal siblinghood, to help us all help one another to get enough control over our invented technological servants to keep them from controlling us. Until we solve that problem (and the destructive powers of technology are so damnably efficient, we had better hurry!) our kind of verbalizing bodies has purpose aplenty.

Insofar as that cultural emphasis comes to take over, if it does, to that extent you will be surviving the immediacy of your epoch-making book in its sheerly "ideological" dimension. But in the universality of its poetic dimension, it will go on being what it is, namely, the symbolic constituting of an epoch, human every step of the way.

Time's about up. But I'd like to add some odds and ends in

parting. Richard Lewis's recollections in the *Carleton Miscellany* document the existence of a friendly nonracial "we" of which your "me" was a part, in Bennington days when Stanley Hyman and Shirley Jackson were being very lively there. The demands local to your story ruled out that biographical strand in which not only did *we* back you, but you could and did get us to look for traces of unconscious Nortonism in our thinking (plus our not shelling out funds to a black institution in commemoration of a saintly dead daughter).

The difference between an epoch-making book and the day's news is this: The news ceases to be news, but the book goes on reconstituting its epoch. Whereas at the time of the writing it grew out of its background, in being read now it both reconstructs its time and takes on a universal poignancy.

Best luck, to you and Fanny both,
K. B. [Kenneth Burke]

Notes

This essay began as a short letter from Mr. Burke to Mr. Ellison and has been expanded for the present volume.—Ed.

1. Ralph Ellison, *Invisible Man* (New York: Random House, 1952), 26. Subsequent references are cited in text as *IM*.

2. The references cited in this paragraph are to Melvin Dixon's "O, Mary Rambo, Don't You Weep" and R. W. B. Lewis's "The Ceremonial Imagination of Ralph Ellison," which appeared in the Winter 1980 issue of *Carleton Miscellany*.

Ellison's Zoot Suit

LARRY NEAL

◆　◆　◆

W ELL, THERE IS ONE THING that you have to admit. And that is, dealing with Ralph Ellison is no easy matter. It is no easy task to fully characterize the nature of Ellison's life and work. He cannot be put into any one bag and conveniently dispensed with. Any attempt to do so merely leads to aesthetic and ideological oversimplifications. On the surface, over-simplifications may appear pragmatic and viable but, in the long run, they weaken us. To overlook the complex dimensions of a man's ideas, character, and personality is to do great disservice to the righteous dissemination of knowledge.

Much of the criticism directed against Ellison is personal, over-simplified, and often not based on an analysis of the man's work and ideas. A great deal of the criticism emanates from ideological sources that most of us today reject.

To be concise, much of the anti-Ellison criticism springs from a specific body of Marxist and black neo-Marxist thought. The literary term used to designate this body of thought is called "social realism." Some of Ellison's most virulent critics have been social realists.

One of the most famous of social realists' attacks was the subject of a literary exchange between Ellison and Irving Howe, a liberal left-winger and former editor of *Dissent* magazine. In an essay published in the fall 1963 issue of *Dissent*, Howe accused James Baldwin and Ralph Ellison of abandoning the task of the Negro writer. That task Howe proposed to be the militant assertion of Negro freedom. In his assault upon Baldwin and Ellison, Howe evoked Richard Wright as the embodiment of the truest, most relevant exponent of black freedom in fiction. Howe, the knowing white boy, praised Wright for his penchant toward what is termed "protest" literature and castigated both Ellison and Baldwin for their failure to carry on the "protest" tradition as exemplified by Wright's *Native Son*.

Ellison wrote an excellent rebuttal to Howe's piece, titled "The World and the Jug."[1] Ellison attacked Howe's attempt to rigidly circumscribe the role of the black writer. He asserted the essential differences in outlook between himself and Richard Wright. Where Wright, in *Black Boy*, saw black life "void of hope" and bare of tradition, Ellison countered with a very positive vision of Afro-American life. For Ellison, black people did not exhibit a tradition void of hopes, memories, and personal attachments. They were, instead, profoundly human and blessed with a strong, spiritually sustaining culture. "The World and the Jug" is a finely balanced essay, mean, but eloquently controlled.

Underlying this exchange between Ellison and Howe is the recurring question of the writer's role, especially in the context of the struggle for human liberation. Marxism puts forth the idea that all literature is propaganda, or becomes propaganda when it enters the social sphere. And, as propaganda, it is implicitly a reflection of class attitudes. The role of the revolutionary writer in the Marxist context is, therefore, to extol the virtues of the proletariat, to sharpen its class consciousness in order that it may overthrow the ruling classes and finally take control of the "means of production."

Richard Wright was especially influenced by the Marxist ideas he encountered in the thirties. As a young writer he had joined the John Reed Club in Chicago and was very active in Communist cultural activities. Coming from Mississippi, where he had seen and experienced racial oppression, he sincerely believed that it was his duty to use his writing as a weapon against that oppression. All of his writing, up to and including his masterwork, *Native Son*, is informed by his belief in social revolution. Following Lenin's idea that the revolutionary vanguard must expose the corruption in the capitalist system, all of Wright's fictional landscapes, with the exception of *The Long Dream*, tend to be very bleak and humorless. Excellent social realist that he was, he was skillful at depicting in exact detail the impact of the material world on both the oppressed and the oppressors alike. Now Wright has gone the way of the ancestors, but he is still a major influence in contemporary black writing. At least we are still feeling the influence of a certain kind of "protest" writing that appears highly reminiscent of Wright, even though most of it does not begin to approach Wright's high level of artistic achievement.

What Ralph Ellison was doing in his exchange with Irving Howe was defending his right to his (Ellison's) own personal vision, while trying not to fall into the bag of depreciating Wright: "Must I be condemned because my sense of Negro Life was quite different?" (*S&A*, 119). Ellison asks this question, fully aware that there is an ideological contingent lying in wait to pounce on him for not carrying on in the tradition of Wright. But, ironically, it was Wright himself who rejected the sectarian Marxism of the American Communist party. Dig his essay in Arthur Koestler's book *The God that Failed*. And in the foreword to George Padmore's *Pan-Africanism or Communism*, Wright implies that the black man operates on the premise of a personal nationalism, and not along fixed ideological lines:

The Negro's fundamental loyalty is, therefore, to *himself*. His situation makes this inevitable. [Am I letting awful secrets out of the bag? I'm sorry. The time has come for this problem to be stated clearly so that there is no possibility of further misunderstanding or confusion. The Negro, even when embracing

Communism or Western Democracy, is not supporting ideologies; he is seeking to use *instruments* (instruments owned and
controlled by men of other races!) for his own ends. He stands
outside of those instruments and ideologies; he has to do so,
for he is not allowed to blend with them in a natural, organic
and healthy manner.] (13)

Like Wright, Ellison was also active in the literary Left of the
late thirties and early forties. And also like Wright, Ellison rejected
sectarian Marxism. As far as I can perceive, Ellison had never
really internalized Marxism in the first place. This appears to be
the case even when he was writing in the left-wing *New Masses*.
His work appears always to have been striving for a penetration
into those areas of black lifestyle that exist below the mere depiction of external oppression. He had read Marx, though, as
should anyone who is interested in those ideas operative in today's
world. But luckily for us, his work never took on the simplistic
assertions of the literary Marxist.

Therefore, Ellison's clearly articulated break with naturalism
must also be seen in light of his previous awareness that hard-
core ideologues, particularly Communists, represented an awesome threat not only to his artistic sensibility, but to his "national" sensibility as well. And it is amazing how fantastically true
Ellison's initial impulses have been. If Harold Cruse's *Crisis of the
Negro Intellectual* has any one theme that demands our greatest
attention, it is his clear analysis of the detrimental role that the
left wing has played in our struggle for self-determination and
liberation. Ellison himself is also aware, and this awareness un-
derlies the following remarks he made in an interview that was
published in the March 1967 issue of *Harper's* magazine. He is
speaking to several young black writers:

They fostered the myth that Communism was twentieth-
century Americanism, but to be a twentieth-century American
meant, in their thinking, that you had to be more Russian
than American and less Negro than either. That's how they

lost the Negroes. The Communists recognized no plurality of interests and were really responding to the necessities of Soviet foreign policy and when the war came, Negroes got caught and were made expedient in the shifting of policy. Just as Negroes who fool around with them today are going to get caught in the next turn of the screw. ("Stern Discipline," 88)

Ellison has not been forgotten by his enemies both in the white Left and the black Left. The Communists were the first to lead the attack against Ellison when *Invisible Man* appeared in 1952. Since then, we have read or heard a number of attacks emanating from black writers who trace their literary lineage from the so-called progressive movements of the thirties and forties. In this connection, the interested reader should dig Harold Cruse's section on Ellison in *The Crisis of the Negro Intellectual*. Cruse's book seems theoretically out of focus in many instances, because it walks such a precarious line between a weakly defined nationalism and a strained neo-Marxism. But, in my opinion, he is strictly on the case when he enters the "debate" between Ellison and his detractors. Here I refer to Cruse's account of the anti-Ellison attack that occurred at a writers' conference at the New School in 1965. Leading the charge against Ellison were Herbert Aptheker, a leading theoretician of the Communist party; John Henrik Clarke, the editor of several significant anthologies; and John O. Killens, the novelist. Cruse asserts that the writers gathered at the conference were not properly prepared to cope with the questions posed by Ellison's critical and aesthetic methodology. Further, he asserted that "the radical left wing will never forgive Ellison for writing *Invisible Man*" (Cruse, 505–511).

Why? The answer is quite simple. The literary Left, both white and Negro, were fuming over Ellison's rejection of white-controlled left-wing politics, his harsh depiction of the Communists (called the "Brotherhood" in Ellison's novel), and the novel's obvious rejection of the aesthetics of social realism. The Communist *Daily Worker* of June 1, 1952, for example, published a review of the book under the following headline: "Ralph Ellison's

Novel 'Invisible Man' Shows Snobbery, Contempt for Negro People." The review which followed was written by a Negro left-winger named Abner N. Berry, who opened his piece by stating:

> Written in [the] vein of middle class snobbishness—even contempt—towards the Negro people, Ellison's work manipulates his nameless hero for 439 pages through a maze of corruption, brutality, anticommunism slanders, sex perversion and the sundry inhumanities upon which a dying social system feeds.

And on the aesthetic level he asserted:

> There are no *real* characters in *Invisible Man*, nor are there any *realistic* situations. The structure, the characters and the situations are *contrived* and resemble *fever fantasy*. . . . In effect, it is 439 pages of contempt for humanity, written in an *affected, pretentious*, and *other worldly* style to suit the king pins of world white supremacy. (Emphasis mine, naturally)

Therefore, along with making the unpardonable sin of obliquely attacking the party through his characterization of the Brotherhood in his novel, Ellison was also being attacked for having developed a new aesthetic universe, one that was seeking to develop its own laws of form and content. Social realism, particularly Marxist socialist realism, does not allow for the free play of fantasy and myth that Ellison was attempting in his novel. Marxist social realism essentially posits the view that the details of a work of art should be predicated on fairly simple structural lines. A work should extol the virtues of the working classes, but the extolling should take place along party lines. Hence, not only is the writer's aesthetic range controlled, but his political range as well. And to further worsen matters, this aesthetic ideology is nearly Victorian in the extreme. It seems to emanate from a very square vision of social realities.

Here is John O. Killens in the June 1952 edition of the newspaper *Freedom*, commenting on *Invisible Man*:

Mix a heavy portion of sex and a heavy, heavy portion of violence, a bit of sadism and a dose of redbaiting (Blame the Communists for everything bad) and you have the making of a bestseller today.

Add to this decadent mixture of a Negro theme with Negro characters as Uncle Toms, pimps, sex perverts, guilt-ridden traitors—and you have a publisher's dream.

But how does Ellison present the Negro people? The thousands of exploited farmers in the South [are] represented by a sharecropper who made both his wife and daughter pregnant. The main character of the book is a young Uncle Tom who is obsessed with getting to the "top" by pleasing the Big, Rich White folks. A million Negro veterans who fought against fascism in World War II are rewarded with a maddening chapter [of] crazy vets running hogwild in a down home tavern. The Negro ministry is depicted by an Ellison character who is a Harlem pastor and at the same time a pimp and a numbers racketeer.

The Negro people need Ralph Ellison's *Invisible Man* like we need a hole in the head or a stab in the back.

It is a vicious distortion of Negro life.[2]

It is remarkable how similar were Berry's and Killens's reactions to this novel. They easily could have been written by the same person. But this is supposed to be 1970. And I would like to believe that we can read *Invisible Man* with more intellectual freedom than is apparent in Abner Berry's and John O. Killens's presumably sincere, but extremely flaccid critical remarks. Especially today, when the major concerns ramified throughout Ellison's life and work are still very relevant to our contemporary search for new systems of social organization and creative values. Ellison's vision, in some respects, is not that far removed from the ideas of some of the best black writers and intellectuals working today. That's why I wince somewhat when I reread the following statement that I made in the afterword to *Black Fire*: "The things that concerned Ellison are interesting to read, but contemporary Black youth feel another force in the world today. We know who we are, and are not invisible, *at least not to each other*. We are not Kafkaesque creatures stumbling through a white light of confusion and absurdity" (652).

My statements represent one stage in a long series of attempts, over the past several years, to deal with the fantastic impression that Ellison's work has had on my life. It is now my contention that of all the so-called older black writers working today, it is Ralph Ellison who is the most engaging. But the major issue separating many young black writers from a Ralph Ellison appears to have very little to do with creative orientation, but much more to do with the question of political activism and the black writer. Ellison's stance is decidedly nonpolitical: "[The novel] is *always* a public gesture, though not necessarily a political one" (*S&A*, 110). (We'll come back to this later.) And further, there is a clearly "aristocratic" impulse in his stance, an understandable desire not to be soiled by the riffraff from all kinds of ideological camps. As we have already noted, Ellison, like Wright, was active in left-wing literary circles in the late thirties and early forties. There must have been some psychological torments for him then, since we can glean, even from his early writings, a distinctly "nationalistic" orientation that must have, at times, been at odds with the party line. Why should this have caused problems?

The answer is very simple. Most serious writers should understand it: The left wing, particularly the Communist party, represented one of the main means by which a young black writer could get published. There were perhaps other routes through the Establishment. But for a young black writer checking out the literary happenings in 1937 (Ellison was about twenty-three years old when he wrote his first piece for *New Challenge*, a black, left-oriented magazine), the party was very attractive. After all, was not Richard Wright on that side of the street? And did not the Communist party seem very amenable to young black talent? I hope that I am not exaggerating, but it seems that, from this perspective, the whole literary atmosphere, for a black writer, seems to have been dominated by the Left.

Never having been a hard-core ideologue in the first place,

Ellison appears to have been exceedingly uncomfortable as a leftist polemicist. Some of his journalistic writing for the Communist-oriented *New Masses* strains for political and social relevancy, just as some of ours does. But you can perceive another kind of spirit trying to cut through the Marxist phrase-mongering, another kind of spirit trying to develop a less simplistic, more viable attitude toward not only the usable content of Afro-American culture in America, but more important, a sense of the *meaning* of that culture's presence and its manifestations as they impinged upon "white culture." One isolatable political tendency that begins to emerge at the end of Ellison's Marxist period is a nascent, loosely structured form of black nationalism.

But Ellison was always clever. As Ellison himself notes in the *Harper's* interview quoted earlier, he never wrote the "official type of fiction." "I wrote," he says:

> what might be called propaganda—having to do with the Negro struggle—but my fiction was always trying to be something else: something different even from Wright's fiction. I never accepted the ideology which the *New Masses* attempted to impose on writers. They hated Dostoevski, but I was studying Dostoevski. . . . I was studying [Henry] James. I was also reading Marx, Gorki, Sholokhov, and Isaac Babel. I was reading everything, including the Bible. Most of all, I was reading Malraux. . . . This is where I was really living at the time. . . . Anyway, I think style is more important than political ideologies. ("Stern Discipline," 86)

But there is even a counter-Marxist thrust below the surface of his early political writings. This counterthrust manifests itself in Ellison's concern with folk culture and lifestyle. So that in the midst of his political writings, it is possible to see him groping for a unique cultural theory, one that is shaped on the basis of cultural imperatives integral to to the black man's experience in America. For example, 1943 found Ellison as the managing editor of the *Negro Quarterly*. The editor was Angelo Herndon, a black intellectual of the radical Left. Herndon had been arrested in the

South for engaging in union activities. The *Negro Quarterly* appears to have been the last attempt on the part of black intellectuals of that period to fashion an ideological position that was revolutionary but not totally dominated by the white Marxist Left.

But there was a war going on in 1943. When the war began, America found itself on the side of the Allied Forces, Britain and France. It was also allied with the Russians against the fascist German state. Now that socialist Russia was under attack, American Communists began to concentrate on the war effort. In the interim between the Russo-German Pact of 1939 and the formal entry of Russia into the war, there had been a significant shift in party policy with respect to the "Negro question." Now that Russia was under attack, the Nonaggression Pact abrogated, the Communist party was urging its American chapter to deemphasize the struggle for Negro liberation and instead to concentrate on the war effort. It correctly reasoned that excessive political activism among black people would only slow down the industrial war machinery, thus endangering Russia by impeding the progress of the Allied struggle in Europe. All of this put left-wing black intellectuals in a trick.

Their international perspective forced them to acknowledge the awesome threat that fascism posed to human progress. But they were also acutely aware that an atmosphere of racism and fascism also existed here in America. Then there was the question of Japan. Many black people felt a vague sense of identification with the powerful Asian nation and secretly wished that it would overcome the white Western powers. And there were other attitudes which grew out of the specific situation of racism in America.

A significant item in this regard is an unsigned editorial that appeared in the *Negro Quarterly* in 1943 which, from the import of its style and content, is believed to have been written by Ralph Ellison. The editorial addresses itself to the conflicting attitudes held by black people toward the war effort. Black people were being segregated in the armed services, and, because of racism, were not even getting an opportunity to make some bread in the war-related industries. It was the latter situation which had led to A. Philip Randolph's 1941 threat to march on Washington for jobs and fair employment. Under Randolph's pressure, President Franklin D. Roosevelt was forced to sign Executive Order 8802, which was supposed to guarantee black people equal access to jobs in the war industries. Under these circumstances, it is easy to understand why there were, among black people, such conflicting attitudes toward the war.

Ellison's writings enumerated these attitudes. They ranged from apathy to all-out rejection of war. Addressing himself to this attitude of rejection in the editorial mentioned earlier, Ellison stated that it sprang from a "type of Negro nationalism which, in a sense, is admirable; it would settle all problems on the simple principle that Negroes deserve equal treatment with all other free human beings." But Ellison concluded that this attitude of total rejection of the war effort was too narrow in scope. It was not just a case of "good white men" against "bad white men." The Negro, he strongly asserted, had a natural stake in the defeat of fascism, whether it was national or international. He further proposed that there was another manifestation of "Negro nationalism" that was neither a "blind acceptance" of the war nor an "unqualified rejection" of it. This attitude is

> broader and more human than the first two attitudes; and it is *scientific* enough to make use of *both* by *transforming* them into *strategies of struggle*. It is committed to life, it holds that the main task of the Negro people is to work unceasingly toward creating those democratic conditions in which it can live and recreate itself. It believes the historical role of Negroes to be that of integrating the larger American nation and compelling it untiringly toward true freedom. And while it will have none of the slavishness of the first attitude, it is imaginative and flexible enough to die if dying is forced upon it. (Emphases mine)

Somehow we are involved here with an attempt at ideological reconciliation between two contending trends in Afro-American thought, that is, the will toward self-definition, exclusive of the overall white society, and at the same time the desire not to be counted out of the processes of so-called American democracy. This is the precarious balancing act that Ellison is forced to perform while he tries to cut through the ideological prison in which he finds himself encased. He attacks Negro leaders for not having group consciousness and calls for a "centralization" of Negro political power.

But as we proceed to read the editorial, we begin to encounter the Ellison who would be himself and write one of the most important novels in history. Toward the end of this editorial, with its carefully balanced blend of Marxism and Negro nationalism, we find Ellison making the following blatantly non-Marxist statement:

> A third major problem, and one that is indispensable to the centralization and direction of power, is that of learning the meaning of the *myths* and *symbols* which abound among the Negro masses. For without this knowledge, leadership, no matter how correct its program, will fail. Much in Negro life remains a *mystery*; perhaps the *zoot suit conceals* profound political meaning; perhaps the symmetrical frenzy of the Lindy-hop conceals clues to great potential powers—if only Negro leaders would solve this *riddle*. On this knowledge depends the effectiveness of any slogan or tactic. For instance, it is obvious that Negro resentment over their treatment at the hands of their allies is justified. This naturally makes for a resistance to our stated war aims, even though these aims are essentially correct; and they will be accepted by the Negro masses only to the extent that they are helped to see the bright start of *their own* hopes through the *fog* of their daily experiences. The problem is *psychological*; it will be solved only by a Negro leadership that is aware of the psychological attitudes and incipient forms of action which the black masses *reveal* in their emotion-charged *myths, symbols,* and wartime *folk-lore.* Only through a skillful and wise manipulation of these centers of repressed social energy will Negro resentments, self-pity and indignation be channe-

lized to cut through temporary issues and become transformed
into positive action. This is not to make the problem simply
one of words, but to recognize . . . that words have their own
vital importance. (Emphases mine)

There is a clear, definite sense of cultural nationalism at work
here. These statements represent an especial attempt on the part
of Ellison to get past the simplistic analysis of folk culture brought
to bear on the subject by Marxist social realists. For rather than
locating the mechanisms for organizing political power totally in
an analysis of the black man's class structure, Ellison turns Marxism on its head, and makes the manipulation of cultural mechanisms the basis for black liberation.[3] Further, these statements
set into motion a host of themes which are elaborated upon in
his later work, particularly his cultural criticism. Here also we get
snatches of a theory of culture. And some aspect of this theory
seems to imply that there is an unstated, even noumenal set of
values that exists beneath the surface of black American culture.
These values manifest themselves in a characteristic manner,
or an *expressive style*. The Lindy-hop and the zoot suit are, therefore,
in this context not merely social artifacts, but they, in fact, mask
deeper levels of symbolic and social energy. Ellison perceives this
theory as the instrumental basis for a new kind of Negro leader:

They [the leaders] must integrate themselves with the Negro
masses; they must be constantly alert to new concepts, new
techniques and new trends among peoples and nations with
an eye toward appropriating those which are valid when tested
against the reality of Negro life. By the same test they must
be just as alert to reject the faulty programs of their friends.
When needed concepts, techniques or theories do not exist
they must create them. Many new concepts will evolve when
the people are closely studied in action.

To some extent, this kind of perception shapes many of the
characters in *Invisible Man*. Rinehart comes to mind in this con-

nection. However, there is a specific allusion to the ideas enunciated in this 1943 editorial in the following passage from Ellison's novel:

> What about those fellows waiting still and silent there on the platform, so still and silent they clash with the crowd in their very immobility, standing noisy in their very silence; harsh as a cry of terror in their quietness? What about these three boys, coming now along the platform, tall and slender, walking stiffly with swinging shoulders in their well-pressed, too-hot-for-summer suits, their collars high and tight about their necks, their identical hats of black cheap felt set upon the crowns of their heads with a severe formality above their conked hair? It was as though I'd never seen their like before: Walking slowly, their shoulders swaying, their legs swinging from their hips in trousers that ballooned upward from cuffs fitting snug about their ankles; their coats long and hip-tight with shoulders far too broad to be those of natural western men. These fellows whose bodies seemed—what had one of my teachers said of me?—"You're like one of these African sculptures, distorted in the interest of design." Well, what design and whose?[4]

To the protagonist, they seem like "dancers in a funeral service." (This episode follows the death of Tod Clifton.) Their black faces are described as being "secret." They wear "heel-plated shoes" and rhythmically tap as they walk. They are said to be "men outside of historical time." That is to say, no current theory of historical development accurately describes them. Yet there is a gnawing and persistent feeling, on the part of the unnamed protagonist, that the boys may hold the key to the future liberation. And as he grasps the implications of this idea, he is emotionally shaken:

> But who knew (and now I began to tremble so violently I had to lean against a refuse can)—who knew but they were the *saviors*, the *true leaders*, *the bearers* of something precious? The *stew-*

ards of something uncomfortable, burdensome, which they
hated because, living outside of history, *there was no one to applaud
their value* and they themselves failed to understand it. (*IM*, 333;
emphases mine)

Ellison's 1943 remarks in the *Negro Quarterly* concerning black
cultural compulsives were cloaked in the language of politics. But
they implicitly penetrate way beyond the sphere of politics. It is
obvious from the foregoing passage that he thought enough of
the concept of hidden cultural compulsives in black American
life to *translate* them into art. Further, as we have noted, the concept is rather non-Marxist in texture and in substance. It probably
represents, for him, a "leap" not only in political consciousness
but in aesthetic consciousness as well. As a result of his experiences with hard-core ideological constructs, Ellison came to feel
that politics were essentially inhibiting to an artist, if they could
not be subsumed into art. Perhaps, this is what he means when
he says in the *Harper's* interview: "Anyway, I think style is more
important than political ideologies" ("Stern Discipline," 86).

I am not sure whether I fully concur with Ellison on this
point. But there is something in his stance that specifically relates
to the current black arts movement. The current movement is
faced with some of the same problems that confronted Ellison.
Only the historical landscape has changed, and the operational
rhetoric is different.

I don't think I am exaggerating when I say that some form of
nationalism is operative throughout all sections of the black community. The dominant political orientations shaping the sensibilities of many contemporary black writers fall roughly into the
categories of cultural nationalism and revolutionary nationalism.
That is to say, as writers, we owe whatever importance we may
have to this current manifestation of nationalism. I, for one, tend
to believe this is a good situation in which to be. It provides an
audience to which to address our work, and also imports to it a
certain sense of contemporaneity and social relevance.

But we are going to have to be careful not to let our rhetoric
obscure the fact that a genuine nationalist revolution in the arts

will fail, if the artistic products of that revolution do not encounter our audiences in a manner that demands their most
profound attention. I'm talking about a black art that sticks to
the ribs, an art that through the strength of all of its ingredi-
ents—form, content, craft, and technique—illuminates something specific about the living culture of the nation, and, by extension, reveals something fundamental about man on this
planet.

Therefore, we have to resist the tendency to "program" our
art, to set unnatural limitations upon it. To do so implies that
we ultimately don't trust the intelligence of the national laity,
and consequently feel that we must paternally guide them down
the course of righteous blackness. So very often we defuse the
art by shaping it primarily on the basis of fashionable political
attitudes. There is a tendency to respond to work simply on the
sensation it creates.[5] If black art is to survive, in the national sense,
it's gonna need more supporting it than a cluster of new clichés.

Translating Politics into Art

There is quite a discussion about the nature of history in Ellison's
Invisible Man. Along with the obvious theme of identity, the nameless narrator is constantly in search of a "usable past." In order
to arrive at an understanding of the complex dimensions of his
American experience, Ellison plunged deep into the murky world
of mythology and folklore, both of which are essential elements
in the making of a people's history. But Ellison's history is non-
dialectical. The novel attempts to construct its own universe,
based on its own imperatives, the central ones being the shaping
of a personal vision, as in the blues, and the celebration of a
collective vision as is represented by the living culture. And it is
the living culture, with all of its shifting complexities, which constitutes the essential landscape of the novel. The unnamed narrator questions the "scientific" history of the Brotherhood and,
in one of the most intense sections of the novel, asks the following question: "What if Brother Jack were wrong? What if history

was a gambler, instead of a force in a laboratory experiment, and the boys his ace in the hole? What if history was not a reasonable citizen, but a madman full, of paranoid guile . . . ?" (*IM*, 333).

This discourse follows the death of Tod Clifton, a man who had previously been described as having fallen "outside of history." Tottering between contending political forces, that is, the rigid dogmas of the Brotherhood and the emotionally compelling rhetoric of Ras the Exhorter, Tod attempts to leap outside historical time altogether. And he ultimately leaps to his death.

Churning way beneath the surface of the novel's narrative is a fantastically rich and engaging mythic and folkloristic universe. Further, this universe is introduced to us through the music of Louis Armstrong, whose music, then, forms the overall structure for the novel. If that is the case, the subsequent narrative and all of the action which follows can be read as one long blues solo. Critic Albert Murray, a close associate of Ellison's, put it this way:

> *Invisible Man* was *par excellence* the literary extension of the blues. Ellison had taken an everyday twelve-bar blues tune (by a man from down South sitting in a manhole up North in New York, singing and signifying about how he got there) and scored it for full orchestra. This was indeed something different and something more than run-of-the-mill U.S. fiction. It had new dimensions of rhetorical resonance (based on lying and signifying). It employed a startlingly effective fusion of narrating realism and surrealism, and it achieved a unique but compelling combination of the naturalistic, the ridiculous, and the downright hallucinatory. (*Omni Americans*, 167)

What is important about Murray's observation here is that it isolates, in *Invisible Man*, a unique aesthetic. There has been much talk of late about a "black aesthetic," but there has been, fundamentally, a failure to examine those elements of the black experience in America which could genuinely constitute an aesthetic. With no real knowledge of folk culture—blues, folk songs, folk narratives, spirituals, dance styles, gospels, speech, and oral history—there is very little possibility that a black aesthetic will be realized in our literature.

Ellison, however, finds the aesthetic all around him. He finds it in memories of his Oklahoma background. He finds it in preachers, blues singers, hustlers, gamblers, jazzmen, boxers, dancers, and itinerant storytellers. He notes carefully the subtleties of American speech patterns. He pulls the covers off the stereotypes in order to probe beneath the surface where the hardcore mythic truth lies. He keeps checking out style. The way people walk, what they say, and what they leave *un*said. If anyone has been concerned with a "black aesthetic" it has certainly got to be Ralph Ellison. And even if you disagree with Ellison's political thrust these days, you have to dig his consistent concern for capturing the essential truths of the black man's experience in America.

And where are these essential truths embodied, if not in the folk culture? Do not Stagalee, High John the Conqueror, John Henry, Shine, and the Signifying Monkey reveal vital aspects of our group experience? Or has the current "rediscovery" of African culture obscured the fact that however disruptive slavery must have been to our original African personalities, our fathers and mothers intuitively understood what aspect of it could be rescued and reshaped? And did not this reshaping indicate a *willed* desire to survive and maintain one's own specific outlook on life? Didn't it exhibit a willed desire to survive in the face of danger? What kind of people were they in their weaknesses and their strengths? Haven't we read their slave narratives and listened carefully to their songs? And hasn't the essential spirit that they breathed into these expressions continued to manifest itself in all meaningful aspects of our struggle? We must address ourselves to this kind of humanity because it is meaningful and within our immediate reach. To do so means understanding something essential about the persistence of tradition, understanding the manner in which values are shaped out of tradition, and—what's more important—understanding the values whose fundamental function was to bind us together into a community of shared feelings and memories in order that we might survive.

Ellison's protagonist, when confronted with possible expulsion from his southern Negro college, suffers deeply at the thought of losing his regional roots. In his longing for a sustainable image of the world that has created him, he transforms an "ordinary" housemother into a ritual goddess. Dig. Here is your black aesthetic at its best:

Ha! to the gray-haired matron in the final row. Ha! Miss Susie, Miss Susie Gresham, back there looking at that co-ed smiling at that he-ed——listen to me, the bungling bugler of words, imitating the trumpet and the trombone's timbre, playing thematic variations like a baritone horn. Hey! old connoisseur of voice sounds, of voices without messages, of newsless winds, listen to the vowel sounds and the crackling dentals, to the low harsh gutturals of empty anguish, now riding the curve of a preacher's rhythm I heard long ago in a Baptist church, stripped now of its imagery: No suns having hemorrhages, no moons weeping tears, no earthworms refusing the sacred flesh and dancing in the earth on Easter morn. Ha! singing achievement. Ha! booming success, intoning. Ha! acceptance, Ha! a river of word-sounds filled with drowned passions, floating, Ha! floating, Ha! floating, Ha! with wrecks of unachievable ambitions and stillborn revolts, sweeping their ears, Ha! ranged stiff before me, necks stretched forward with listening ears, Ha! a-spraying the ceiling and a-drumming the dark-stained after rafter, that seasoned crossarm of tor-turous timber mellowed in the kiln of a thousand voices; playing, Ha! as upon a xylophone; words marching like the student band, up the campus and down again, blaring triumphant sounds empty of triumphs. Hey, Miss Susie! the sound of words that were no words, counterfeit notes singing achievements yet unachieved, riding upon the wings of my voice out to you, old matron, who knew the voice sounds of the Founder and knew the accents and echo of his promise; your gray old head cocked with the young around you, your eyes closed, face ecstatic, as I toss the word-sounds in my breath, my bellows, my fountain, like bright-colored balls in a water spout——hear me, old matron, justify now this sound with your dear old nod of affirmation, your closed-eye smile and bow of recognition, who'll never be fooled with the mere content of words, not my words, not these pinfeathered flighters that stroke your lids till they flutter with ecstasy with but the mere echoed noise of the promise. And after the singing and outward marching, you seize my hand and sing out quavering, "Boy, some day you'll make the Founder proud!" Ha! Susie Gresham, Mother Gresham, guardian of the hot young women on the puritan benches who couldn't see your Jordan's water for their private steam; you, relic of slavery whom the campus loved but did not understand, aged, of slavery, yet bearer of something warm and vital and all-enduring, of which in that island of shame we were not ashamed—it was to you on the final row I directed my rush of sound, and it was you of whom I thought with shame and regret as I waited for the ceremony to begin. (IM, 88–89)

This poetic narrative is the prelude to the ceremony in which Rev. Homer Barbee, taking the role of tribal poet, ritually consecrates the memory of the Founder. His speech is permeated with myth. The Founder's image is not merely locked into legitimate history, it bobs and weaves among acts, half-remembered truths, and apocrypha. The Founder is perceived by Barbee as a culture hero bringing order out of chaos, bringing wisdom to bear upon fear and ignorance. He is compared to Moses, Aristotle, and Jesus. He is called, by Homer Barbee, "prophet," "godly man," "the great spirit," and "the great sun." In his hardships and moments of danger, he is helped by strange emissaries, one of whom, Barbee says, may have come "direct from above." Another of the Founder's helpers is an old slave who is ridiculed by the town's children:

He, the old slave, showing a surprising knowledge of such matters—*germology* and *scabology*—ha! ha! ha!—he called it, and what youthful skill of the hands! For he shaved our skull, and cleansed our wound and bound it neat with bandages stolen from the home of an unsuspecting leader of the mob, ha! (*IM*, 94)

Barbee makes his audience, composed primarily of black college students, identify with the Founder. No, in fact, under the spell of the ritual sermon, they must *become* the Founder. They must don the mask of the god, so to speak. All of these details are said to be remembered by the students, yet Barbee has a compulsive need to reiterate them, to recharge them with meaning by reconsecrating them. His essential role, as ritual priest, is to keep before them the "painful details" of the Founder's life. These are memories that his young audience must internalize, and share fully, if they are to ever realize themselves in the passage from adolescence into maturity. And this is the function of folk culture. This is what Ellison sensed in the blues. In an essay entitled "Richard Wright's Blues," he notes:

> The blues is an impulse to keep the painful details and episodes of a brutal experience alive in one's aching consciousness, to finger its jagged grain, and to transcend it, not by the consolation of philosophy but by squeezing from it a near-tragic, near-comic lyricism. As a form, the blues is an autobiographical chronicle of personal catastrophe expressed lyrically. (*S&A*, 78–79)

In "Blues People," a review of Imamu Baraka's (LeRoi Jones's) book, he makes this statement about the role of the blues singer:

> Bessie Smith might have been a "blues queen" to the society at large, but within the tighter Negro community where the blues were part of the total way of life, and a major expression of an attitude toward life, she was a priestess, a celebrant who affirmed the values of the group and man's ability to deal with chaos.[6]

Blues represent a central creative motif throughout *Invisible Man* from the hero's "descent" into the music at the beginning of the novel. The blues allow Trueblood to face up to himself after the disastrous event of making his daughter pregnant. The blues inform the texture of much of the novel's prose:

> My stomach felt raw. From somewhere across the quiet of the campus the sound of a guitar-blues plucked from an out-of-tune piano drifted towards me like a lazy, shimmering wave,

like the echoed whistle of a lonely train, and my head went over again, against a tree, and I could hear it splattering the flowering vines. (*IM*, 122)

And at another point the hero contemplates the meaning of this blues lyric:

> She's got feet like a monkey
> Legs
> Legs, Legs like a maaad
> Bulldog . . . (*IM*, 134)

"What does it mean?" he thinks:

And why describe anyone in such contradictory words? Was it a sphinx? Did old Chaplin-pants, old dusty-butt, love her or hate her; or was he merely singing? What kind of woman could love a dirty fellow like that, anyway? And how could even *he* love her if she were as repulsive as the song described? . . . I strode along, hearing the cartman's song become a lonesome, broad-toned whistle now that flowered at the end of each phrase into a tremulous, blue-toned chord. And in its flutter and swoop, I heard the sound of a railroad train highballing it, lonely across the lonely night. He was the Devil's son-in-law, all right, and he was a man who could whistle a three-toned chord. . . . God damn, I thought, they're a hell of a people! And I didn't know whether it was pride or disgust that suddenly flashed over me. (*IM*, 134–35)

Why this emphasis on folklore and blues culture? In a 1970 issue of the *College Language Association* (*CLA*) *Journal*, George Kent supplies an answer which many of those who consider themselves nationalists should well consider:

Offering the first drawings of a group's character, preserving situations repeated in the history of the group, describing the boundaries of thought and feeling, projecting the group's wisdom in symbols expressing its will to survive, embodying those values by which it lives and dies, folklore seemed, as Ellison described it, basic to the portrayal of the essential spirit of black people.[7]

Ellison's spiritual roots are, therefore, deep in the black American folk tradition. I think that this awareness of specifically black contributions to the so-called mainstream of American life gives him a fundamental certainty that no matter how much he praises the writers of the white West, he is still himself: Ralph *Waldo* Ellison. Much of Ellison's concern with the major literary figures of Europe and America emanates from his sincere belief that it is the duty of every writer, black or white, to be fully aware of the best that has ever been written. For Ellison that has never meant *becoming* a white man. It meant bringing to bear on literature and language the force of one's own sensibility and modes of feeling. It meant learning the craft of fiction, even from white artists, but dominating that craft so much that you don't play like the other feller any more. That trumpet you got in your hand may have been made in Germany, but you sure sound like my Uncle Rufus whooping his coming-home call across the cotton fields. But you got to master the instrument first, Ellison might say. I would agree to that, but add this: you got to somehow master *yourself* in the process.

If there is any fundamental difference I have with Ellison, it is his, perhaps unintentional, tendency to imply that black writers should confine their range of cultural inquiry strictly to American—and European—subject matter. For a man who was not exactly parochial about his search for knowledge to subtly impose such attitudes on young writers is to deny the best aspects of his own development as an artist.

Young writers, on the other hand, should not fall for any specious form of reasoning that limits the range of their inquiry strictly to African and Afro-American subject matter. A realistic movement among the black arts community should be about the *extension* of the *remembered* and a *resurrection* of the *unremembered*; should be about an engagement with the *selves* we know and the *selves* we have forgotten. Finally, it should be about a synthesis of the conglomerate of world knowledge; all that is meaningful and moral and that makes one stronger and wiser, in order to live as fully as possible as a human being. What will make this knowledge ours is what we do with it, how we color it to suit our specific needs. Its value to us will depend upon what we bring to bear upon it. In our dispersal, we can "dominate" Western culture or be "dominated" by it. It all depends on what you feel about yourself. Any black writer or politician who does not believe that black people have created something powerful and morally sustaining in their four hundred or so years here has declared himself a loser before the war begins. How would we create, even fight, denying the total weight of our particular historical experience *here* in America.

I must emphasize the word "total" because, as Ellison and Albert Murray often explain, there is a tendency among American sociologists and black creative intellectuals to perceive our history in purely pathological terms. For example, Don L. Lee makes a statement in *Ebony* magazine to the following effect: If you don't know about rats and roaches, you don't know about the black experience. Why define yourself in purely negative terms, when you know that your very life, in its most profound aspects, is not merely a result of the negative? We are not simply, in *all* areas of our sensibilities, merely a set of black reactions to white oppression. And neither should our art be merely an aesthetic reaction to white art. It has finally got to exist as good art also, because in terms of the development of a national art, excellent art is, in and of itself, the best propaganda you can have. By now, we should be free enough to use any viable techniques that will allow us to shape an art that breathes and is based essentially on our own emotional and cultural imperatives.

Ellison, however, almost overwhelmingly locates his cultural, philosophical, and literary sensibility in the West. That's his prerogative, and that prerogative should be protected. But being so-called free individuals, at least on the question of whom one accepts as "literary ancestors," it is possible to extend one's vocabulary and memory in any manner one chooses. It's already being done in music; Coltrane, Sun Ra, Pharaoh Sanders, and Leon Thomas indicate devices, procedures, functions, attitudes, and concerns that are not vividly indicated in Euro-American culture. They indicate a synthesis and a rejection of Western musical theory at the same time, just as aspects of Louis Armstrong's trumpet playing indicated, in its time, a respect for the traditional uses of the instrument, on the one hand, and, on the other, to the squares, it indicated a "gross defilement" of the instrument. I recall once reading an article about a son of A. J. Sax, the Belgian instrument maker, who said something to the effect that he didn't believe his father intended for the instrument to be played the way jazz musicians were playing it. Yeah, you can take the other dude's instruments and play like your Uncle Rufus's hog callings. But there is another possibility also: *You could make your own instrument.* And if you can sing through that instrument, you can impose your voice on the world in a heretofore-unthought-of manner.

In short, you can create another world view, another cosmology springing from your own specific grounds, but transcending them as your new world realizes itself.

All black creative artists owe Ellison special gratitude. He and a few others of his generation have struggled to keep the culture alive in their artistic works. We should not be content with merely basking in the glow of their works. We need what they have given us. But the world has changed. Which is as it should be. And we have changed in the world. Which is quite natural. Because everybody and everything is change. However, what Ellison teaches us is that it is not possible to move toward meaningful creative ends without somehow taking with you the accumulated weight of your forebears' experiences.

What I think we have to do is to understand our roles as synthesizers: the creators of new and exciting visions out of the accumulated weight of our Western experience. We must also deeply understand the specific reasons, both historically and emotionally, that cause many of us to *feel* that there is a range of ideas beyond those strictly of the West. To be more precise, no philosophical, political, or religious attitude in the world today,

Western or Eastern, fully provides the means of mankind's spiritual and psychic liberation. No one system of ethics, oriental or occidental, exists in harmony with the social world from which it springs. Why?

Perhaps it is because the one central component of man's sensibility which would allow him to survive on human terms has never been allowed to flower. And that is the artistic sensibility which essentially defines man as a spiritual being in the world. That is because politicians have never accepted the idea that art was simply a public gesture, hence not political. Therefore, Ellison is incorrect when he says to Irving Howe: "I would have said that it [the novel] is always a public gesture, though not necessarily a political one." This statement is only half-true. The novel is *both* a public gesture *and* a political gesture. As Ellison knows, burning a Cadillac on the White House lawn[8] is a public gesture, but it is amusingly political also. The minute a work of art enters the social sphere, it faces the problem of being perceived on all kinds of levels, from the grossly political to the philosophically sublime. It just be's that way, that's all. And Marx hasn't a thing to do with it. But Marxists implicitly understand the relationship between a work's public character and its political character, however minute a work's political characteristics might be. And that is why totalitarian and fascist regimes must suppress all genuine art. "Who is that fool babbling all kinds of ghosts and chimera out of his eyes, ears, hands, feet, and mouth? We can't understand him. He must certainly be our enemy."

In a system of strategies, of statement, and counterstatement, art is just one other element in the ring, even when it dons an elaborate mask and pretends not to be saying what it really says. *Invisible Man* is artistically one of the world's greatest novels; it is also one of the world's most successful "political" novels. It is just that Ellison's politics are ritualistic as opposed to secular. Ellison's manipulation of rhetorical imagery in *Invisible Man* is enough to blow the average politician off the stand.

The poet, the writer, is a key bearer of culture. Through myth, he is the manipulator of both the collective conscious and unconscious. If he is good, he is the master of rhetorical imagery.

And, as such, he is much more psychically powerful than the secular politician. And that is why he is, to some extent, in some societies, feared and suppressed by secular politicians. Sometimes, he is suppressed even by the laity who must finally embrace his art, if it is to live. But the suppression of art, whether it occurs in the West or in the East, whether it occurs under capitalism or socialism, is detrimental to man's spiritual survival. Without spirit, the substance of all of his material accomplishments means essentially nothing. Therefore, what we might consider is a system of politics and art that is as fluid, as functional, and as expansive as black music. No such system now exists; we're gonna have to build it. And when it is finally realized, it will be a conglomerate, gleaned from the *whole* of all of our experiences.

Later now:
A cool *asante*
in the hey y'all,
habari gani to yo' mamma,
this has been your sweet Poppa Stoppa
running the voodoo down.

Notes

1. Ralph Ellison, "The World and the Jug," in *Shadow and Act* (New York: Random House, 1964). Quotations from this essay and others in *Shadow and Act* are cited in the text as *S&A*.

2. John O. Killens, *Freedom*, June 1952, 7. Killens's comments are reprinted in Harold Cruse, *The Crisis of the Negro Intellectual* (New York: William Morrow & Co., 1967), 235.

3. See Maulana Karenga's seven criteria for culture in *The Quotable Karenga* (US), 1967. Note that Maulana makes one of the seven criteria for culture Mythology, and another important one Creative Motif. See also Cruse, *Crisis of the Negro Intellectual*.

4. Ralph Ellison, *Invisible Man* (New York: Random House, 1952), 332–33. Subsequent references are cited in the text as *IM*.

5. For example, Sam Greenlee's novel *The Spook Who Sat by the Door*

(New York: R. W. Baron, 1969), is an atrocious novel. It lacks style and conscious sense of craft. It is clearly more of a "manual" than a "revolutionary" novel. Its major premise is excellent, but flawed by Greenlee's inability to bring it off. Its "revolutionary content" is never firmly rooted in a form that is sustaining below the mere surface of graphic detail. Where Greenlee could have written a great novel, one both excellently written and revolutionary in stance, he blew the challenge by a glib adherence to militancy.

6. Ellison's review of *Blues People* (*Shadow and Act*, 257) is stringently critical, and at times a little beside the point. What he really seems to be doing here is castigating LeRoi Jones for not writing the book that he (Ellison) would have written. The specific thrust of *Blues People* was never really analyzed. Of course Ellison is capable of analyzing the specific ideas in *Blues People*, but he just wanted to write his own essay on the blues. And his essay is worthwhile and meaningful, too.

7. See George E. Kent, "Ralph Ellison and Afro-American Folk and Cultural Tradition," *College Language Association (CLA) Journal* 13 (1970): 256–76.

8. See Ellison's short story "It Always Breaks Out," *Partisan Review,* Spring 1963: 13–28.

Works Cited

Berry, Abner N. Review of *Invisible Man* by Ralph Ellison. *Daily Worker,* June 1, 1952.

Cruse, Harold. *The Crisis of the Negro Intellectual.* New York: William Morrow & Co., 1967.

Ellison, Ralph. *Invisible Man.* New York: Random House, 1952.

———. "It Always Breaks Out." *Partisan Review,* Spring 1963: 13–28.

———. *Shadow and Act.* New York: Random House, 1964.

———. "A Very Stern Discipline." Interview with Steve Cannon, Lennox Raphael, and James Thompson. *Harper's* 234 (March 1967): 76–95.

Karenga, Maulana. *The Quotable Karenga.* (US: n.p.), 1967.

Murray, Albert. *The Omni Americans.* New York: Random House, 1970.

Neal, Larry. Afterword in *Black Fire: An Anthology of Afro-American Writing.* Edited by LeRoi Jones and Larry Neal. New York: William Morrow & Co., 1968.

Wright, Richard. Foreword to George Padmore's *Pan-Africanism or Communism.* New York: Roy Publishers, 1956.

Ellison's Vision of *Communitas*

NATHAN A. SCOTT, JR.

◆ ◆ ◆

FROM THE TIME of its first appearance in the spring of 1952 Ralph Ellison's *Invisible Man* has been thrusting itself forward, ever more insistently with the passage of each year, as a commanding masterpiece in the literature of American fiction—and, now that it has had a career of a half-century, all that I want here to try to do is to suggest something of what it is that accounts for the kind of powerful claim that it continues to exert upon us.

Ours is, of course, a period marked by an efflorescence of fictional talent on the American scene more notable surely than any comparable European insurgency. Yet, in its representative expressions, it is a talent, for all its variety, that—in such writers as William Gass and John Barth and Donald Barthelme—often chooses to dwell (as the title of a book on recent American fiction by the English critic Tony Tanner says) in a City of Words. Bellow and Styron and Updike and certain others, in their commitment to the traditional arts of narrative, remain sufficiently unreconstructed as to conceive the novel to be a mode of feigned history, but they, though retaining a large and devoted readership, may not embody what Matthew Arnold called "the tone of the centre." For those who are advancing the new poetics of fiction take it for granted (as William Gass says) "that literature is language, that stories and the places and the people in them are merely made of words as chairs are made of smoothed sticks and sometimes of cloth or metal tubes," and thus, since "there are no events but words in fiction,"[1] they think of the novelistic craft as simply an affair of putting words together in new and surprising combinations—which record nothing other than the event of the writer's having done certain interesting things with language itself. So charmed is the new literature with its own verbal universe of metaphor and metonymy that it refuses any deep involvements with the empirical, verifiable world of actual fact, preferring instead what Conrad long ago called the "prolonged hovering flight of the subjective over the outstretched ground of the case exposed." And though the analogical surprises of a John Barth, the shaped rhythms of a William Gass, the "pricksongs and descants" of a Robert Coover, and the entropic auguries of a Thomas Pynchon may all present one or another kind of piquant *divertissement*, they are very clearly not informed by the kind of intentionality that looks toward finding new stratagems wherewith to give a liberating "shape and . . . significance to the immense panorama of . . . anarchy which is contemporary history": which is perhaps to say that they do not seek (in Yeats's great phrase) to hold "reality and justice in a single thought."

The kind of *dandysme* which often reigns now has in recent years been denominated by literary academicians specializing in *Tendenz* as "post-modernism," but a part of the immense appeal that belongs to a figure like Ralph Ellison is surely an affair of his fidelity to the ethic of classic modernism. For the great masters of the past century—Joyce and Lawrence and Mann and Faulkner—were indeed proposing to do what T. S. Eliot in his famous review of *Ulysses* (in the issue of the *Dial* for November 1923) descried as Joyce's intention: namely, to give a "shape and . . . significance to the immense panorama of . . . anarchy which is contemporary history." *The Magic Mountain* and *The Death of Virgil*,

Women in Love and *The Sun Also Rises, The Sound and the Fury* and *Man's Fate* are books that strike us today as having a remarkable kind of weight and contemporaneity, because they are, as it were, taking on the age: with a fierce kind of audacity, they seem to be intending to *displace* a daunting world, to clear a space for the human endeavor and thus to keep open the door of the future. Clearly, the novelists at work in these texts are fascinated with the gesticulatory possibilities inherent in the words, but they are writers who conceive the words they deploy to be ultimately something more than signs merely of grammatical connection. And thus they are not content with the kind of *in*verisimilitude by which the new avant-garde is so greatly bewitched, for they intend to show the very age and body of the time, its form and pressure; in short, the rites and ceremonies and plots and arguments of their fictions are organized toward the end of envisaging new forms of life for the soul, and it is just in this that one element of the genius of twentieth-century modernism lies.

Now it is in this line that Ralph Ellison stands. Immediately after *Invisible Man* first appeared in 1952, the astonishing authority of its art quickly brought it to the forefront of the literary scene, and this at a time when, under the new influence of Henry James, so many representative American writers of the moment—such as Jean Stafford and Frederick Buechner and Isabel Bolton and Monroe Engel and Mary McCarthy—were choosing to seek their effects by the unsaid and the withheld, by the dryly ironic analogy and the muted voice. In the early 1950s Ellison, like Faulkner and Penn Warren, was particularly notable for being unafraid to make his fiction howl and rage and hoot with laughter over "the complex fate" of the *homo Americanus*: indeed, the uninhibited exhilaration and suppleness of his rhetoric were at once felt to be a main source of the richness of texture distinguishing his extraordinary book. Yet the kind of continuing life that his novel has had is surely to be accounted for in terms not of sheer verbal energy alone but, more principally, in terms of the cogency of systematic vision that it enunciates. And though something like this has frequently been remarked, what is essential in the basic stress and emphasis of the novel has just as frequently been mis-reckoned, no doubt largely because the book has so often been construed as having an import related exclusively to the experience of black Americans.

The protagonist of *Invisible Man* is, of course, a young black man (unnamed) who must pick his perilous way through the lunatic world that America has arranged for its Negro minority. In the beginning, he is what the white masters of the southern world in which he grows up were once in the habit of calling "a good Negro": he has cheerfully accepted all the promises of that Establishment, so much so that the oily-tongued and cynical president of his college, Dr. Bledsoe, has singled him out as his special ward. But, unhappily, on a certain day he unintentionally exposes a visiting white trustee from the North to the local Negro gin-mill and to the incestuous entanglements of a Negro farmer's family in the neighborhood—and, as a result, is ousted from the college, as a punishment for his having allowed a donor of the institution to see what visiting white patrons are not supposed to see.

He then moves on to New York, there to journey through the treacherous byways of an infernally labyrinthine world, as he seeks to make contact with whatever it is that may authenticate his existence. The executive powers ordain that, being black, he shall be "invisible," and thus his great central effort becomes that of wresting an acknowledgment, of *achieving* visibility. He gets a job in a Long Island paint factory, and there he becomes involved—again, inadvertently—as a scab in labor-violence. Soon afterward, however, he is taken up by "the Brotherhood" (i.e., the Communist party), after he is heard to deliver an impassioned and a quite spontaneous speech one winter afternoon, as he finds himself part of a crowd watching the eviction of an elderly Negro couple from their Harlem tenement flat. The assignment he is given by his new confreres is that of *organizing* the sullenness of Harlem. But he soon discovers that the Negro's cause is but a pawn being used by the Brotherhood to promote its "line." So, after a furious race riot in the Harlem streets, he in utter disillusionment dives through a manhole, down into a cellar, for a period of "hibernation." He has tried the way of "humility," of

being a "good Negro"; he has tried to find room for himself in
American industry, to become a good cog in the technological
machine; he has attempted to attach himself to leftist politics—
he has tried all those things by means of which it would seem
that a Negro might achieve visibility in American life. But, since
none has offered a way into the culture, he has now chosen to
become an underground man. All his reversals have been due to
the blackness of his skin: so now, at last, he decides to stay in his
cellar where, by way of a tapped line, he will steal the electricity
for his 1,369 bulbs from Monopolated Light and Power and dine
on sloe gin and vanilla ice cream and *embrace* "The Blackness of
Blackness."

Yet Ellison's protagonist, unlike so many of his counterparts
in African-American fiction, is in the end by no means one *merely*
wounded. True, he twice tells us, in the accent of Eliot's *East
Coker*—first in the prologue, and again at the end of his narrative—that his "end is in . . . [his] Beginning." And so it is, for his
last state—since it is an underworld, a place of exile, of dislodg-
ment and expatriation—is in a way his first. But it is an underworld that *he* has *illuminated*. "Step outside the narrow borders of
what men call reality and you step into chaos . . . or imagination,"
(576) he says. When, that is, you step outside the domesticated
and the routinized, you may step into chaos, since the definition
of the world, as he has discovered, is possibility—the very infi-
niteness of which may be defeating, unless by dint of a feat of
imagination some transcendence may be realized. And since, as
it would seem, the protagonist-narrator conceives art itself to be
the definition of such a transcendence, he—amidst the misrule
and confusion of a demented world—has undertaken to form
the lessons he has learned into a story, to "put it [all] down,"
and thereby (like another young man who became an artist) to
forge in the smithy of his own soul the uncreated conscience of
his native land. His story ends in a cellar because, having constantly been told that it is in some such hovel that he belongs,
this *eiron* has chosen mockingly to descend, then, into a Harlem
basement where, if he cannot have visibility, he can at least have
vision—and where he can produce out of his abysmal pain a po-

etry that, as he says, "on the lower frequencies . . . [may] speak for you"—*le lecteur*.

The book presents, as the late Alfred Kazin suggested some years ago, one of the most deeply engaging studies in modern literature in "the art of survival."[2] And in relation to everything with which its young anti-hero must reckon Ellison displays a notable mastery. His reader finds himself, indeed, utterly immersed in all the concrete materialities of African-American experience: one hears the very buzz and hum of Harlem in the racy, pungent speech of his West Indians and native hipsters; one sees the fearful nonchalance of the zootsuiter and hears the terrible anger of the black nationalist on his street-corner platform; and all the *grotesquerie* in the novel's account of a dreary little backwater of a remote southern Negro college has in it a certain kind of empirically absolute rightness. The book is packed full of the acutest observations of the manners and idioms and human styles that comprise the ethos of black life in America, and it gives us such a sense of social fact as can be come by nowhere in the manuals of academic sociology—all this being done with the ease that comes from enormous expertness of craft, from deep intimacy of knowledge, and from love.

Yet, deeply rooted as the novel is in the circumstances of Negro life and experience, it wants on its "lower frequencies" to speak about a larger condition, and, indeed, when Ellison is taken (as he too often is) to be a barrister seeking on behalf of the black multitudes to impose a certain racial affidavit on the American conscience, what is most deeply prophetic in the testimony brought forward by his novel is by way of being obscured. Nor is it at all inapposite to consider the authorial performance conveyed by *Invisible Man* as reflecting a prophetic intention, at least not if one thinks of prophetism in something like the terms proposed by the distinguished anthropologist, the late Victor Turner.

Turner's theory of culture, based in large part on his extensive field-researches among the Ndembu people of northwest Zambia, entails an elaborate scheme which he developed in numerous writings but most fully in three major books, *The Forest of Symbols* (1967), *The Ritual Process* (1969), and *Dramas, Fields, and Metaphors*

(1974). His starting-point is the concept of the "liminal phase" advanced by the Belgian ethnographer Arnold van Gennep in his classic work of 1908, *Les Rites de Passage*. Van Gennep, in working out the logic of "transition" rites, remarked three phases into which they invariably fall and which he identified as, first, separation, then margin (or *limen*, the Latin signifying "threshold"), and then reaggregation. That is to say, the neophyte first undergoes some detachment or dislocation from his established role in a social structure or cultural polity—whereupon he finds himself as a novice in a "liminal" situation in which he is neither one thing nor another, neither here nor there, neither what he was nor yet what he will become. Then, in the third phase, the passage is completed by his reincorporation into a social or religious structure: no longer is he invisible by reason of his divestment of status and role, for, once again, he finds himself with acknowledged rights and obligations vis-à-vis those others who with him are members in whatever body it is to which they jointly belong.

Now Turner is careful to remark that "liminars" are, in most human communities, by no means the only *déclassés*, for always there are various "outsiders" (shamans, monks, priests, hippies, hoboes, gypsies) who either by ascription or choice stand outside the established order, just as there are also various kinds of "marginals" (migrant foreigners, persons of mixed ethnic origin, the upwardly and downwardly mobile) who may be "simultaneously members . . . of two or more groups whose social definitions and cultural norms are distinct from, and often even opposed to, one another."[3] But, though at many points he is strongly insistent on these distinctions, at many others he seems to be treating "outsiderhood" and "marginality" as merely special modes of "liminality," and it appears for him to be the decisive antipode to "aggregation."

What Turner is most eager to remark, however, is the wrongheadedness of regarding liminality as a merely negative state of privation: on the contrary, as he argues, it can be and often is an enormously fruitful seedbed of spiritual creativity, for it is precisely amid the troubling ambiguities of the liminar's *déclassement* that there is born in him a profound hunger for *communitas*. And he prefers the Latin term, since he feels "community" connotes an ordered, systemized society—whereas the liminar's yearning is not for any simple kind of social structure but rather, as he says, for that spontaneous, immediate flowing from *I* to *Thou* of which Martin Buber is our great modern rhapsode.[4] Which is to say that the liminar thirsts for *communitas*: this is what the naked neophyte in a seclusion lodge yearns for: this is what the dispossessed and the exiled dream of: this is what "dharma bums" and millenarians and holy mendicants and "rock" people are moved by—namely, the vision of an *open* society in which all the impulses and affections that are normally bound by social structure are liberated, so that every barrier between I and thou is broken down and the wind of *communitas* may blow where it listeth.

Moreover, Turner conceives it to be the distinctive mission of the prophet to lift *communitas* into the subjunctive mood: he is the liminal man *par excellence* whose special vocation, as a frontiersman dwelling on the edges of the established order, is to puncture "the clichés associated with status incumbency and role-playing"[5] and to fill for his contemporaries the open space of absolute futurity with a vision of what the theologians of Russian Orthodoxy call *sobornost*—which is nothing other than that "catholicity," that harmony, that unanimity, that free unity-in-diversity, which graces the human order when a people gives its suffrage to the "open morality" (as Bergson would have called it) of *agape*.

Now it is when *Invisible Man* is regarded in its relation to the experiential realities addressed by Victor Turner that its special kind of prophetic discernment may perhaps be most clearly identified. True, its narrator is a young black man encumbered with all the disadvantages that American society has imposed on his kind. But his very last word to the reader—*mon semblable, mon frère!*—records his conviction that, "on the lower frequencies," he, in the story he tells about himself, is speaking about a condition that embraces not just his ancestral kinsmen but the human generality of his age. Which suggests that what is most essentially problematic in his situation is not merely his blackness but, rather, something else, and it is this which needs now to be defined.

One of Ellison's critics speaks of how frequently his novel is by way of coming to an end and then having once more to start itself up again,[6] and something like this is surely the case: at least, it may be said that the persistent rhythm of the novel is an affair of the protagonist's drifting into a relation with one or another of the various trustees of social power and then either digging in his heels or taking flight, when the connection threatens to abrogate his freedom. After he is expelled from his college, he takes to New York the various letters of introduction Dr. Bledsoe has provided, and it is his eventual discovery of the cruel dispraise that these sealed letters from the malignant old man have actually conveyed that leads him to think: "Everyone seemed to have some plan for me, and beneath that some more secret plan." And so indeed it is: wherever he turns, he finds himself dealing with those—whether it be Bledsoe or Mr. Norton or the Reverend Homer A. Barbee or the owner of the Long Island paint factory or Brother Jack—who are eager to map out a design for his life and to convert him into a kind of automaton of their own schemes. They may be agents of religion or education or industry or radical politics, but, at bottom, they are (as Tony Tanner says) "mechanizers of consciousness"[7]—and each is prepared to say something like what Bledsoe says in reference to his college: "This is a power set-up, son, and I'm at the controls." In fact, this young *picaro* does at last himself realize that all his various proctors and patrons have been "very much the same, each attempting to force his picture of reality upon me and neither giving a hoot in hell for how things looked to me." But he is unflagging in his refusal of obedient service to the organizers and manipulators: he wants to be free of that great alien force that we call Society. So, in the logic of the novel, his exemplary role is related not merely to the disinherited African-American but, far more basically, to that "disintegrated" or "alienated" consciousness which, as Hegel reminds us in the *Phenomenology of Mind*, is distinguished by its antagonism to "the external power of society" and which, in the modern period, is not simply here or there—but everywhere.

But, in his liminality, Ellison's young knight does not choose merely to pour scornful laughter on the social establishment, in the manner of Rinehart, for, *isolé* though he is, he remains totally in earnest. There comes a moment when, though having separated himself from the Brotherhood, he is nevertheless hunted by the partisans of the West Indian black nationalist, Ras the Exhorter, who conceives the interracialism of the Brotherhood to be a fearfully mischievous confusion of "the blahk man" and who is unrelenting in his pursuit of him who has been its chief spokesman in Harlem. So, by way of hurriedly arranging a scanty disguise, our principal purchases some darkly tinted spectacles and a flamboyant hat, and immediately he is mistaken on the streets for a man named Rinehart of whom he has never heard—and whom he never sees. One evening there suddenly emerges from a Lenox Avenue subway exit a large, blowsy prostitute reeking of "Christmas Night perfume" who for a moment takes him to be her Man: "Rinehart, baby, is that you? . . . Say, you ain't Rinehart, man . . . git away from here before you get me in trouble." And, as he swings on, a few moments later he is hailed by a couple of hipsters who take him to be Rinehart the numbers man: "Rinehart, poppa, tell us what you putting down." Then a group of zoot-suiters greets him: "Hey now, daddy-o." And, again, in an Eighth Avenue tavern he is taken to be Rinehart by the barkeeper: "What brand you drinking tonight, Poppa-stopper?" Some larcenous policemen expecting a pay-off summon him from, their patrol car to a curb and, when he denies that he is Rinehart, the response flung back at him is "Well, you better be by morning." Then, again, outside a storefront church he is greeted by two aging, pious drones as "Rever'n Rinehart," and they offer him assurances about how zealously they are collecting money for his building fund. And, after many such encounters, he begins to marvel at this extraordinary personage—"Rine the runner and Rine the gambler and Rine the briber and Rine the lover and Rinehart the Reverend." Indeed, he is at once fascinated by the virtuosity of this remarkable changeling—and, in a way, unhinged by the abyss of infinite possibility opened up by his glimpse of the "multiple personalities" worn by this black Proteus.

But, no, not for him the way of this wily rascal who deals

with the intractabilities of social circumstance by simply mocking them in the cultivation of an extravagant histrionism. No, Ellison's protagonist is a liminar who, though separated from the established orders of the world, is yet not estranged from himself. And thus he yearns for an authentic existence, not for Rinehart's world of no boundaries at all but for something like a New Jerusalem, where no man is an island and where Love is the name behind the design of the human City.

He is unable to descry at any point on the horizon the merest prospect, however, of this Good Place. And so at last he descends into an underground world. He is floundering about one night through Harlem streets inflamed by a savage race riot (carefully orchestrated by the Brotherhood itself), and, in his abstracted anguish at the sheer futility of this lunatic paroxysm, he stumbles into some black *enragés* who, being suddenly angered by the sight of his briefcase, are about to set upon him, when he lifts the cover of a manhole and plunges down into a coal cellar below. There he finds a narrow passage that leads into a "dimensionless room," and this he elects to occupy as the site of his "hibernation."

This liminar in his cellar bears no resemblance, however, to that bilious and exacerbated little cypher whose portrayal in Dostoievski's *Notes from the Underground* has made him one of the great modern archetypes of the Underground Man. Ellison's hero has been "hurt to the point of abysmal pain, hurt to the point of invisibility," not only by American racism but by all those "mechanizers of consciousness"—by Bledsoe as well as by Mr. Norton, by Brother Jack as well as by Ras the Exhorter—whose great "passion [is] to make men conform to a pattern." Yet, in his hibernation, he realizes that, for all the vehemence with which he has taken a stand " 'against' society," he still wants to defend "the principle on which the country was built." As he says, "I defend because in spite of all"—though "I sell you no phony forgiveness"—"I find that I love." He harbors no love for those who are moved by a "passion toward conformity," for, as he insists, "diversity is the word." "Life is to be lived, not controlled." So the dream by which he is enheartened in his basement room is the dream that we shall "become one, and yet many": it is the dream of *communitas*. And it is in the eloquence with which the novel projects this vision for the human future that it proves (in the terms I have taken over from Victor Turner) its prophetic genius—and its special relevance to the American situation of our own immediate present. For, given the furious assertiveness that distinguishes the various racial and ethnic particularisms making up our national society today, ours (as one thoughtful observer remarked some years ago) is a country representing something like "pluralism gone mad." One of our great needs as a people is to recover a sense of common purpose and of a common destiny that overrides our "atomized world of a thousand me-first . . . groupings" of one kind or another.[8] And it is the reminder in this connection that Ellison's novel brings that gives its testimony just now a special poignance.

BUT NOW IT should also be remarked that Ellison's essays are often being controlled by the same vision of *communitas* that guided *Invisible Man*. "The way home we seek," he says in "Brave Words for a Startling Occasion" "is that condition of man's being at home in the world which is called love." In short, he took it for granted that the regulative norm to which our social and cultural life are accountable is what the *koinē* Greek of the New Testament denominates as *agape*. But he had a clear sense of how infinitely difficult any full realization of this ultimate norm is. For he conceived the American scene to be marked, above all else, by its diversity, its fluidity, its complexity. And this diversity, this fluidity, in Ellison's analysis, breeds a profound unease. It is the essay in *Going to the Territory* entitled "The Little Man at Chehaw Station" that presents one of the central statements of his diagnosis. He says:

> Beset by feelings of isolation because of the fluid, pluralistic turbulence of the democratic process, we cling desperately to our own familiar fragment of the democratic rock, and from such fragments we confront our fellow Americans in that combat of civility, piety, and tradition which is the drama of

American social hierarchy. Holding desperately to our familiar turf, we engage in . . . [a] ceaseless contention. . . .

The rock, the terrain upon which we struggle, is itself . . . a terrain of ideas that, although man-made, exert the compelling force of the ideal, of the sublime; ideas that draw their power from the Declaration of Independence, the Constitution, and the Bill of Rights. We stand, as we say, united in the name of these sacred principles. But, indeed, it is in the name of these same principles that we ceaselessly contend, affirming our ideals even as we do them violence.[9]

The trouble is, he suggests, that "for many our cultural diversity is as indigestible as the concept of democracy in which it is grounded." And the nineteenth-century metaphor that likened the country unto a great "melting pot" is today noisily rejected "in the name of the newly fashionable code word 'ethnicity'." "Most amazingly, these attacks upon the melting pot are led by the descendants of peasants, or slaves, or inhabitants of European ghettos—people whose status as spokesmen is a product of that very melting of hierarchical barriers they now deny." But, of course, implicit in this denial of the kind of cultural integration for which the melting pot was once a generally accepted metaphor is a sadly misdirected "effort to dismiss the mystery of American identity (our unity-within-diversity) with a gesture of democracy-weary resignation." Indeed, as Ellison reminds us, "we are, all of us—white or black, native-born or immigrant—members of minority groups" who have *become* Americans by opportunistically appropriating one another's cultures:

The Pilgrims began by appropriating the agricultural, military, and meteorological lore of the Indians—including much of their terminology. The Africans, thrown together from numerous ravaged tribes, took up the English language and the biblical legends of the ancient Hebrews and were "Americanizing" themselves long before the American Revolution. . . .

Everyone played the appropriate game. The whites took over any elements of Afro-American culture that seemed use-

ful: the imagery of folklore, ways of speaking, endurance of
what appeared to be hopeless hardship, and singing and dancing—including the combination of Afro-American art forms
that produced the first musical theater of national appeal—
the minstrel show.[10]

And so it has gone throughout the entire course of American
history: we have always been a "nation of nations" whose people
have been "constantly moving around and, culturally, rubbing off
on one another": this is how "Englishmen, Europeans, Africans,
and Asians *became* Americans." Which is to say that the distinc-
tiveness of the whole American enterprise would be unimaginable
apart from the common dedication to *communitas* by which our
national tradition has been so singularly marked.

In the autumn of 1979 the poet Michael Harper mounted a
great celebration at Brown University that was called the Ralph
Ellison Festival. In the course of that happy occasion Ellison delivered a major address which he included in the collection of
his essays that appeared in 1986, its title being that which he
bestowed on this volume, *Going to the Territory*. And here again he
speaks of "the mystery which haunts American experience, . . .
the mystery of how we are many and yet one." He invites us to
consider how impossible it is, given the pluralistic character of
our society, for "any one group to discover by itself the intrinsic
forms of our democratic culture. This has to be a cooperative
effort, and it is achieved," he says, "through contact and communication across our divisions of race, class, religion, and region." Moreover, he suggests that "the process of synthesis
through which the slaves took the music and religious lore of
others and combined them with their African heritage in such
ways as to create their own cultural idiom" is a quite typical case
of how all groups dwell in such a pluralistic society as our own:
"no one group has managed to create the definitive American
style": each group seeks "the homeness of home" by appropriating
"those styles which provide them with a feeling of being most in
harmony with the undefined aspects of American experience,"

and thus we find ways"of naming, defining, and creating a consciousness of who and what we have come to be." In short, we
feed and fatten on *communitas*.

It is this note which is being struck again and again in many
of the essays in *Going to the Territory*, as well as in many of the pieces
in his collection of 1964, *Shadow and Act*. On nothing is he quicker
to pour scorn than on any kind of cultural sectarianism or racial
particularism that threatens to break the various mutualities that
constitute the fundamental glue holding a polymorphous society
together. For to fence off oneself or one's group from all the rich
diversity of human experience and endeavor that distinguish the
American scene is (if I may borrow a term once used by Robert
Penn Warren in a brief essay on Ellison) to forswear that "school
of imagination" through whose disciplines Americans of whatever
background stand their best chance, their only chance of learning
who they most truly are. Indeed, this is perhaps the most fundamental lesson that Ellison's achievement at once in his fiction
and his essays enforces upon us, that "no man is an island," that
we are members one of another, and that we derive our deepest
nourishment from the total body of which we are all parts. It is
in such unity, embracing and nurturing but not overriding diversity, that, as his young protagonist in *Invisible Man* wants to say
in his basement room, we may rediscover "the principle on which
the country was built" and to which it is finally answerable—
communitas.[11]

Notes

1. William H. Gass, *Fiction and the Figures of Life* (New York: Vintage
Books, 1972), pp. 27, 30.

2. Alfred Kazin, *Bright Book of Life: American Novelists and Storytellers from
Hemingway to Mailer* (Boston: Little, Brown, 1973), p. 246.

3. See Victor Turner, *The Ritual Process* (Ithaca, N.Y.: Cornell University Press, 1977), p. 127.

4. See Martin Buber, *I and Thou*, trans. Ronald Gregor Smith (Ed-
inburgh: Clark, 1937).

5. *The Ritual Process*, p. 128.

6. See Marcus Klein, *After Alienation: American Novels in Mid-Century* (Cleveland, New York: World, 1964), pp. 107–109.

7. Tony Tanner, *City of Words: American Fiction, 1950–1970* (New York: Harper and Row, 1971), p. 53.

8. Meg Greenfield, "Pluralism Gone Mad," *Newsweek*, August 27, 1979, p. 76.

9. Ralph Ellison, *Going to the Territory* (New York: Random House, 1986), pp. 16–17.

10. Ibid., pp. 27–28.

11. The last paragraph of this essay was written by Professor Scott in 2003 expressly for this volume.

Ralph Ellison, Race, and American Culture

MORRIS DICKSTEIN

❖   ❖   ❖

IN THE STANDARD VIEWS of American culture after the war, and especially of the 1950s, the arts and intellectual life turned deeply conservative, reflecting the imperatives of the cold war, the migration to the suburbs, the new domesticity, and the rise of McCarthyism. A small academic industry has sprung up, linking every cultural development of the postwar period to the clenched mind-set of the cold war. At the same time, it has been more and more evident that the facile contrast between the fifties and the sixties is based on a deep simplification. The fifties were a far more restless, dynamic, and contradictory period than we have generally allowed. It can be easily shown how the roots of the sixties lay in the new energies of the postwar years, when writers, along with jazz musicians, abstract painters, and maverick filmmakers, contributed to a creative ferment that matched the growth of the economy and the spread of American influence. Working just outside the mainstream, often seemingly apolitical, these writers and artists helped shape a counterculture focused on the youthful dropout, the rebel without a cause, the disgruntled outsider who embodied new cultural values: improvisation, spontaneity, an experimental attitude.

This last phrase comes not from the Beats but, surprisingly, from Ralph Ellison describing his 1952 novel *Invisible Man* as he accepted the National Book Award. It may be hard to imagine Ellison, always so correct and elegant in his personal demeanor, as any kind of radical, or as a forerunner of the counterculture. Moreover, no black writer was more warmly welcomed by the literary establishment or more reviled by his young successors when the catchwords of black nationalism took hold in the 1960s and '70s. Even before then, left-wing critics like Irving Howe had indicted Ellison and James Baldwin for turning their backs on the militant traditions of black anger associated with their mentor, Richard Wright.

Baldwin's damaging depiction of *Native Son* in his 1949 manifesto, "Everybody's Protest Novel," and again two years later in "Many Thousands Gone," dealt a major blow to Wright's reputation. It cleared the ground for writing that was far more personal than Wright's, more metaphysical, more concerned with individual identity, including sexual identity. Neither Baldwin nor Ellison ever challenged one essential conviction of Wright's, that the experience of African Americans was deeply conditioned by the traumatic effects of racial separation and discrimination. But this alone, they insisted, was insufficient to account for the varied ways that blacks had accommodated to their treatment and the complex lives they had shaped for themselves.

In his controversial 1963 essay "Black Boys and Native Sons," Howe looked approvingly at Baldwin's recent shift toward protest writing in *The Fire Next Time*. "Like Richard Wright before him, Baldwin has discovered that to assert his humanity he must release his rage." He accuses Ellison, however, of ending his only novel with a "sudden, unprepared and implausible assertion of unconditioned freedom," as if the Invisible Man in his basement hole spoke, without irony, for Ellison himself. Baldwin's newfound militance did little to endear him to the young black firebrands of the sixties, who attacked or dimissed him, and it seriously damaged his work, which at its best was grounded in introspection, not angry rhetoric. But Ellison responded to Howe and Baldwin—and, by implication, to his own later black critics—in a celebrated essay, "The World and the Jug," in which he wittily disparaged Baldwin for "out-Wrighting Richard" and minimized his own oedipal relationship to the author of *Native Son*. "Wright was no spiritual father of mine," he wrote. "I rejected Bigger Thomas as any *final* image of Negro personality" (something Wright himself had never intimated). Ellison explored the relationship more affectionately in a lecture about Wright a few years later, revealing how close he was to his mentor at least until 1940.

In essays like these, Ellison picked up where Baldwin faltered, insisting on the variety and complexity of black life and the range of influences, from Hemingway and T. S. Eliot to jazz, that had been enriching for black artists. Ellison was immune to the destructive force of black nationalism, perhaps because he had already reimagined it so well in *Invisible Man*. Black anger and black pride were only part of the broad constellation of Ellison's novel, which ranges over the whole terrain of African-American life, from folklore and dialect to urban hustling and pan-Africanism. This was why he reacted so strongly to Howe's well-argued but prescriptive essay. It seemed to confine the black writer to a path of anger, protest, and victimization. To a man who cherished his creative freedom, who had aspired to write the Great American Novel, this was a much narrower role than the one he wished to play.

The issue of freedom identified by Howe would become the keystone not only of Ellison's creative work but of his radical rethinking of the role of race and culture in American life. Howe, with his affinity for the European social novel, with his political commitments and his sense of the tragic, spoke up for the conditioned life, insisting that harsh circumstances define and limit the options available to individuals, especially those at the bottom of the social ladder. Ellison, on the other hand, was determined that his fiction and essays would reflect the widest range of encounters, the most abundant opportunities for self-making—in other words, a larger, more various American reality as he had known it.

Ellison's novel had already sent up every kind of ideological current in black life, from the Marxism of the thirties to Black Power notions that would only flourish more than a decade later. Born in Oklahoma in 1914, not long after its transition from Indian territory to statehood, Ellison had studied music at Tuskegee Institute between 1933 and 1936 before migrating to Harlem, where he began to write under Richard Wright's insistent prodding. Thus he not only knew Negro life in the West, in the South, and in the largest northern ghetto, but was exposed (at Tuskegee) to the accommodationist ideas of Booker T. Washington ("the Founder"), which he would wickedly satirize throughout *Invisible Man*. All these, including his close links with the Harlem branch of the Communist party are among the autobiographical strands from which his novel is loosely woven. But these experiences appear even more directly in the essays which, as we now can see, form a major part of Ellison's literary legacy.

When Ellison first brought together his essays, reviews, lectures, and interviews in 1964 in *Shadow and Act*, they were gratefully received as revealing adjuncts to his novel, and as a promissory note for the fiction yet to come. A second collection, *Going to the Territory*, appeared with almost no fanfare in 1986. But well before the *Collected Essays* of 1995, it became clear that this impressive prose was not simply an assortment of personal opinions but a major body of cultural criticism that had inspired other black intellectuals and had begun to influence the national outlook on race, as Wright had done for the 1940s and Baldwin had done for the 1950s and early 1960s.

What once looked tame or apolitical in Ellison's work—his emphasis on identity, freedom, and the vast potential for diversity in American life—has come to seem more radical than the political criticism that rejected it; this too has become part of our revised view of the postwar years. The key to Ellison's approach is his way of exploring his double consciousness, his sense of identity as a Negro and as an American. His answer to Baldwin's question, "Do I really *want* to be integrated into a burning house?" would surely have been, "Yes, because it's *my* house." And because not all of it is burning, not all the time: the property is still rich with undeveloped possibilities.

Of all African-American writers and intellectuals, Ellison stakes the greatest claims—not for a separate black culture or literary tradition, but for an inestimably great role within *American* culture. He acknowledges a debt to Jewish-American writers, but insists that they did not escape provinciality until they saw their experience in wider terms as part of the crazy quilt of American culture, by treating their protagonists as representative Americans, not simply as archetypal Jews.

Where others pay lip service to "diversity," Ellison shows in fascinating detail how different currents have merged into the mainstream of our culture—not simply how Anglo-Saxon culture was altered by the folkways and speech of outsiders but how the children of immigrants and slaves adapted remote customs to their own usage. Cultural appropriation is the great theme of Ellison's essays, which explore the mixed origins and improvisational strategies of both black and American identity. Through a half century of lecturing and writing, Ellison never tired of describing how different cultural forms, high and low, classical and vernacular, eastern and western, northern and southern, were braided together into an authentic American creativity. In the varied traditions of early Du Bois, Dewey, Randolph Bourne, Horace Kallen, and Alain Locke, Ellison's is a classically pluralist defense of cultural diversity. In a revealing tribute to Locke, Ellison stressed the danger of becoming "unconsciously racist by simply stressing one part of our heritage," the genetic, racial part:

> You cannot have an American experience without having a black experience. Nor can you have the technology of jazz, as original as many of those techniques are, without having had long centuries of European musical technology, not to mention the technologies of various African musical traditions. . . .
>
> What I am suggesting is that when you go back you do not find a pure stream; after all, Louis Armstrong, growing up in New Orleans, was taught to play a rather strict type of military

music before he found his jazz and blues voice. Talk about cultural pluralism! It's the air we breathe; it's the ground we stand on.

Part of Ellison's story was about how a culture could be created by people who were neither free nor equal—by despised immigrants or oppressed slaves. In one example, he describes how slaves adapted European dance fashions brought over by their masters:

> First the slaves mocked them, and then decided, coming from dancing cultures, that they could do them better—so they went on to define what is surely the beginnings of an American choreography.

He goes on to show that what began in rags in the slave yards eventually found its way into Negro dance halls and juke joints until it finally reached the stage. In Ellison's picture, popular and vernacular culture, located at the fringes of the social hierarchy, provides the pores through which the main body of culture breathes and renews itself. Blacks had "the freedom of experimentation, of trying out new things no matter how ridiculous they might seem," because "there was no one to take them too seriously." Oppression and dislocation had imposed "a great formlessness" on Negro life. They needed to experiment, to develop a new language, because they were forced into tight corners where they *had* to improvise, to recreate themselves, and because the cultural mainstream reflected no honest images of their own lives—or mirrored them only in distorted or one-dimensional forms, as in minstrel culture or in Hollywood movies.

To Ellison, white Americans have always "suffered from a deep uncertainty as to who they really are." On one hand this led them to seek a unified identity by scapegoating "outsiders." But the same national uncertainty gives these outsiders exceptional leverage—politically, to recall the majority to its professed ideals; culturally, to work within the many popular forms of expression that make America different from an old and traditional culture.

"On this level," says Ellison, "the melting pot did indeed melt, creating such deceptive metamorphoses and blending of identities, values, and life-styles that most American whites are culturally part Negro American without even realizing it." And he shows how, beginning as far back as *Huckleberry Finn*, the black presence led to "certain creative tensions" that had a decisive effect on the high culture as well.

In the opening piece of his second collection, "The Little Man at Chehaw Station," Ellison wrote a definitive (if idealized) meditation on the American audience, which he saw embodied in the little man behind the stove at a small railroad station near Tuskegee—the random individual whose judgment matters, who sees through the bogus performance, whose culture is at once eclectic and classical, popular yet demanding. If *Invisible Man* had a single ideal reader, it would be this man, completely ordinary yet protean and adventurous. "Possessing an American-vernacular receptivity to change, a healthy delight in creative attempts at formalizing irreverence, and a Yankee trader's respect for the experimental, he is repelled by works of art that would strip human experience—especially American experience—of its wonder and stubborn complexity." This figure is the artist's creative conscience—the surprisingly knowledgeable, innately skeptical Everyman. Whether such a man actually exists, for Ellison he is a paradigm of democratic life, in which culture and education have spread through mysterious channels and "certain assertions of personality, formerly the prerogative of high social rank, have become the privilege of the anonymous and the lowly."

Such a man can also become the agent rather than simply the consumer of culture; in a different guise he reappears later in the essay as a classic "American joker," a cool ghetto customer who performs some astonishing bits of personal theater before delighted onlookers outside Ellison's home on Riverside Drive. After describing this street-smart character's antics, including his flamboyant dress and body language, Ellison calls him "a home-boy bent on projecting and recording with native verve something of his complex sense of cultural identity." This man—or Ellison's projection of him—represents culture as pragmatic improvisation, for he is putting together his own personality out of bits and pieces of different traditions. Making himself up as he goes along, he demonstrates "an American compulsion to improvise upon the given." He "was a product of the melting pot and the conscious or unconscious comedy it brews." To Ellison, Americans have "improvised their culture as they did their politics and institutions: touch and go, by ear and by eye; fitting new form to new function, new function to old form." This emphasis on improvisation links Ellison not only to the counterculture of the 1950s, but to a wider American tradition that extends from Emerson and pragmatism to jazz and picaresque fiction—the *Huck Finn*-style road novels, steeped in the vernacular, that made a breakthrough for many fifties writers. It also connects him, as Ross Posnock shows in his new book *Color & Culture*, to postmodern, antiessentialist notions of identity.

In this account of our eclectic forms of self-invention, Ellison is at once expounding the technique of *Invisible Man*, situating it within American culture, and perhaps explaining why it was so hard for him to complete his second novel. Two years later he developed these ideas in an autobiographical lecture, "Going to the Territory," the title piece of the same collection. Here Ellison gave one of the most forceful descriptions of how our culture and identity have been shaped by a constant process of cultural assimilation. The very title alludes to Huck Finn's metaphor for reclaiming his freedom. Recalling his own school days in Oklahoma, not long after the territory had become a state, Ellison describes young Negroes learning European folk dances, a sight which some might find "absurd" but to him is part of a salutary process of appropriating the Other, making creative use of what seems alien. Rather than expressing "a desire to become white," we were narrowing "the psychological distance between them and ourselves," as well as "learning their dances as an *artistic* challenge." This skill, this discipline, would be the black children's secret weapon as well as their key to an unnoticed freedom— "our freedom to broaden our personal culture by absorbing the culture of others," something that could develop and grow even "within our state of social and political unfreedom."

For Ellison himself this was a special gift, for it introduced him "to the basic discipline required of the artist." Ellison's musical education would shape his vision of American literature as the cultural expression of democracy, an ongoing process of transformation mediated by the vernacular. He sees the vernacular not simply as "popular or indigenous language," but as a "dynamic *process* in which the most refined styles of the past are continually merged with the play-it-by-eye-and-by-ear improvisations which we invent in our efforts to control our environment and entertain ourselves." On one level this is a demotic version of Eliot's "Tradition and the Individual Talent,"with its account of how the tradition is constantly being altered by new voices and creative departures. On another level it's a well-articulated example of a fluid and functional pragmatic aesthetic within a democratic culture.

Far from treating the vernacular as a dumbing-down of high culture, a view common among critics of popular culture in the 1950s, Ellison sees it as part of an ongoing process of self-renewal. "While the vernacular is shy of abstract standards," he says, "it still seeks perfection in the form of functional felicity. This is why considerations of function and performance figure so prominently in the scale of vernacular aesthetics." This, of course, is a description of jazz, for Ellison the very epitome of how vernacular artists refine and transform traditional materials. But it applies equally well to a writer like Twain, who showed how to turn regional speech into art "and thus taught us how to capture that which is essentially American in our folkways and manners."

Ellison's versions of Twain, of jazz and the blues, and of his own early musical education are also accounts of the creative process that shaped *Invisible Man* and made it an archetypal American novel. In his previously mentioned 1953 speech accepting the National Book Award, Ellison gives prime importance to the book's "experimental attitude," that phrase out of the pragmatist lexicon that would apply equally well to a modernist or a jazz aesthetic. Explaining why he turned away from the spare language of naturalism, he notes that "despite the notion that its rhythms were those of everyday speech, I found that when compared with the rich babel of idiomatic expression around me, a language full of imagery and gesture and rhetorical canniness, it was embarrassingly austere." In its place he sought a language and form that were richer, more varied, and more mysterious, full of word-play and allusion, metaphoric in plot as well as verbal style, so as to convey the fluidity and complexity of the world as he had experienced it. With its protean form and exuberant style, *Invisible Man* would exemplify the vernacular process through which American culture had explored its contradictions, including its racial conflicts.

One of Ellison's most strongly held views was that race itself is hardly more than a mystification, that skin color and blood kinship are of little help in explaining the complexity of human culture. Ellison's aim is to put aside "the insidious confusion between race and culture." Whether seen as a source of pride (by nationalists), of shame (by racists), or of solidarity (by communal boosters), race alone determines little about what human beings can achieve. It is not a fate to which individuals have been ineluctably condemned, nor an essence that defines or delimits them. In his response to Irving Howe, he complains that "Howe makes of 'Negroness' a metaphysical condition, one that is a state of irremediable agony which all but engulfs the mind." Ellison's pragmatic response—to Howe, to Baldwin, to white supremacists and black nationalists alike—is that identity is fashioned rather than given, created rather than determined by biology or social statistics. "It is not skin color which makes a Negro American but cultural heritage as shaped by the American experience."

For Ellison the construction of identity is analogous to the hard work of making art, involving a mixture of personal discipline and subtle cultural influences. In *Invisible Man* he gives us an anonymous protagonist with no identity except what others are continually trying to impose on him, no strategy except his eagerness to please. In the whole spectrum of postwar fiction he is the ultimate outsider, telling his story from his underground lair. But through most of the novel he is also the man who most wanted to be an insider, to fit in and to be accepted. The novel's episodic structure, prismatic language, and fluid technique reflect the process through which he tests and gradually sheds these imposed definitions, with all the illusions that came with them.

Like Voltaire's Candide, whose experience continually belies his teacher's insistence that this is "the best of all possible worlds," Ellison's protagonist is an unshakable innocent, immature, eager to get ahead, trained in the habits of deference and humility through which blacks in America had traditionally gotten by. But life itself tells him otherwise, beginning with the death of his grandfather, who, after a long, quiet, humble existence, calls himself a spy and a traitor in the enemy's country, and urges him to "overcome 'em with yeses, undermine 'em with grins, agree 'em to death and destruction." Near the end of the book, the hero bitterly determines to do just that: "I'd let them swoller me until they vomited or burst wide open.... I'd yes then until they puked and rolled in it. All they wanted of me was one belch of affirmation and I'd bellow it out loud. Yes! Yes! YES! That was all anyone wanted of us, that we should be heard and not seen, and then heard in one big optimistic chorus of yassuh, yassuh, yassuh!"

The whole novel is a test of his grandfather's double message of humility and enmity, seeming accommodation and inner resistance—the first of many bits of advice he takes in without fully understanding them. Like the heroes of other picaresque novels, the young man is less a full-blooded character than a convenience of a symbolic, often surreal plot. Ellison uses narrative as a free-wheeling vehicle for ideas, word-play, wild satire, ideological burlesque, and striking realistic detail. His grandfather's words serve as a chorus or leitmotif recurring from episode to episode. The novel is tied together by many other such texts that reappear musically, a theme and variations marking the stages of the narrator's progress. Another text like this is "To Whom It May Concern—Keep This Nigger-Boy Running," which he understands to be the message he carries as he tries to make his way in the world. At every step he's given the illusion of progress only to keep running in place, to get nowhere. He needs to break with received messages, socially ascribed roles, conventional restraints, and respectable ambitions in order to come into his own.

The typical bildungsroman is about the passage from innocence to experience, a process that turns the naive or callow protagonist into the substantial person who narrates the book. The hero of *Invisible Man*, however, ends up nowhere, in a state of articulate hibernation, in some well-lit Dostoevskyan hole in the ground, not in Harlem but in some "border area" where he can see without being seen. The novel is not about the shaping of a life but the unshaping of illusions, about breaking through to a new awareness of what you can do and be. When the hero eventually puts his innocence behind him—the naiveté he had resumed in nearly every episode—it is not to make a life but to shed all the false lives for which he had been pointlessly striving. Along with the "running" metaphor, this suggests *Invisible Man*'s kinship to other picaresque fiction of the 1950s, such as *The Catcher in the Rye*, *On the Road, Lolita*, and *Rabbit, Run*. In these novels, the protagonist's deepest need is not to become a success, to settle into an ordered life, but to escape the one he already has—not to take on responsibility but to slough it off. Like Holden Caulfield, Ellison's hero eventually sees through the phoniness of nearly everyone around him, the fakery inherent in social role-playing. He rejects the 1950s mantra of maturity, the demand for affirmation, and reaches for something that makes him an outsider, even a pariah. He wants to live his discontent, even if it is only half understood.

One thread of *Invisible Man* is Ellison's lively mockery of every kind of respectability, black or white, corporate or communist, middle class or working class. The good white citizens who organize the "battle royal" are lechers and sadists, treating the black boys like gladiators in a Roman arena. At college the young man tries but fails to live by the visionary ideals of the Founder and Dr. Bledsoe. Expelled, he learns what those so-called ideals really add up to—a way of manipulating whites into thinking that you serve and respect them. Up north, he seeks help from a trustee of the college named Emerson—the names in the book are broadly symbolic—but is disabused by the man's fretful son. He is a spoof of a well-meaning white liberal—patronizing, neurotic, and self-absorbed; he urges the young man to study another Emerson's ideas about self-reliance, and seeks plaintively to be his friend, but ends up asking him to become his valet.

Each episode is dominated by a false God exacting tribute, a would-be mentor trying to determine his path. "Everyone seemed to have some plan for me, and beneath that some more secret plan." At the paint factory he is under the authority of an old Uncle Tom, Lucius Brockway, underpaid, overqualified, submissive to whites, vicious to other blacks especially those connected with the union. After an explosion reminiscent of Fritz Lang's sci-fi masterpiece *Metropolis*, he enters a surgical "white" world and is subjected to surreal experiments by men probing his sense of reality. In trying to deprive him of his identity, to lobotomize him, they unwittingly open him up to a new, more fluid sense of identity that will flourish in the big city.

At the other extreme are the few characters who nurture him without an agenda of their own, or simply help open his eyes. Trueblood's tragicomic tale of incest introduces him to the earthy world of the shacks and sharecropper cabins that lie outside the purview of the respectable college. When he shows this world to one of the white trustees, he is cast out—for introducing a touch of reality onto a painted set. Another helpful figure is the vet who echoed his grandfather's advice as the young man headed north: "Play the game, but don't believe in it—that much you owe yourself." In Harlem he boards with Mary, whose maternal concern is as anchored and authentic as Trueblood's ribald comedy of love and lust. She is a warm-hearted specimen of the common people, the substratum of personal reality that social theories ignore or suppress. The hero's mentors claim to be putting him in touch with history, but it is only a conveyor belt toward an unwanted future, an abstract process that takes no account of his wishes or needs. "Look at me! Look at *me!*" he finally shouts, in what could be the motto for the whole novel. "Everywhere I've turned somebody has wanted to sacrifice me for my good—only *they* were the ones who benefited."

In one of the novel's richest scenes, he buys baked yams from a Harlem street vendor and is flooded with nostalgia for the home he left behind, a distant pastoral world he has been taught to rise above. Yet going back to this early world is no answer. He *must* see its value—must accept the common life, the sensory plenitude from which he sprang—but also must put it behind him. Just as the college is the false Eden from which he had to fall in order to become himself, Mary's home is only a temporary shelter from the swirl of the city streets. Eating the yams makes him not only homesick but reflective. "What a group of people we were, I thought. Why, you could cause us the greatest humiliation simply by confronting us with something we liked." This leads him to a delicious fantasy in which he accuses Bledsoe of being "a shameless chitterling eater! . . . of relishing hog bowels!"

> Bledsoe would disintegrate, disinflate! With a profound sigh he'd drop his head in shame. He'd lose caste. The weekly newspapers would attack him. The captions over his picture: *Prominent Educator Reverts to Field-Niggerism.* . . . In the South his white folks would desert him. . . . He'd end up an exile washing dishes at the Automat.

This goes on much longer—it's the kind of wild riff that marks the hero's moments of recognition—and it leads to a moral: "to hell with being ashamed of what you liked." But the mind keeps turning, and within a page or two he begins to see the limits of the yam view of life. "Continue on the yam level and life would be sweet—though somewhat yellowish. Yet the freedom to eat yams on the street was far less than I had expected upon coming to the city. An unpleasant taste bloomed in my mouth now as I bit the end of the yam and threw it into the street; it had been frostbitten." In the end he typically resolves his conflict with an outrageous pun, "I yam what I am."

This yam scene is one of several turning points at the center of the book. It's preachy—Ellison is always making his points— yet full of the sensory exuberance that gives this novel its gusto. Much of the commentary on the novel has focused on the brilliant set-pieces of the first half, especially the Trueblood episode, making up a darkly comic American equivalent of *The Pilgrim's*

Progress. But readers have sometimes stumbled over the seemingly overlong Brotherhood sections that follow, which are clearly based on Ellison's (and Wright's) experiences with the Communist party. It is only here, however—and in the Harlem riots that follow—that Ellison begins to pull the many threads together, bringing the novel to its exhilarating conclusion. Just as the hero must leave Mary behind, he must give up the sanctuary of the Men's House, a temple of hollow propriety and foolish dreams and ambitions. (The Men's House is Ellison's version of the Harlem Y, where he stayed when he first came to the city in 1936.) By dumping the foul contents of a cuspidor over the head of a Baptist reverend whom he takes for Bledsoe, the hero throws away the crutch that protected him from a world "without boundaries"—from the fluid reality of Harlem and the city. If in earlier episodes he is slowly shedding illusions, only to deal with new ones right afterward, now he gradually yields to the flux as he comes to recognize and relish his own invisibility. In his own way he enacts the process of self-making described in Ellison's (and Emerson's) essays.

The narrator's growth of awareness, his willingness to go with the urban flow, is played out through metaphors, such as the images of blindness and vision that run through the whole novel: the blindfolded boys at the battle royal, the college sermon about the Founder by the blind preacher Barbee, the torn photograph of a boxer who had been blinded in the ring, and finally the glass eye of Jack, the Brotherhood leader, which pops out at an unfortunate moment and reminds us of the limits of *his* vision. In the Brotherhood the young man learns to see beyond race, as Richard Wright did, but he is mocked and chastised when what he sees doesn't fit the current line. The Brotherhood liberates him at first, introducing him to a wider world, giving him both work to do and a fully developed set of ideas, along with a sense of hope, a solidarity with others. But finally, like every other institution, it tries to impose its outlook on him. The Brotherhood pretends to a scientific grasp of history; it claims to know what Harlem needs better than Harlem itself. But this is ultimately exposed as another example of whites patronizing blacks—

and of inflexible organizations stifling spontaneity and individuality.

As the novel's epilogue makes clear, Ellison is giving us a black-accented version of the anticonformist discourse of the 1950s, the social critique of the lonely crowd and the organization man. But because he is black, the narrator is faceless in a special and vivid way. He is invisible because no one really *sees* him; the Brotherhood recruits him but does not want him to think. "You made an effective speech," they tell him. "But you mustn't waste your emotion on individuals, they don't count. . . . History has passed them by." They object when he makes any appeal to color, yet he wonders whether he is being used simply because he's black. "What was I, a man or a natural resource?"

The second half of *Invisible Man* is also closely linked to mid-century novels and memoirs of disillusionment with communism, including Koestler's *Darkness at Noon*, the suppressed second half of Wright's *Black Boy*, and the collective volume *The God that Failed*, which included both Koestler and Wright along with Ignazio Silone and others. Since Ellison was young and marginal to the Harlem branch of the party and Wright was famous and central to it, it's fair to assume that this part of *Invisible Man* is heavily indebted to Wright's experiences, as described in both *American Hunger* and Ellison's "Remembering Richard Wright." There Ellison expresses gratitude to Wright for his willingness to confide in him about his problems with the party, "especially his difficulty in pursuing independent thought." When Ellison's narrator is brought up on trial, the charges echo those directed against Wright—that he trusts his own judgment over the party's, that he speaks *for* blacks rather than *to* them, that he is too concerned with race. *Invisible Man* takes us far beyond the anticommunist confessional, however; the young man's disillusionment is part of a much larger process of casting off misconceptions and exploring his own identity.

When the narrator decides that his political patrons are simply white men with yet another plan for him, he realizes that even in the Brotherhood he needs to live a double life. He learns to live within a shifting sense of who he actually is. Standing before an audience on his party assignment, decked out in a new suit and a new name, he experiences a sense of vertigo, as if caught with his identity down. He fears that he might forget his name, or be recognized by someone in the audience. "I bent forward, suddenly conscious of my legs in new blue trousers. But how do you know they're your legs?. . . . For it was as though I were looking at my own legs for the first time—independent objects that could of their own volition lead me to safety or danger." He feels that he is standing simultaneously at opposite ends of a tunnel, both in the old life he has left behind and in a new world that's still disturbingly vague and unformed:

> This was a new phase, I realized, a new beginning, and I would have to take that part of myself that looked on with remote eyes and keep it always at the distance of the campus, the hospital machine, the battle royal—all now far behind. Perhaps the part of me that observed listlessly but saw all, missing nothing, was still the malicious, arguing part; the dissenting voice, my grandfather part; the cynical, disbelieving part—the traitor self that always threatened internal discord. Whatever it was, I knew that I'd have to keep it pressed down.

Like so much else in the novel, this at once exemplifies and parodies Emersonian notions of self-transformation. As a spokesman for the Brotherhood, the narrator is shedding his old skin, exercising his power over language and people. Yet he is also simply playing another assigned role, keeping the dissenting parts of himself "pressed down." With a flash of panic he sees that "the moment I walked out upon the platform and opened my mouth I'd be someone else." But he also senses that he could become simply a party hack with an assumed name, someone arbitrarily forced to deny his past.

Only when he puts on dark green glasses and is everywhere taken for Rinehart, the hustler and trickster, the man of many faces and roles, is he willing to step outside history, acknowledge his invisibility, and yield to the fluidity of the world around him. Both the Brotherhood and the nationalists—personified by Ras the Exhorter, with his impassioned Garveyite rhetoric of racial pride—are locked into the hard lines of history as they each see it. Only Rinehart, who is everywhere and nowhere at once, can negotiate the chaos of the ghetto, the boundary-free world of modern urban identity:

> Could he be all of them: Rine the runner and Rine the gambler and Rine the briber and Rine the lover and Rinehart the Reverend? Could he himself be both rind and heart? What is real anyway?. . . . His world was possibility and he knew it. He was years ahead of me and I was a fool. The world in which we lived was without boundaries. A vast seething, hot world of fluidity, and Rine the rascal was at home. Perhaps *only* Rine the rascal was at home in it.

This is the novel's version of the malleable, self-fashioned identity that Ellison invokes in his essays, a way of stepping out of imposed roles or shaping them to your needs. His friend Tod Clifton, the poster boy for the Harlem Brotherhood, has turned his back on the organization and plunged out of history. In midtown he hawks Sambo dolls, whose fine strings symbolize how he himself felt manipulated. After Tod is shot down by a policeman, the narrator pursues a less suicidal way of reclaiming his individuality. Rinehart, the man of the city, provides him with a clue. "My entire body started to itch, as though I had been removed from a plaster cast and was unused to the new freedom of movement." He sees that compared to the South, where everyone knew him, the urban world can offer him freedom. "How many days could you walk the street without encountering anyone you knew, and how many nights? You could actually make yourself anew. The notion was frightening, for now the world seemed to flow before my eyes. All boundaries down, freedom was not only the recognition of necessity, it was the recognition of possibility."

MANY OF THE midcentury works of deradicalization convey a wounded quality, a sense of apocalyptic combat, as in Whittaker

Chambers's *Witness* (1952), or a deep sense of loss, as in much of *The God that Failed*. Many former radicals portrayed communism as a lost or spoiled idealism, something precious they would never be able to recover. But a heady exhilaration spills over in the last hundred pages of *Invisible Man*, the thrill of a man reclaiming his own life—the food that embarrassed him, the experiences that formed him, the music "that touched upon something deeper than protest, or religion." What does the Brotherhood know of "the gin mills and the barber shops and the juke joints and the churches . . . and the beauty parlors on Saturdays when they're frying hair. A whole unrecorded history is spoken there." For these people it was not the Brotherhood but Rinehart, with his dodges and disguises, his endlessly resourceful maneuvers, that represented "a principle of hope, for which they gladly paid. Otherwise there was nothing but betrayal."

The narrator reasserts his solidarity with those who lie outside history, the "transitory ones": "birds of passage who were too obscure for learned classification, too silent for the most sensitive recorders of sound." As in his recognition of a world "without boundaries," Ellison, through his character, is expressing his commitment to becoming an artist, at once shaping his own identity and keeping in touch with common experience. The Brotherhood's line, like other white views of Negro life, is enjoined from above, not experienced from below. "It was all a swindle, an obscene swindle. They had set themselves up to describe the world. What did they know of us, except that we numbered so many, worked on certain jobs, offered so many votes, and provided so many marchers for some protest parade of theirs." As he recognizes how he's been used, his Dostoevskyan sense of humiliation helps him repossess his own experience:

> I began to accept my past and, as I accepted it, I felt memories welling up within me. It was as though I'd learned suddenly to look around corners; images of past humiliations flickered through my head and I saw they were more than separate experiences. They were me; they defined me. I was my experiences and my experiences were me, and no blind men, no

matter how powerful they became, even if they conquered the world, could take that, or change one single itch, taunt, laugh, cry, scar, ache, rage or pain of it.

Through images of sight and insight, he gives us what seems like the novel's actual point of origin, the writer's own moment of recognition that catapulted him from the blindness of politics, ideology, and sociological abstraction to a grasp of the complexity of his own experience. Suddenly, all his old mentors merge into a single figure trying to bend him to their will—an external force that he must overthrow. "I looked around a corner of my mind and saw Jack and Norton and Emerson merge into one single white figure. They were very much the same, each attempting to force his picture of reality upon me and neither giving a hoot in hell for how things looked to me. I was simply a material, a natural resource to be used." This is Ellison's declaration of independence, his personal emancipation proclamation. The thrill he feels in writing it we also feel in reading it, not least because it provides the novel with such a strong formal resolution.

Did Ellison imagine that ordinary people, especially black people, could find freedom in the same way, as some artists can, by recognizing that reality and identity are malleable, that they are free to create themselves? He believes that blacks have a culture, a way of life, in which they already have done so. He dislikes deterministic visions of entrapment like the portrait of Bigger Thomas in *Native Son*, and insists that Richard Wright, in creating Bigger, had not done justice to his own wide experience. But Ellison's emphasis is always on *imaginative* freedom within political and social *un*freedom, within limits that can be only partly transcended. Writing about *The Great Gatsby* he describes "the frustrating and illusory social mobility which forms the core of Gatsby's anguish," yet he argues that the novel's black readers could not make Gatsby's mistakes. Accepting the National Book Award for *Invisible Man*, Ellison, despite his feeling that social mobility can be "illusory," appealed to the shape-changing figure of Proteus as his paradigm for coping with America's "rich diversity and its almost magical fluidity and freedom." In his essays he tells us repeatedly that the effort that creates art—that requires craft, discipline, and a mastery over reality—is the same as the process that shapes individual identity and ultimately culture itself.

In one of many discursive texts set into *Invisible Man*, the narrator remembers a literature teacher's comments on Stephen Dedalus in Joyce's *Portrait of the Artist*:

> Stephen's problem, like ours, was not actually one of creating the uncreated conscience of his race, but of creating the *uncreated features of his face*. Our task is that of making ourselves individuals. The conscience of a race is the gift of its individuals who see, evaluate, record.... We create the race by creating ourselves and then to our great astonishment we will have created something far more important: We will have created a culture.

Since *Invisible Man* is in many ways modeled on Joyce, and since Joyce himself highlights the word *race*, this is an especially momentous statement of purpose. *Invisible Man* is linked not only to the postwar discourse of anticommunism but to the closely related defense of liberal individualism and cultural pluralism in the work of social critics like Lionel Trilling, Reinhold Niebuhr, and Arthur Schlesinger, Jr. The case Trilling makes for the inwardness and complexity of art as against ideology is echoed by both Baldwin and Ellison. Yet Ellison gives it a radical, not a conservative edge. His arguments for the diversity of both black and American life, for a cultural rather than a strictly political approach, for discipline and self-mastery, and for an acceptance of complexity and contradiction have in recent years provided black artists and intellectuals like his close friend Albert Murray, Toni Morrison, Michael Harper, Wynton Marsalis, James Alan McPherson, Stanley Crouch, Gerald Early, and Henry Louis Gates, Jr., with a vigorous alternative to both black nationalism and Marxism.

Powerful as Ellison's essays are, his novel is even more impressive, a veritable *Ulysses* of the black experience, rich with folklore, verbal improvisation, mythic resonance, and personal history, in his words, "a raft of hope, perception and entertainment" that does justice to the variety of African-American life. Though a novel of the civil rights years, its perspective is neither integrationist nor rights-oriented but cultural. As angry as any text of black nationalists, it charts an odyssey through a whole way of life, a study of attitudes rather than abuses, deliberately written, as he recalled much later, in a voice of "taunting laughter," in a tone "less angry than ironic."

The novel is rich with moments that are neither realistic nor allegorical but emblematic, such as the yam-eating scene or the hero's one-man uprising at the Men's House or the splendid vision of Ras on a great black horse, dressed in the garb of an Abyssinian chieftain, with fur cap, shield, and cape ("a figure more out of dream than out of Harlem"). Ras makes great speeches, but when the narrator, defending himself, throws a spear that locks his jaws together, Ellison is doing something that few other postwar novelists could get away with—creating a charged image that is at once an event, a metaphor, and a statement. Baldwin in "Notes of a Native Son" had looked at the Harlem riots of 1943 through the lens of his own family history; Ellison, no less effectively, makes them emblematic of all the crosscurrents of African-American life.

In the typology of *Invisible Man*, Marcus Garvey foreshadows the Black Panthers, thirties Marxism anticipates post-sixties Marxism, and a midcentury conception of America's cultural diversity, marked by a fluid, malleable sense of identity, proves remarkably germane to an end-of-century debate over pluralism and multiculturalism. After steering us through every kind of emotional and ideological excess, Ellison's work represents the triumph of the center, the victory of moderation. Summing up every ideology roiling the turbulent waters of black life, Ellison wrote a great ideological novel, perhaps the single best novel of the whole postwar era, at once his own inner history and the complex paradigm of a whole culture.

Works Cited

Ellison, Ralph. *Invisible Man*. New York: Random House, 1957.

————. "Alain Locke." In *The Collected Essays of Ralph Ellison*, ed. John F. Callahan. New York: Random House, 1995.

————. "Brave Words for a Startling Occasion." In *The Collected Essays of Ralph Ellison*, ed. John F. Callahan. New York: Random House, 1995.

————. "Going to the Territory." In *The Collected Essays of Ralph Ellison*, ed. John F. Callahan. New York: Random House, 1995.

————. "The Little Man at Chehaw." In *The Collected Essays of Ralph Ellison*, ed. John F. Callahan. New York: Random House, 1995.

————. "The World and the Jug." In *The Collected Essays of Ralph Ellison*, ed. John F. Callahan. New York: Random House, 1995.

Howe, Irving. "Black Boys and Native Sons." In *A World More Attractive*. New York: Horizon, 1963.

The Rules of Magic

Hemingway as Ellison's "Ancestor"

ROBERT G. O'MEALLY

♦　♦　♦

We get changes of identity, often symbolized—
in strict obedience to the rules of magic—by the
changing of one's name, as the new synthetic
character is felt to require a corresponding verbal
change; or there is a formal choice of "ancestors,"
as one in meeting the exigencies of his present,
proposes to coerce the future by a quasi-mystical
revising of the past.

Kenneth Burke
Attitudes toward History

True jazz is an art of individual assertion within
and against the group. Each true jazz moment (as
distinct from the uninspired commercial performance) springs from a contest in which each artist challenges all the rest; each solo flight, or improvisation, represents (like the successive
canvases of a painter) a definition of his identity:
as individual, as member of the collectivity and
as a link in the chain of tradition.

Ralph Ellison
Shadow and Act

THERE HAS BEEN much ado about Ralph Ellison's complex debt to Richard Wright. Ellison himself shifts back and
forth uncomfortably. He comes closest to explaining his own un-

easiness in the face of any simplistic formulation of his literary paternity when he reminds his readers of his own father's untimely death and of his ambivalent feelings about the stepfathers who took his place. When he met Wright the last thing Ellison wanted was another father.[1] But then again it is Ellison who calls the name of father when invoking the images of certain favorite "ancestors," notably William Faulkner and Ernest Hemingway.[2] In some ways, the Faulkner example is as easy to see as the Wright: in Ellison's fiction one hears a voice as deeply southern as Faulkner's—a voice as rich and as quick with exalted southern lies, told with conversational jam-session style as well as with poetic eloquence. In both writers, too, one finds the shared impulse for technical experimentation along with a shared vision of the human plight, and of man's capacity to overcome.

Yet it is Ernest Hemingway whom Ellison most emphatically chooses as his own, even pitting him against Wright. Why was Wright "family" and Hemingway a chosen "ancestor"? In 1964 Ellison wrote:

Not because he [Hemingway] was white or "accepted." But because he appreciated the things of this earth which I love and which Wright was too driven or deprived or inexperienced to know: weather, guns, dogs, horses, love *and* hate and impossible circumstances which to the courageous and dedicated could be turned into benefits and victories. Because he wrote with such precision about the processes and techniques of daily living that I could keep myself and my brother alive during the 1937 Recession by following his descriptions of wing-shooting; because he knew the difference between politics and art and something of their true relationship for the writer. Because all that he wrote—and this is very important—was imbued with a spirit beyond the tragic with which I could feel at home, for it was very close to the feeling of the blues, which are, perhaps, as close as Americans can come to expressing the spirit of tragedy. . . . But most important, because Hemingway was a greater artist than Wright, who although a Negro like myself, and perhaps a great man, understood little if anything of these, at least to me, important things. Because Hemingway loved the American language and the joy of writing, making the flight of birds, the loping of lions across an African plain, the mysteries of drink and moonlight, the unique styles of diverse peoples and individuals come alive on the page. Because he was in many ways the true father-as-artist of so many of us who came to writing during the late thirties [3]

The essay from which this excerpt comes tries to refute the "segregated" idea that black artists must depend on other black artists as prime models and teachers. Ellison brings home his rhetorical point by preferring Hemingway, in whose work one finds no admirable Afro-American characters: instead one finds wisecracks about background "niggers" with flashing smiles. But Ellison's point is not "merely" rhetorical. Ellison has changed his mind about Hemingway, and then changed it again. In his essays and fiction, one finds the younger writer steadily conjuring with Hemingway-like forms and ideas. Although his writing "voice" has remained his own since 1944, throughout his career Ellison has played Hemingway riffs, somewhat like a jazz player improvising on blues chords—or playing with and then against a jam session "gladiator." Sometimes the Hemingway influence on Ellison is obvious, sometimes not. But for Ellison, Papa Hemingway never completely disappears.

To point out that segregation, particularly in Oklahoma, was neither absolute nor, ironically, without certain benefits, Ellison recalls that as a youngster he read Hemingway while waiting his turn in Negro barbershops in Oklahoma City.[4] Probably what he first saw were the feature stories and "letters" which Hemingway wrote for *Esquire* almost every month during the thirties: dispatches from Europe, Africa, and the West Indies concerning, for the most part, war, bullfights, hunting, boxing, fishing, and, inevitably, the struggle to create good art.[5] But by 1933, when Ellison left Oklahoma to study music at Tuskegee, Hemingway also had published his greatest stories and novels[6] as well as *Death in the Afternoon*. It seems likely that in the local library (also segregated) or in the homes of friends, young Ellison saw some of this

Hemingway work, too. In Hemingway's writing, Ellison would easily recognize the frontierlike Michigan, not so unlike the territory just beyond the limits of Oklahoma City. Both places had Indians, vast open spaces, and good areas to fish and hunt. And like Hemingway, Ellison played high school football and could readily identify with the undefeated sportsmen of *Men without Women* (1927) and *Winner Take Nothing* (1933).

In the beginning, Ellison, a fledgling trumpet player, was claimed by the music of Hemingway's sentences. When the literal meanings escaped him, Ellison could get a sense of what Hemingway was up to by the sheer pitch and rhythm of his writing.[7] And later he related Hemingway's understated but allusive style to jazz:

> Jazz was eclectic . . . at its best. . . . It made the whole world of music, of sound, its own. And it took what it needed from those areas. You hear references to opera, to church music, to anything, in something by Louis Armstrong or any other jazzman of the thirties, forties, or fifties. So this acquaintance with jazz made me quite aware that allusions to ideas and to other works of art were always turning up in Hemingway. (Garrett, 224)

Although he has said that while he was in college Eliot's *Waste Land* "initiated the search" for the sources of literature, Ellison also found that Hemingway's style, especially "the what-was-not-stated in the understatement, required study" (Garrett, 223). Like the blues, Hemingway's style implied a great deal more than was expressed outright (*S&A*, 245).

In Hemingway's fiction what was implied was a heroic attitude toward life's troubles and changes, a resiliency and steadfastness which as an adult Ellison also would connect with the blues. He would not spell it out, but Hemingway could make his reader feel "that some great crisis of courage had occurred and just was not said," notes Ellison. "And I related this to jazz" (Garrett, 223–24). In 1945, Ellison wrote of the blues: "Their attraction lies in this, that they at once express both the agony of life and the possibility of conquering it through sheer toughness of spirit.

They fall short of tragedy only in that they provide no scapegoat but the self" (*S&A*, 94). In this spirit, Hemingway's heroes endure with stoicism so much unmeaning agony and terror that Albert Murray calls Hemingway not just a blues writer but "an honorary Negro," a title Hemingway once chose for himself (Murray, "Storyteller," 14). Indeed, what Ellison has written about the blues is also true of certain heroes in Hemingway: "The blues voice . . . mocks the despair stated explicitly in its lyric, and it expresses the great human joke directed against the universe, that joke which is the secret of all folklore and myth: that though we be dismembered daily we shall always rise up again."[8] Ellison describes Jake Barnes, the wounded survivor and narrator of *The Sun Also Rises* (a novel Murray says could just as well be called "Jake's Empty Bed Blues," "Blues for Lady Brett," or even "Rocks in My Bed" ["Storyteller," 16]), in terms that express an extreme version of the blues hero's plight and challenge: "Ball-less, humiliated, malicious, even masochistic, he still has a steady eye upon it all and has the most eloquent ability to convey the texture of his experience."[9]

In the late 1930s, Ellison reached around those writers of the new Negro Renaissance, much of whose work he felt was stained by the "moribund" influence of Carl Van Vechten, and chose Hemingway as a model. Hemingway was simply a "greater writer than the participants in the Negro Renaissance," said Ellison in 1967.[10] Hemingway had spotted the "so-called 'Jazz Age' [as] a phony, while most Negro writers jumped on the illusory bandwagon when they, of all people, should have known better" ("Stern Discipline," 90). Ellison perceived the Hemingway hero's feeling of being at odds with American society to be quite similar to the feeling of blacks. The Hemingway hero held "an attitude springing from an awareness that they lived outside the values of the larger society, and *I* feel that their attitudes came closer to the way Negroes felt about the way the Constitution and the Bill of Rights were applied to us" (93). In this context Hemingway again evokes for Ellison the world of jazz:

> I believe that Hemingway in depicting the attitudes of athletes, expatriots [sic], bullfighters, traumatized soldiers, and impotent

idealists, told us quite a lot about what was happening to that most representative group of Negro Americans, the jazz musicians—who also lived by an extreme code of withdrawal, technical and artistic excellence, rejection of the values of respectable society. They replaced the abstract and much betrayed ideals of that society with the more physical values of eating, copulating, loyalty to friends, and dedication to the discipline and values of their art. ("Stern Discipline," 93)

Looking back from the vantage point of the sixties (and taking a shot at any black nationalist critics who might be listening), Ellison was quoted as overstating the case by saying that Hemingway "tells us more about how Negroes feel than all the writings done by those people mixed up in the Negro Renaissance" (90).

In the mid-1930s, when he first put his trumpet aside and began writing "in earnest," he chose Hemingway (along with Wright) as a principal guide. In 1937, Ellison started reading Hemingway with a writer's eye, trying to learn his sentence structure and his means of organizing a story. He went about the task of learning to write with Hemingway-like intensity and singleness of purpose, and refused for a time even to attend musical performances for fear of being sidetracked (see Ellison and Hersey interview). Like a young musician practicing *études* (or like an apprentice photographer learning to compose a picture by looking at a master's photographs through a camera lens), Ellison would copy certain Hemingway stories in longhand, "in an effort to study their rhythms, so as not just to know them but to possess them."[11]

A member of the Federal Writers Project (1936–1939), Ellison interviewed many black New Yorkers and tried to get their stories on paper. Here Hemingway proved useful. Ellison would listen to his Harlem informants' talk and "very often," he recalls, "I was able to get it on paper by using a kind of Hemingway typography, by using the repetitions. I couldn't quite get the tone of the sounds in, but I could get some of the patterns and get an idea of what it was like." Thus he could avoid "falling into the transcription of dialect," which he had found unsatisfactory in

Wright's fiction (McPherson, "Indivisible," 59). Quite unlike
Wright, who, in a typical piece of dialogue in *Uncle Tom's Children*
(1938) has Aunt Sue say, "Ahma ol woman n Ah wans yuh t tell
me the truth."[12] Project Worker Ellison records the words of a
Harlem yarn spinner in this way:

> I hope to God to kill me if this aint the truth. All you got to
> do is to go down to Florence, South Carolina, and ask most
> anybody you meet and they'll tell you it's the truth. . . .
>
> Florence is one of these hard towns on colored folks. You
> have to stay out of the white folks way; all but Sweet. That
> the fellow I'm fixing to tell you about. His name was Sweet-
> the-monkey. I done forgot his real name, I caint remember it.
> But that was what everybody called him. He wasn't no big guy.
> He was just bad. My mother and my grandmother used to say
> he was wicked. He was bad all-right. He was one sucker who
> didn't give a dam bout the crackers. Fact is, they got so they
> stayed out of *his* way. I caint never remember hear tell of any
> them crackers bothering that guy. He used to give em trouble
> all over the place and all they could do about it was to give
> the rest of us hell.
>
> It was this way: Sweet could make hisself invisible. You don't
> believe it? Well here's how he done it. Sweet-the-monkey cut
> open a black cat and took out its heart. Climbed a tree back-
> wards and cursed God. After that he could do anything. The
> white folks would wake up in the morning and find their stuff
> gone. He cleaned out the stores. He cleaned up the houses.
> Hell, he even cleaned out the dam bank! He was the boldest
> *black* sonofabitch ever been down that way. And couldn't no-
> body do nothing to him.[13]

In this passage Ellison was obviously practicing how to capture
the sounds of vernacular speech without distracting the reader
with a thicket of misspellings and apostrophes.

Impressed particularly by the Oklahoman's ability to talk about
Hemingway, Wright had invited Ellison to contribute to *New Challenge* magazine in 1937. Ellison's first review, which pinpointed the

need for "greater development in technique" ("Creative and Cultural Lag," 91), and his short story "Hymie's Bull" (which did not appear because the magazine folded) were both stamped in the Hemingway mold. With poetic directness and rhythmic style, the young reporter Hemingway had written in 1922 about fishing the Rhone Canal:

> It is a good walk in to Aigue. There are horse chestnut trees along the road with their flowers that look like wax candles and the air is warm from the heat absorbed from the sun. The road is white and dusty, and I thought of Napoleon's grand army, marching along it through the white dust on the way to the St. Bernard pass and Italy. Napoleon's batman may have gotten up at sun up before the camp and sneaked a trout or two out of the Rhone Canal for the Little Corporal's breakfast. And before Napoleon, the Romans came along the valley and built this road and some Helvetian in the road gang probably used to sneak away from the camp in the evening to try for a big one in one of the pools under the willows. In the Roman days the trout perhaps were not as shy. (*By-Line*, 35)

And in a feature story entitled "A Congress Jim Crow Didn't Attend" (1940), Ellison's report for *New Masses* on the National Negro Congress, one overhears Hemingway's cadences and deadpan tone in the face of dramatic action which is deliberately detailed. Ellison writes:

> Outside of Baltimore we began passing troupes of cavalry. They were stretched along the highway for a mile. Young fellows in khaki with campaign hats strapped beneath their chins, jogging stiffly in their saddles. I asked one of my companions where they were going and was told that there was an army camp near by. Someone said that I would find out "soon enough" and I laughed and said I was a black Yank and was not coming. (5)

Later in the same piece, Ellison describes the conference meeting hall in Hemingway terms:

The auditorium had that overwhelming air usually associated
with huge churches, and I remembered what André Malraux
once said about the factory becoming for the workers what
the cathedral was, and that they must come to see in it not
ideal gods, but human power struggling against the earth. (7)

In 1932 Hemingway wrote: "If a writer of prose knows enough
about what he is writing about he may omit things that he knows
and the reader, if the writer is writing truly enough, will have a
feeling of those things as strongly as though the writer had stated
them" (*Death*, 192). Hemingway's famous use of understatement
intrigued young Ellison, but early on he had serious doubts that
it was a style he wanted to incorporate into his own writing. In
his 1940 review for *New Masses* of Langston Hughes's first autobiography, *The Big Sea*, Ellison takes Hughes to task for understating
the meanings of too many experiences. Radical Ellison's objections
were not just political but artistic:

In his next book . . . we hope that besides the colorful incidents,
the word pictures, the feel, the taste, and smell of his experiences, Langston Hughes will tell us more of how he felt and
thought about them. For while the style of *The Big Sea* is
charming in its simplicity, it is a style that depends upon understatement for its most important effects. Many *New Masses*
readers will question whether this is a style suitable for the
autobiography of a Negro writer of Hughes's importance; the
national and class position should guide his selection of techniques, and method should influence his style. In the style of
The Big Sea too much attention is apt to be given to the esthetic
aspects of experience at the expense of its deeper meanings.
Nor—this being a world in which few assumptions may be
taken for granted—can the writer who depends upon understatement to convey these meanings be certain that they do
not escape the reader. To be effective the Negro writer must
be explicit; thus realistic; thus dramatic. . . . When Hughes
avoids analysis and comment, and, in some instances, emotion,
a deeper unity is lost. This is that unity which is formed by
the mind's brooding over experience and transforming it into

conscious thought. Negro writing needs this unity, through which the writer clarifies the experiences of the reader and allows him to recreate himself. ("Stormy Weather," 20)

Contrast this appraisal of Hughes's self-portrait with an early statement (preceding the novel's publication by four years) by Ellison of his intentions for *Invisible Man*'s hero: "I am attempting to create a character who possesses both the eloquence and the insight into the interconnections between his own personality and the world about him to make a judgment upon our culture."[14] He did not want his book to be narrowly topical, but rather he wanted it to state its case explicitly and to draw fairly definite conclusions about the state of the nation. He did not want to "explain his book away" (*à la* the naturalists), but he did want his ideas made clear. And although Invisible Man is a simple man (even a naive simpleton) during most of Ellison's novel, eventually he wakes up and is more able than Hughes of *The Big Sea*, or virtually any Hemingway character, to express what he's gone through, and to do so in precise, comprehensive terms.

In 1940, Ellison went so far as to declare that although the "hardboiled" Hemingway style was successful for conveying American violence ("a quality as common to Negro life as to the lives of Hemingway characters")[15] it nonetheless had a "negative philosophical basis" ("Prize Fighter," 26–27). This was Ellison's most stinging criticism of work by the writer he had idealized. Even after starting on *Invisible Man*, Ellison's dissatisfaction with Hemingway seemed to center on what went unstated or understated in Hemingway's prose. In the mid-1940s Ellison expressed concern about the fact that no fully drawn blacks appear in Hemingway's work; how did he feel then about black freedom, and about the black American's tragic quest for equality? Ellison had begun to feel that the concern for the Negro and for the values which his presence connoted in American fiction were not just *unspoken* by Hemingway, they were *nonexistent*. "It is not accidental," wrote Ellison in 1946, "that the disappearance of the human Negro from our fiction coincides with the disappearance of deep-probing doubt and a sense of evil" (*S&A*, 35). Perhaps Hemingway was not so much the spokesman for the 1920s Lost Generation as he was "a product of a tradition which arose even before the Civil War—that tradition of intellectual evasion for which Thoreau criticized Emerson in regard to the Fugitive Slave Law and which has been growing swiftly since the failure of the ideals in whose name the Civil War was fought" (*S&A*, 36). Rather than probing "the roots of American culture" Hemingway "restricted himself to elaborating his personal style." This narrow naturalist explored neither society nor morality, but instead indulged in "working out a personal problem through the evocative, emotion-charged images and ritual-therapy available through the manipulation of art forms." If freedom was still at issue, it was solely *personal* freedom; and if the writing involved rituals, they were cynical rituals of defeat:

> Beneath the dead-pan prose [wrote Ellison], the cadences of understatement, the anti-intellectualism [lies] the concern with every "fundamental" of man except that which distinguishes him from the animal. . . . Here is the twentieth-century form of that magical rite which during periods of great art has been to a large extent public and explicit. Here is the literary form by which the personal guilt of the pulverized individual of our rugged era is expiated: not through his identification with the guilty acts of an Oedipus, a Macbeth or a Medea, by suffering their agony and loading his sins upon their "strong and passionate shoulders," but by being gored with a bull, hooked with a fish, impaled with a grasshopper on a fishhook; not by identifying himself with human heroes, but with those who are indeed defeated. (*S&A*, 39–40)

Flashing technique for its own sake, this writing, like the stereotype in literature, conditions the reader to complacent inaction, said Ellison. "And when I read the early Hemingway," wrote Ellison, "I seem to be in the presence of a Huckleberry Finn who . . . chose to write the letter which sent Jim back into slavery" (40).

Ellison's own fiction since 1944 shows that he has remained

dissatisfied with understatement as a technique to express his own sense of the American scene. In addition to its other problems, the clipped phrases of the understated speaker did not compare, he wrote in 1953, with "the rich babel of idiomatic expression" which he heard in New York, and which he had known in the South. Robert Penn Warren has written that Hemingway's "short, simple rhythms, the succession of coordinate clauses, the general lack of subordination—all suggest a dislocated and ununified world. The figures who live in this world live a sort of hand-to-mouth existence perceptually, and conceptually. Subordination implies some exercise of discrimination—the shifting of reality through the intellect. But in Hemingway we see a Romantic anti-intellectualism."[16]

The author of *Invisible Man* sifts through reality in sentences which, in their driving complexity, often echo Faulkner or Wright more than they do Hemingway. The reality Ellison wished to project in fiction was so "mysterious and uncertain and ... exciting," he said, that it would "burst ... the neatly understated forms of the novel asunder" (*S&A*, 104). In 1955, Ellison told a symposium of writers that his former mentor's laconic characters may have expressed the disillusionment of the postwar era, but when the Depression hit and "reality was ripping along," Hemingway's images no longer were adequate as a guide for confronting experience.[17] Hemingway had produced fiction that was ultimately too provincial to escape its particular setting and time. Yet, surprisingly, in the same discussion, Ellison also spoke up in defense of Hemingway. He "links up pretty close to Twain," he said ("What's Wrong," 495).

This linkage with Twain, which, for Ellison, spells adherence to the American novel's greatest themes and most characteristic forms—this sense of belonging to the national literary canon encompassing nineteenth-century prose masters along with contemporary stylists—is the theme of most of Ellison's literary essays from the fifties on. And his connection of Hemingway with Twain signaled that Ellison had begun again to change his mind about what was implied "beneath the dead-pan cadences" of Hemingway's prose. By 1957 he was back squarely in Hemingway's corner. "Neither the American fiction of the twenties nor of the fifties," wrote Ellison "can be understood outside the perspective provided by the nineteenth century." For it was in the nineteenth century that Emerson, Thoreau, Whitman, Melville, Twain, James, and Crane (among others, of course, but this is the line of nineteenth-century writers that Ellison usually marshals) wrote explicitly about American democracy and the lingering problem of freedom and unfreedom as it centered on the man beneath the social hierarchy, the Negro. With the great nineteenth-century themes in mind, Ellison now read *A Farewell to Arms* as an ironic comment upon and ultimately a ringing affirmation of the "sacred assumptions" of American life:

> For as I read Hemingway today [1957] I find that he affirms the old American values by the eloquence of his denial; makes his moral point by stating explicitly that he does not believe in morality; achieves his eloquence through denying eloquence; and is most moral when he denies the validity of a national morality which the nation has not bothered to live up to since the Civil War. ("Society," 74)

The confusion about Hemingway's motives—about what went unsaid in his fiction—stemmed not from a failure on the author's part, Ellison now argued, but on the part of his readers and his less skilled and less moral imitators. "For although it is seldom mentioned," wrote Ellison, "Hemingway is as obsessed with the Civil War and its aftermath as any Southern writer" (74). When Hemingway's Nick or Jake took to the woods for a round of fishing or hunting (and when Frederic declared his separate peace), they turned their backs on a society whose ideals had become so tarnished that they preferred to set up frontier outposts (like Huck and Jim's raft) where the values of freedom and friendship could be upheld, if only in a short space and time. What went unstated in Hemingway then was a firm belief in the American social ideals of liberty and democracy.

Obviously, Ellison's changed view of Hemingway's content was linked with a changed view of his style. What in the forties Ellison had begun to put down as Hemingway's decadent "morality of craftsmanship," he now described as Hemingway's fineness of technique. This was not dry gear shifting for kicks, but careful maneuvering of the reader into a full and moral perspective on life in our time. True enough, most of Hemingway's readers and imitators forgot all about the moral dimension of American life and literature, misreading Hemingway and using his work as a model for their own escapist and self-indulgent fantasies. But the writer's technique itself, said Ellison in 1957, has moral implications, despite all abuses by poor writers. Even when "the question of the Sphinx was lost in the conundrums" of perfectly turned phrases, the Hemingway-inspired emphasis on the value of technique reminded readers that "literature, to the extent that it is art, is *artificial*" ("Society," 78). This reminder that literature is manmade is a moral reminder insofar as it helps the reader recall that language can be seductive, therapeutic, even magical. However beckoning it may be, though, it can express falsehood as well as truth. This awareness of literature as rhetoric serves as a warning for all readers to remain on guard as critics, ever aware that the most alluring fiction—be they novelistic, historical, or religious—are skillful acts of word-magic, brightly inviting castles of language. It is up to the reader to read with enough perspicuity to decide what is true and right, and to set the rest aside.

By the 1960s and 1970s, Ellison would extend this metaphor of "morality of craftsmanship" (now an encomium)[19] in important ways. For the writer, he said, "craft under the pressure of inspiration" is the crucial formula:

> It's one thing to have a feeling, an insight, to hear in your mind's ear a rhythm, or to conceive an image. It is the *craft*, the knowledge of what other people have done, of what has been achieved by those great creators of the novel which gives you some idea of the possibility of that image, that nuance, that rhythm, that dramatic situation. It's not dry technique or craft that I'm talking about; it's craft which makes it possible for you to be more or less conscious of what you are doing

and of the tools that you have to work with. (WGBH-TV interview)

Repeatedly, Ellison uses the example of the medical doctor to discuss the responsibility of the writer.[20] A physician misdiagnosed his own mother's illness and caused her untimely death. A surgeon's slip killed Bennie Moten, then at the top of his career as a jazz bandleader, and his fans wanted to lynch his careless doctor. Writers, in Ellison's view, also have lives in their hands and thus bear a social (at times Ellison uses the word *sacred*) responsibility to know what they are doing. In 1942, Hemingway had compared the writer's calling to that of the priest:

> A writer should be of as great probity and honesty as a priest of God. . . . A writer's job is to tell the truth. His standard of fidelity to the truth should be so high that his invention, out of his experience, should produce a truer account than anything factual can be. For facts can be observed badly; but when a good writer is creating something, he has time and scope to make of it an absolute truth. (*Men at War*, xv)

Ellison elaborates on this insight, observing that not only must the moral writer always do the best work he can, but when "you [writers] describe a more viable and ethical way of living and denounce the world or a great part of society for the way it conducts its affairs and then write in a sloppy way or present issues in a simplistic or banal way, then you're being amoral as an artist" ("Through a Writer's Eyes," B3). Since writers provide "disastrously explicit" images, ones which influence readers in their search for the meanings of their lives, then false images, or images faultily projected by inadequate craft, can cause confusion, dismay, and even death.

The writer's task, Ellison has said, is to do nothing less than to help create reality. "While fiction is but a form of symbolic action," he wrote in 1982, "a mere game of 'as if,' therein lies its true function and its potential for effecting change. For at its most serious . . . it is a thrust toward a human ideal. And it approaches that ideal by a subtle process of negating the world of things as given in favor of a complex of manmade positives."[21] Isn't that just wishful thinking, though? Aren't you "expressing your own hopes and aspirations for Negroes, rather than reporting historical reality?" he was asked in an interview in 1967. "But hope and aspiration are indeed important aspects of the reality of Negro American life, no less than that of others," he replied. "Literature teaches us that mankind has always defined itself *against* the negatives thrown it by society and the universe. . . . Let's not forget that the great tragedies not only treat of negative matters, of violence, brutalities, defeats, but they treat them within a context of man's will to act, to challenge reality and to snatch triumph from the teeth of destruction" ("Stern Discipline," 84). The writer imbued with the proper sense of his craft's "sacredness" knows that his job is to provide readers with strategies for confronting the chaos of the contemporary world—or, in Kenneth Burke's phrase often quoted by Ellison, to provide the reader with necessary "equipment for living."[22]

Which brings us to *Invisible Man*—Ellison's most comprehensive piece of "equipment for living." How does Hemingway figure there? *Invisible Man*, like most of the heroes of Ellison's short stories, is an intelligent and sensitive youngster, a brown-skinned cousin of Nick Adams, straining toward manhood in a world full of the blues. And certain of *Invisible Man*'s controlling metaphors mirror images and actions in Hemingway's work: notably the metaphors of life as a war, a game, or a fight (or a prizefight, or even a bullfight)—life as an encounter between the individual and the forces set against him. Like the old waiter of "A Clean, Well-Lighted Place," Invisible has been through a lot, and needs plenty of light (in the case of Ellison's character, 1,369 filament bulbs) to feel secure in the threatening world. Furthermore, *Invisible Man* itself comprises a classic defense of art that recalls defenses by Aristotle, Plato, and Shelley; but more specifically it is framed in terms that bring to mind Hemingway's descriptions of fighters, sportsmen, and writers as artists who assert their values and skills against encroachments by fakers, fools, and unfeeling power brokers, and sometimes by killers. Invisible Man, like Hemingway's apprentice heroes, learns at last to confront his experience directly, and he earns the perspective that it takes to do what Jake Barnes can do—to tell his troubling tale with the force and eloquence of an artist. Ellison informs his reader that almost as soon as he first heard, in his mind's ear, the words "I am an invisible man," the voice sounded "with a familiar timbre of voice": unmistakably black American, ringing with blues-toned irony.[23] Just as *The Sun Also Rises* makes us wonder how Jake achieves his ironic voice, his truce with his grim reality, this novel traces Invisible Man's achievement of a voice with which to state (and thus to overcome) the trouble he has seen.

In one of the novel's key passages, Invisible Man hears his grandfather's deathbed words, spoken to Invisible's father:

> "Son [the old man said], after I'm gone I want you to keep up the good fight. I never told you, but our life is a war and I have been a traitor all my born days, a spy in the enemy's country ever since I give up my gun back in the Reconstruction. Live with your head in the lion's mouth. I want you to overcome 'em with grins, agree 'em to death and destruction, let 'em swoller you till they vomit or bust wide open. . . . Learn it to the younguns," he whispered fiercely; then he died. (*IM*, 13–14)

To unlock the full meaning of these magic words, the puzzled grandson must journey through hundreds of pages of hard and contradictory living. What he finally discovers is that life *is* a war, and it is a war wherein to be a good soldier, snapping to attention and obeying all orders, is to work against one's people and oneself. In this cosmic war the first step toward victory involved more than learning the techniques of warfare; it involved getting oriented by realizing that things "ain't what they used to be," and that they are not even what they seem now. It involved having a mature perspective on oneself, on one's ideals, and on one's enemies, in whose very camp one must dwell. In short, the key was to become *conscious* in a profound sense: resigned like a blues-man to a life of war.

Significantly, the war the grandfather refers to is linked, in his dying speech, with the American Civil War.[24] Although he has long since given up his gun, he tells his son to "learn it to the younguns," the grandchildren a generation removed from the Civil War. The point, as Ellison has said repeatedly from beyond the text, is that the Civil War continues in America. The issues of property versus human rights; individual, state, and sectional autonomy versus the power of the union; and a sheaf of other definitively American political and economic issues—centering on the abiding problem of Negro freedom—remain unresolved. American life, to paraphrase the old man, is a civil war in which the black man (and everyone) must fight, over and over again, to be free. Part of becoming conscious involves seeing, as Invisible eventually does, that his problem is not unique: "It goes a long way back, some twenty years." And it goes back still further, at least back to the nineteenth century when the Civil War was fought and when, for a brief moment during Reconstruction, Americans tried to live up to the implications surrounding that clash. "The writer is forged in injustice as a sword is forged," wrote Hemingway.[25] And a war, especially a civil war, can make or break a writer, he said. In Hemingway, code heroes are often soldiers at war who must test themselves not just in theory but in the real world of intense, dangerous action. The Civil War in the background of *Invisible Man* (surfacing especially in allusions to Douglass and to other nineteenth-century writers and erupting in the riot at the novel's climax) helps to forge Invisible's con-sciousness as a man of eloquence who is able "to make a judg-ment about our culture."

Conditioning by the mass media blinds today's readers to the fact that *Invisible Man* is an extraordinarily violent novel, so violent that Ellison wondered if antiviolence commentators would snipe at the book. Fights occur in scene after scene—hand-to-hand battles, which rehearse the background struggle of the continuing civil war. Invisible's fight with the "blind" white man in the prologue, the yokel's fight with the prizefighter of scientific method, the battle-royal free-for-all, the Golden Day fisticuffs, Invisible against Lucius Brockway, Tod and Invisible versus Ras, and Tod versus the cops are just some of the novel's main fights. Several allusions are made to the Johnson and Jeffries fight—that symbolic encounter between the races. At one point Bledsoe promises to help Invisible because the young man shows ire and "the race needs smart, disillusioned fighters":

> Therefore [Bledsoe goes on] I'm going to give you a hand— maybe you'll feel that I'm giving you my left hand after I've struck you with my right—if you think I'm the kind of man who'd lead with his right, which I'm most certainly not. (*IM*, 112)

Up north, the Brotherhood meetings were generally as noisy and smoky as smokers or prizefights, the reader is told; in fact, Invisible's first speech is made in the very auditorium where, significantly enough, a popular fighter had lost his vision in the ring. Each of these physical fights, brawls, and prizefights has its own symbolic meaning. But one can say that in the world of *Invisible Man* the struggle for meaning and endurance is not only metaphysical but physical. The would-be hero must put his own body on the line, and only if he has the resiliency, the strength, and the technical skill can he avoid a whipping—or, if he cannot avoid a whipping, he can at least know what it's for. Lacking science and quickness, the prologue yokel prevails through sheer strength and inspired timing:

> The fighter was swift and amazingly scientific. His body was one violent flow of rapid rhythmic action. He hit the yokel a hundred times while the yokel held up his arms in stunned surprise. But suddenly the yokel, rolling about in the gale of boxing gloves, struck one blow and knocked science, speed and footwork as cold as a well-digger's posterior. The smart money hit the canvas. The long shot got the nod. The yokel had simply stepped inside of his opponent's sense of time. (*IM*, 7)

The Invisible Man, the comic yokel for most of the novel, is battered by swift and scientific battlers in scene after scene. In time, of course, he learns that to prevail he must have science *and* power—and an alert sense of what time it is; he must be both *hare* and *bear*. But he finds out that either way, life will give him a thrashing to remember.

What he learns, too, is the Hemingway lesson: that he is caught up in a violent game which, like the fight game, attains a certain grace when played well. The banished Golden Day inmate (one of the crazy war veterans) gives some advice on how life's game is played:

> "For God's sake, learn to look beneath the surface," he said. "Come out of the fog, young man. And remember you don't have to be a complete fool in order to succeed. Play the game, but don't believe in it—that much you owe yourself. Even if it lands you in a strait jacket or a padded cell. Play the game, but play it your own way—part of the time at least. Play the game, but raise the ante, my boy. Learn how it operates, learn how you operate. . . . You might even beat the game. . . . Down here they've forgotten to take care of the books and that's your opportunity." (*IM*, 118)

Here Ellison defines the "they" against which Invisible's most strenuous fight must be waged: "They?" says the vet. "Why the same *they* we always mean, the white folks, authority, the gods, fate, circumstances—the force that pulls your strings until you refuse to be pulled any more. The big man who's never there, where you think he is" (*IM*, 118). To an extent it is the *"nada y pues nada"*[26] that Hemingway's heroes struggle against, the sense of dissolution and meaninglessness and the excruciating pain threatening the prizefighter Jack in Hemingway's "Fifty Grand" (*Fifth Column*, 398–424), the ever-ready opponent that threatens to sock you blind. Then, too, more than for Hemingway, Ellison's "big man who's never there" is Clio, he is History.

Ellison's "they" is nonetheless comparable to the bull which

Hemingway's matadors must confront, and which, in the symbolic language of *Invisible Man*, the "youngun" from the South must learn to bring down. Hemingway's *Death in the Afternoon* comprises a handbook of bullfighting and a prose-poem on the poetics of the *toreo*. It teaches that the bullfight is not so much a game (or fair contest between equals) as it is a tragedy and a ritual. It is the tragedy of the bull which, whether goring or even killing its opponent or not, is doomed to die. (A bull that bests its matador has no more value as a fighter because the experience of winning makes it too skillful an opponent for the next matador to have the slightest chance against, so successful bulls also meet "death in the afternoon" of their first and last bullfight.) This tragic drama celebrates the doomed bull's best qualities. With the exuberance of the aficionado, Hemingway describes the magnificence of the fighting bull:

> Bulls in Spain have been known to charge a motor car and even, getting onto the tracks, to stop a train, refusing to back up or leave the track when the train stopped and when, with much blowing of the whistle the train finally advanced, charging the engine blindly. A really brave fighting bull is afraid of nothing on earth. . . . [He] can turn on his feet almost as a cat does. (*Death*, 109)

And furthermore:

> The bravery of a truly brave bull is something unearthly and unbelievable. The bravery is not merely viciousness, ill-temper, and the panic-bred courage of a cornered animal. The bull is a fighting animal and when the fighting strain has been kept pure and all cowardice bred out he becomes often, when not fighting, the quietest and most peaceful acting in repose, of any animal. It is not the bulls that are the most difficult to handle that make the best bullfights. The best of all fighting bulls have a quality, called nobility by the Spanish, which is the most extraordinary part of the whole business. The bull is

a wild animal whose greatest pleasure is combat and which
will accept combat offered to it in any form, or will take up
anything it believes to be an offer of combat. (*Death*, 113)

It takes a good bull for the matador to do his job well. Slow or
cowardly bulls, or bulls that have poor eyesight including, Hemingway specifies, one-eyed bulls (*tuertos*) (488), make dull and difficult killing. For the drama to attain the level of tragedy, the
bull must have heroic parts; otherwise its death can seem cruel
or even savagely comic.

Of course, the matador is the other leading character in the
tragedy of the bull. Not only is Hemingway's ideal matador brave,
aggressive, quick, highly skilled, and intelligent; he is an artist. In
his stances, approaches, gestures, and style of luring and evading
and then killing the bull, the bullfighter demonstrates his art.
Though his creations are unpreservable, the matador's work still
has lasting value and his medium is not unlike a sculptor's. Indeed, Hemingway claims to "know no modern sculpture, except
Brancusi's, that is in any way the equal of the sculpture of modern bullfighting" (*Death*, 99). Furthermore, "it is impossible to believe the emotional and spiritual intensity and pure, classic beauty
that can be produced by a man, an animal and a piece of scarlet
serge draped over a stick" (207).

For the aficionado the ultimate meaning of the bullfight de-
volves from the ritual of life and death reenacted in the *toreo*.
Hemingway calls the graceful action of a master bullfighter so
deeply moving

that [it] takes a man out of himself and makes him feel im-
mortal while it is proceeding. . . . [It] gives him an ecstasy, that
is, while momentary, as profound as any religious ecstasy; moving all the people in the ring together and increasing in emotional intensity as it proceeds, carrying the bullfighter with it,
he playing on the crowd through the bull and being moved
as it responds in a growing ecstasy of ordered, formal, passionate, increasing disregard for death that leaves you, when it is
over, and the death administered to the animal that had made

it possible, as empty, as changed and as sad as any major emotion will leave you. (206–7)

In language again quite effectively incongruous for a description of a blood-and-bones bullfight, Hemingway explains:

> The essence of the greatest emotional appeal of bullfighting is the feeling of immortality that the bullfighter feels in the middle of a great faena [maneuver] and that he gives to the spectators. He is performing a work of art and he is playing with death, bringing it closer, closer, closer to himself, a death that you know is in the horns because you have the canvas-covered bodies of the horses on the sand to prove it. He gives the feeling of his immortality, and, as you watch it, it becomes yours. (213)

Conditioned by a long apprenticeship, gored at least once so he knows how to come back from a horn wound, the ideal matador dominates his bull with courage, know-how, and quick reflexes. He stands at the center of a ritual in which man's "grace under pressure," even in the face of violent death, is tested. For Hemingway, he is not just *an* artist; the matador is the prototype of the artist, the idealized human. "Nobody," says Jake in *The Sun Also Rises*, "ever lives their lives all the way up except bullfighters" (10).

Bulls and bullfighting figure in *Invisible Man* in crucial ways. Metaphors that bring to mind the tragedy of the bull, as Hemingway glosses it, are, in fact, central to the novel's meanings. Waking on the morning before he takes his last Bledsoe letter to Emerson (whose son, true to this extent to the nineteenth-century Emerson's ideals, tries to tell him not to be naïve), Invisible feels a wave of nostalgia for the campus he has left behind. Ironically enough, what he recalls about the southern wasteland is a scene of sexual vibrancy in which the bull plays a part: "What were they doing now on campus? Had the moon sunk low and the sun climbed clear? Had the breakfast bugle blown? Did the bellow of the big seed bull awaken the girls in the dorms this morning as on most spring mornings when I was there—sounding clear and full above bells and bugles and early workaday sounds?" (*IM*, 131). Invisible does not, of course, comprehend the irony in this scene. He could not connect his vision of a wasteland and a bull with the world of *The Sun Also Rises*, wherein the wastelanders move aimlessly from scene to scene, unregenerated by the ceremony—the fiesta of the bull.[27]

Before long, Invisible and Tod Clifton are tested as they fight for political power against Ras the Exhorter/Destroyer, or, if you will, Ras the Bull. In a variation on the prologue encounter between the yokel and the scientific fighter, Ras tries to use bull strength against Tod, who maneuvers with speed and fine technique:

> Clifton's arms were moving in short, accurate jabs against the head and stomach of Ras the Exhorter, punching swiftly and scientifically, careful not to knock him into the window or strike the glass with his fists, working Ras between rights and lefts jabbed so fast that he rocked like a drunken bull, from side to side. And as I came up Ras tried to bull his way out and I saw Clifton drive him back and down into a squat, his hands upon the dark floor of the lobby, his heels back against the door like a runner against starting blocks. And now, shooting forward, he caught Clifton coming in, butting him, and I heard the burst of breath and Clifton was on his back and something flashed in Ras's hand and he came forward, a short, heavy figure as wide as the lobby now with the knife, moving deliberately.... [Ras was] panting, bull angry.... "Mahn," Ras blurted, "I ought to kill you. Godahm." (*IM*, 279)

Tod's science is not enough to bring down this thick bull, whose strong and well-timed charge brings him temporary victory. But racial loyalty won't let Ras kill Tod. "You *my* brother mahn.... We sons of Mother Africa, you done forgot?" (278) he says, releasing Tod. But again Invisible (who, in this scene, is less a participant than a witness, like Jake in *The Sun Also Rises*) sees what he's up against. He and the Brotherhood may command science, but the bull sometimes can rush science and bring the house crashing down.

The most capricious and powerful "bull" in *Invisible Man* is not so much a toro as he is a "toy bull terrier," or some sort of bull*dog*. Waiting to give his first speech as a member of the Brotherhood, Invisible recalls his childhood days and a neighborhood bulldog:

> A huge black-and-white dog, log-chained to an apple tree. It was Master, the bulldog; and I was the child who was afraid to touch him, although, panting with heat, he seemed to grin back at me like a fat good-natured man, the saliva roping silvery from his jowls. And as the voices of the crowd churned and mounted and became an impatient splatter of hand claps, I thought of Master's low hoarse growl. He had barked the same note when angry or when being brought his dinner, when lazily snapping flies, or when tearing an intruder to shreds. I liked, but didn't trust old Master; I wanted to please, but did not trust the crowd. Then I looked at Brother Jack and grinned: That was it; in some ways, he was like a toy bull terrier. (*IM*, 255–56)

He had seen it earlier, Jack's resemblance to "a lively small animal, a fyce" (219). But by naming him a *bull*dog, the narrator heightens the irony of the situation. Fyce or toy or terrier—however petite or petty he may be—this bull is muscular, tenacious, and capable of as much quick violence as apparent good humor. That Invisible connects him with "Master" of his childhood increases the irony's tension by yet another notch. When Invisible finally sees through Jack (an unpredictably dangerous one-eyed bull), the black man turns on him saying, "Who are you, anyway, the great white father? . . . Wouldn't it be better if they called you Marse Jack?" (357). Typical of Ellison, no easy equation works here: Jack is fyce, toy bull terrier, bulldog, bull, patron, and slavemaster (and many other things: bear, rabbit, money ["jack"] are just a few). But in this context the important point is that he is Invisible Man's opponent with the bullish power to turn and kill. Invisible's task is to learn how to confront him with style and effectiveness.

Jack takes Invisible to a place in Spanish Harlem "where the neon-lighted sign of a bull's head announced the El Toro Bar" (269). Suddenly Invisible finds himself in a bar from the world of Hemingway. But this is not quite a "clean, well-lighted place" or a muffled "Killers" lunchroom; Ellison fills the room with loaded talk and symbols—even the music is significantly titled. Four beer drinkers argue here in Spanish while "a juke box, lit up green and red, played 'Media Luz' " (269). As Invisible wonders about the purpose of Jack's bringing him to El Toro, he considers the picture behind the bar. Here the allusions to Hemingway become most explicit, as Invisible thinks:

> Before me, in the panel where a mirror is usually placed, I could see a scene from a bullfight, a bull charging close to the man and the man swinging a red cape in sculptured folds so close to his body that man and bull seemed to blend in one swirl of calm, pure motion. Pure grace, I thought, looking above the bar to where, larger than life, the pink and white image of a girl smiled down from a summery beer ad on which a calendar said April One. . . .
>
> "Here, come back," he said, nudging me playfully. "She's only a cardboard image of a cold steel civilization."
>
> I laughed, glad to hear him joking. "And that?" I said, pointing to the bullfight scene.
>
> "Sheer barbarism," he said, watching the bartender and lowering his voice to a whisper. (271)

A moment later, as Jack and Invisible discuss the ideological training session Invisible has just completed, he notices another bullfight scene farther down the bar. In this one "the matador was being swept skyward on the black bull's horns" (271).

"The aficionado, or lover of the bullfight," writes Hemingway, "has this sense of the tragedy and ritual of the fight so that the minor aspects are not important except as they relate to the whole. Either you have this or you have not, just as, without implying any comparison, you have or have not an ear for music" (*Death*, 9). Invisible, who has never been to a bullfight (and whose ear for music also starts out faulty and improves), is by no means an aficionado. But his instincts seem right. He sees the sculptural beauty of the work of the matador close to the bull—so close they "seemed to blend in one swirl of calm, pure motion." And he uses one of Hemingway's key words, "grace," to describe the climax moment of artistic perfection, the moment Hemingway has said brings spiritual and emotional "ecstasy," the moment when man's immortality seems, for an instant, achieved. If these flashes of insight place Invisible on the side of tragic ritual and art, his sighting without comment of the other image, that of the upended matador, shows he still has more naiveté than *aficion*. Presumably he doesn't know what to make of this other side of the bullfighter's art. Hemingway tells us that all bullfighters get gored—it is part of their initiation as seasoned fighters; how one comes back from the injury (tempered and tested or defensive and cowardly) determines one's true mettle as a matador. Seeing the goring scene as a *separate* frame—not part of the continuum in the life of a bullfighter—marks Invisible as a novice: he praises one aspect of the scene but does not see that aspect in relation to the whole bullfight. Nor does he see that this Hemingway bar, with its coded messages against the wall ("where a mirror is usually placed"), is another warning to him. Art and grace are achievable, yes, but there is no way to avoid the slashing test of the horns.

Another twist is that he's sitting at the bar right next to his opponent, One-Eyed Bull Jack. Jack is blind to the art and ritual of the bullfight, terming it "sheer barbarism." He's more perceptive in interpreting the picture of the white girl on the beer ad as "a cardboard image of a cold steel civilization." In fact, his suddenly cleared mood ("as though in an instant he had settled whatever had been bothering him and felt suddenly free" [*IM*, 270]) and his laughter suggest that he perceives in the scene a joke richer than Invisible Man does, a joke reflected by the juxtaposition of the images and the April Fool's Day calendar. In this setting of the El Toro, Jack names Invisible the chief spokesman of the Harlem district. And, as the reader finds out at the novel's end, he's about to set up the Invisible Man as a betrayer of his people, as chief sacrificial victim, number one dupe. In a sense, this seasoned bull is trying to turn the tables on the would-be matador, making him a comic butt for the bull's secret horns. As the hero discovers, it's a "comic-strip world" he's been put in, and Jack, faintly smiling and blind though he may be to tragedy and rituals, manipulates Invisible, using lures, fakery, and force. It's a world where Jack seems to turn gracefully with Invisible one moment but shifts as quickly as a bull to "sweep him sky-ward" in the next.

Symbolically, Invisible Man duels not just with Jack (or the others that try to bull and bully him); in a profound sense he also must confront and master history.[28] "Western culture," wrote Ellison about the challenge of Wright's *Black Boy*, "must be won, confronted like the animal in a Spanish bullfight, dominated by the red shawl of codified experience and brought heaving to its knees" (*S&A*, 93). This confrontation with all of Western culture makes up Invisible's great challenge; and it is directly connected to his quest for identity. In 1973 Ellison spoke of Invisible's situation this way: "His problem is to create an individuality based on an awareness of how it relates to his past and the values of the past" (O'Brien, "Ralph Ellison," 75). Speaking more generally of modern Americans' lack of historical and self-awareness, later in 1973 Ellison said:

> We still do not know who we are. . . . What I have found is that these strings of continuity, these linkages on the basis of ideas and of experiences were automatically—arbitrarily, it seems to me—thrown overboard. And this is disastrous for writers; it's disastrous for *bootleggers*, even. It's disastrous for any sort of human enterprise, because we live one upon the other. We follow, we climb up the shoulders of those who had gone before. ("Alain Locke Symposium," 25–26)

In this book the Invisible Man learns to climb the shoulders of those who have gone before, and to fight off the series of imposed misconceptions of what he has been, and thus of who he is. He rejects not only misstatements of the "facts of the case," but of theoretical schemes in which the facts assume meaning. While theories of "history" abound in *Invisible Man*, Jack and the Brotherhood present the most complete and seductive idea of the way the world turns—the idea whose rejection by Invisible paves the way for his own freedom. Like certain Marxists (but not only them), the Brotherhood sees history as a predictably repeating pattern, a design whose turnings can be precisely charted by proper science. This view of history explains why the "brothers" strive for a style of speech and deduction that is free of emotional charges, mechanical in its accuracy. The "brother with the pipe" loses patience with Jack's figurative speech, saying: "I only wish to point out that a scientific terminology exists. . . . After all, we call ourselves scientists, let us speak as scientists" (232). Jack tells Invisible to take the scientific jargon with a grain of salt. Master ideology, he warns the young man, "but don't overdo it. Don't let it master you. There is nothing to put the people to sleep like dry ideology. . . . Remember too, that theory always comes after practice. Act first, theorize later, that's always a formula, a devastatingly effective one!" (271). Jack's success as a leader depends upon his knowing the dry ideology, and upon his ability to manipulate it to support his larger motive, personal power. "And you don't have to worry about the brothers' criticism," advised Jack. "Just throw some ideology back at them and they'll leave you alone—provided, of course, that you have right backing and produce the required results" (271). The Brotherhood theory of history is an intricate one; but what Invisible learns from Jack (part of whose seductive strategy is to mingle his lies shrewdly with bits of truth) is that political power is the name of the Brotherhood's real game.

History as defined by the Brotherhood is an upwardly spiraling tunnel: one dwells either "inside" or "outside" the irrevocably turning historical chamber. Not without religious overtones, Brotherhood history is also a kind of spirit that can be "born in your brain"; it is a stormy moment that can choose special people for special tasks and "transform" them into servants of history's high calling. Where exactly "the people" figure in this formulation of history is ambiguous. In one scene, the Brotherhood defends them as the righteous soul bearers of history, those who raise up new leaders as they need them, and even reach back into the past and name fallen heroes to direct new turns in history's path; in the next scene, the brothers speak of the people as ignoramuses who need only to be prodded, like cattle. Which simplistic formula Jack uses depends on which ideological point he is throwing out and at whom. But in any case Brotherhood history is a cynical twister which uses, if necessary, or destroys such innocent people as the ones Invisible sees evicted in Harlem. Explaining the scene in merciless terms, Jack describes history as an immutable force, this time as a storm:

> "These old ones," he said grimly. "It's sad, yes. But they're already dead, defunct. History has passed them by. Unfortunate, but there's nothing to do about them. They're like dead limbs that must be pruned away so that the tree may bear young fruit or the storms of history will blow them down anyway. Better the storm should hit them. . . . These people are old. . . . So they'll be cast aside. They're dead, you see, because they're incapable of rising to the necessity of the historical situation." (*IM*, 220)

This godlike history is no respecter of persons, guilty or innocent; it just *moves*, lifting some for a glimpse of salvation, blasting others. With this pseudoreligious, "scientific" formula for history as a cover, Jack targets Harlem for trouble.

Experience eventually teaches Invisible another view of history. "Beware of those who speak of the *spiral* of history," he warns. "They are preparing a boomerang. Keep a steel helmet handy. I have been boomeranged across my head so much that I now can see the darkness of lightness" (5). History repeats, he learns, but not in a neat geometric circle, and if history moves forward or upward, the meaning of the sweep is nonetheless contradictory. "Contradiction," says Invisible, "that . . . is how the world moves: Not like an arrow, but a boomerang" (5). Boomeranging history slashes in unpredictable parabolic patterns, and it can hit and kill others or even blindside its own unsuspecting thrower. Significantly, the boomerang is an instrument of war and of sport. ("Life," we are again reminded that Grandfather says, "is a war"; and as the compulsively talking vet says, it is a game.) It is important too that the boomerang is made and thrown by human hands. In *Invisible Man*, history is revealed as a tale told not by a god or a computer, but by human beings.

Tod Clifton's death brings the message home. This zealot for Brotherhood discovers that the party's conception of history is a malicious lie, that he's been betrayed, used against his people and himself. Unable to face the implications of his discovery, he recoils in despair, he "plunged outside history," as he puts it. Having depended so much on the vision and the values (the view of history) expressed by the Brotherhood, Tod becomes a cynic who "commits suicide" rather than confront a world effaced of meaning. The shock of his cohort's "suicide" makes Invisible realize that the event's significance is open to interpretation and to misinterpretation:

> History records the patterns of men's lives, they say: Who slept with whom and with what results; who fought and who won and who lived to lie about it afterwards. All things, it is said, are duly recorded—all things of importance, that is. But not quite, for actually it is only the known, the seen, the heard and only those events that the recorder regards as important that are put down, those lies his keepers keep their power by. But the cop would be Clifton's historian, his judge, his witness, and his executioner, and I was the only brother in the watching crowd. And I, the only witness for the defense, knew neither the extent of his guilt nor the nature of his crime. Where were the historians today? And how would they put it down? (*IM*, 332)

Not just the cop who shoots Clifton, but the newspapers and the Brotherhood members decide that Clifton is guilty. The Brotherhood even judges that his selling of Sambo dolls makes him a hotheaded fool, a sellout to his people, and a traitor to Brotherhood. But Invisible, who has begun to learn something of the complexity of events and the power of language and ritual, decides to honor Tod at a public funeral. "All right," he thinks, "so we'll use his funeral to put his integrity back together." The funeral oration (not just Invisible's words themselves but "the pattern of my voice upon the air") along with the spontaneous outburst of "Many Thousand Gone" assert that Tod's death was not meaningless. "It was hot downtown and he forgot his history," says Invisible. "He forgot the time and place. He lost his hold on reality." To an extent the death was bleakly comic: "The blood ran like blood in a comic-book killing, on a comic-book day in a comic-book world." But it was also a tragic loss: "Such," says Invisible Man, echoing Hemingway, "was the short bitter life of Brother Tod Clifton" (346).

The presence of some quiet and faddishly dressed black boys on a platform makes Invisible meditate still more on the true design of history:

> What if Brother Jack were wrong? What if history was a gambler, instead of a force in a laboratory experiment, and the boys his ace in the hole? What if history was not a reasonable citizen, but a madman full of paranoid guile and these boys his agents, his big surprise! His own revenge? For they were outside, in the dark with Sambo, the dancing paper doll; taking it on the lambo with my fallen brother, Tod Clifton (Tod, Tod) running and dodging the forces of history instead of making a dominating stand. (*IM*, 333)

Rinehart is "outside history," too. The logical Brotherhood has no place for him in its calculations; it would see him "simply as a criminal." Yet Rinehart not only suggests to Invisible a survival strategy, but his style of living contains yet another lesson about history:

> My God, what possibilities existed! And that spiral business, that progress goo! Who knew all the secrets; hadn't I changed my

name and never been challenged even once? And that lie that
success was a rising *upward*. What a crummy lie they kept us
dominated by. Not only could you travel upward toward success but you could travel downward as well; up *and* down, in
retreat, as well as in advance, crabways and crossways and
around in a circle, meeting your old selves coming and going
and perhaps all at the same time. How could I have missed it
for so long? (*IM*, 385)

With this lesson in mind, Invisible sees that the Brotherhood historians were writing a history that ignored the real experiences
of blacks, among others. Not taking into account the essential
ambiguity (the Rinehartness) of experience—that, for instance,
the ones lowest down in the social hierarchy might be snide
tricksters or even "the bearers of something precious"—the
Brotherhood's formulas were too spare and simple for Harlem.
Nor did they take into account that even painful experiences can
be interpreted in a positive light: "And now," Invisible finally sees,
"all past humiliations became precious parts of my experience,
and for the first time, leaning against that stone wall in the swel-
tering night, I began to accept my past and, as I accepted it, I felt
memories welling up in me. It was as though I'd learned suddenly
to see around corners" (383).

"To see around corners," says Kenneth Burke, "is to gain perspective on one's self and one's situation, to grasp enough of the
true pattern of events to have a handle on the future" (*Attitudes*,
268). More Burke: Invisible Man gains, at last, "perspective by
incongruity,"[29] signaled by Invisible's cryptic words concerning
Rinehart's rascality. "It was unbelievable," thinks Invisible, "but
perhaps only the unbelievable could be believed. Perhaps the
truth was always a lie" (*IM*, 376). Incongruous as it seems, Invisible Man sees the truth of his predicament only when he sees
that, "highly visible" as he is, he is *unseen*. Hence the ironic laughter in his first report: "I am an invisible man." Much "boomeranging" of his expectations taught him the comic nature of
things; his laughter is earned by his encounters with bull-necked
experience.

At the novel's end, the hero has also earned the heroic title, even if he is more a comic than a tragic hero. In his memoirs he looks back on his experience and sees it in ritual terms which recall the rites of initiation, purification, and rebirth one encounters in *The Sun Also Rises* (the English edition of which was entitled *The Fiesta*), *Men without Women, In Our Time*, and Hemingway's essays about hunting and bullfighting. Like many Hemingway characters, Invisible is transformed by witnessing and suffering great violence and caprice. Like the audience at a good bullfight (as reported by Hemingway), readers of *Invisible Man* feel "changed" by Invisible's dances with death. Like a Hemingway bullfighter, Invisible has come close to the bull's horns, he has been upended; and despite his scars, he has come back battling. The novel itself is his act of supreme "grace under pressure," the ultimate Hemingway laurel. By the epilogue he has confronted his tormentors, figured out the magic words and symbols (his grandfather's and those in his suitcase), and endured the wounds of his tragic knowledge. Finally he is freed of his illusions—freed of his imposed names and the imposed schemes of how the world moves. In time, he has stared down fake versions of history. Having learned that history is no more than a fiction, a "lie,"[30] he pieces together his own history, his own "exalted lie."

To Ellison, Hemingway was a guide and a "father-as-artist" in part because he was a worthy sparring partner, a "cooperative antagonist." (Like Hemingway, Ellison has said that he must go toe to toe with the best writers of his time and—to keep the stakes high—with the best writers of all time.) But Ellison also chose Hemingway as his true ancestor because he insisted on telling his "lies" as he himself saw them, despite all precedents and influences, political and otherwise, to tell them any other way. Over and over again his heroes make their forthright stands as artists whose integrity and talent and craft were all they either had or needed to clear a place where they could feel at home in an embattled world. One of his most gifted sons, Ellison, creates in *Invisible Man* a novel as at variance from the Dreiser-Howells-Wright naturalists and realists' work as is *The Sun Also Rises*. In Ellison's book, signs and symbols are presented and meditated upon, but they are never explained away, as Wright's images sometimes are. In this sense Ellison "understates" his case, à la Hemingway; the metaphor of invisibility, for instance, retains its rich mystery. But more like Wright and Faulkner than like Hemingway he is also careful not to be misunderstood, and adds his essay-like epilogue to drive his fictional point home. Invisible Man is not a laconic Hemingway tough guy; he is a talker who says his piece in language more extroverted and southern than Hemingway's characters used. Ellison, in other words, took what he needed from Hemingway without merely copying his style. Still, Invisible Man, much more like Hemingway's Jake and Nick than like Bigger Thomas, takes on the world, body and soul. And at the novel's end, he only wants to last, as Hemingway put it, and to get his work done: to tell his story truer than the facts.

Notes

1. See Steve Cannon, Ishmael Reed, and Quincy Troupe, "The Essential Ellison," 126–59; and Michael S. Harper and Robert B. Stepto, "Study and Experience: An Interview with Ralph Ellison," 417–35.

2. See Albert Murray, *South to a Very Old Place*. When Ellison first met Faulkner in 1953, he introduced himself as one of his sons.

3. Ralph Ellison, *Shadow and Act*, 140–41. All in-text references to the essays in this work appear as *S&A*.

4. Ellison interview, "Introduction: A Completion of Personality," in *Ralph Ellison: A Collection of Critical Essays*, ed. John Hersey, 1–19.

5. See William White, ed. *By-Line: Ernest Hemingway*. Further references in text appear as *By-Line*.

6. I refer to *In Our Time* (1925) and *Men without Women* (1972); *The Sun Also Rises* (1926) and *A Farewell to Arms* (1929); and *Death in the Afternoon* (1932).

7. See George Garrett, "Ralph Ellison," in *The Writer's Voice*, 224.

8. Ellison, "Introduction to Flamenco," 38. Note that this comment on the blues is framed in the context of a discussion of flamenco music and dance.

9. See "Ralph Ellison," *Interviews with Ten Black Writers*, ed. John O'Brien, 68.

10. Ellison interview, "A Very Stern Discipline," 90. Further references in text appear as "Stern Discipline."

11. See Robert G. O'Meally, *The Craft of Ralph Ellison*, 29.

12. Richard Wright, "Bright and Morning Star" (1938), reprinted in Sterling A. eds., Brown et al., *The Negro Caravan*, 110.

13. Ellison, "Folklore," an interview for the Federal Writers Project with Leo Gurley, June 14, 1939, Library of Congress Folklore Archives, Washington, D.C.; reprinted in Ann Banks, *First-Person America*, 244.

14. Ellison, "Ralph Ellison Explains," 145.

15. Ellison, "Negro Prize Fighter," 26–27. Further references cited in text as "Prize Fighter."

16. Robert Penn Warren, introduction to *A Farewell to Arms*, xxvii.

17. See Ellison et al., "What's Wrong with the American Novel?" in *American Scholar* 24:472. Further references in text cited as "What's Wrong."

18. See Ellison, "Twentieth-Century Fiction and the Black Mask of Humanity," *Confluence* (December 1953): 3–21; "Society, Morality, and the Novel," *The Living Novel: A Symposium*, ed. Granville Hicks, 58–91; "The Novel as a Function of American Democracy," *Wilson Library Bulletin* (June 1967): 1022–27. For an excellent analysis of stylistic linkages between Twain and Hemingway, see Richard Bridgman's *The Colloquial Style in America* (New York: Oxford University Press, 1966).

19. Ellison has, through the years, however, remained suspicious of fine technique alone. In "The Novel as a Function of American Democracy," Ellison wrote: "The state of our novel is not so healthy at the moment. Instead of aspiring to project a vision of the complexity, the diversity of the total experience, the novelist loses faith and falls back upon something which is called 'black comedy,' which is neither black or comic. It is a cry of despair. Talent and technique are there; artistic competence is there; but a certain necessary faith in human possibility before the next unknown is not there." *Wilson Library Bulletin* (June 1967): 1027.

20. See Ralph Ellison, "Through a Writer's Eyes." *Washington Post* (August 21, 1973), B3.

21. Ellison, "Introduction," *Invisible Man*, 30th anniversary ed. (New York: Random House, 1982), xix. Further references in text are cited as *IM*.

22. See Kenneth Burke, *Philosophy of Literary Form*, 253–62.

23. See Ellison, *Invisible Man*: the author's introductions in the 30th anniversary ed. and the Franklin Library Ed. (New York: Franklin, 1979).

24. See John F. Callahan, "The Historical Frequencies of Ralph Waldo Ellison," in *Chant of Saints*, 33–52.

25. Quoted by Ellison, *Shadow and Act*, 144.

26. See Ernest Hemingway, "A Clean, Well-Lighted Place," in *The Fifth*

Column and the First Forty-Nine Stories, 477–81. Further references cited in text as *Fifth Column.*

27. See Albert Lee Murray, "*The Waste Land* and *The Sun Also Rises:* A Comparative Study," M.A. thesis.

28. Note Kenneth Burke's definition of *history* as more than a report of past events, but as "man's life in political communities" or the "characteristic responses of people in forming and reforming their communities." *Attitudes toward History,* i.

29. Ibid.; see also Burke, *Permanence and Change: An Anatomy of Purpose,* 146.

30. See Ellison, "The Original 2nd Epithet," in "The Uses of History in Fiction," 69.

Works Cited

Burke, Kenneth. *Attitudes toward History,* 2d ed. Boston: Beacon, 1959.

————. *Permanence and Change: An Anatomy of Purpose.* New York: Republic Books, 1935.

————. *Philosophy of Literary Form,* rev. ed. New York: Vintage, 1957; original edition, 1941.

Callahan, John. "The Historical Frequencies of Ralph Waldo Ellison." *Chant of Saints,* ed. Michael S. Harper and Robert B. Stepto. Urbana: University of Illinois 1979.

Ellison, Ralph. "Alain Locke Symposium." *Harvard Advocate* (Spring 1974): 9–28.

————. "A Congress Jim Crow Didn't Attend." *New Masses* 35 (May 14, 1940) 5–8.

————. "Creative and Cultural Lag." *New Challenge* 2 (Fall (1937): 90–91.

————. "The Essential Ellison." Interview by Steve Cannon, Ishmael Reed, and Quincy Troupe. *Y'Bird Reader* (Autumn 1977): 126–59.

————. "Folklore." Interview for the Federal Writers Project with Leo Gurley, June 14, 1939. Library of Congress Folklore Archives. Reprinted in Ann Banks, ed., *First-Person America.* New York: Knopf, 1980.

————. "Introduction: A Completion of Personality." *Ralph Ellison: A Collection of Critical Essays,* ed. John Hersey. Englewood, N.J.: Prentice-Hall, 1974, 1–19.

————. "Introduction to Flamenco." *Saturday Review of Literature* 37 (December 11, 1954): 38–39.

————. *Invisible Man.* New York: Random House, 1982.

————. "Negro Prize Fighter." *New Masses* 37 (December 17, 1940): 23–27.

————. "The Novel as a Function of American Democracy." *Wilson Library Bulletin* (June 1967): 1022–27.

————. "Ralph Ellison Explains:" *'48 Magazine of the Year* 2 (May 1948): 145.

————. "Ralph Ellison." *Interview with Ten Black Writers*, ed. John O'Brien. New York: Liveright, 1973, 63–77.

————. *Shadow and Act.* New York: Random House, 1964.

————. "Society, Morality, and the Novel." *The Living Novel: Symposium*, ed. Granville Hicks. New York: Macmillan, 1957, 58–91.

————. "Stormy Weather." *New Masses* 37 (September 24, 1940): 20–21.

————. "Study and Experience: An Interview with Ralph Ellison." Michael S. Harper and Robert B. Stepto. *Massachusetts Review* 18 (Autumn 1977): 417–35.

————. "Through a Writer's Eyes." *Washington Post* (August 21, 1973), B3.

————. "Twentieth-Century Fiction and the Black Mask of Humanity." *Confluence* (December 1953): 3–21.

————. "The Uses of History in Fiction." *Southern Literary Journal* 1 (Spring 1969): 57–90.

————. "A Very Stern Discipline." Interview with Steve Cannon, Lennox Raphael, and James Thompson. *Harper's* 234 (March 1967): 76–95.

————. "What's Wrong with the American Novel?" *American Scholar* 24 (Autumn 1955): 464–503.

————. WGBH interview. "Interview with Ralph Ellison." Boston, April 12, 1974. Garrett, George. "Ralph Ellison." *The Writer's Voice.* New York: Morrow, 1973. Hemingway, Ernest. "A Clean, Well-Lighted Place." *The Fifth Column and the First Forty-Nine Stories.* New York: Scribner's, 1938.

————. *Death in the Afternoon.* New York: Scribner's, 1932.

————. *A Farewell to Arms.* New York: Scribner's, 1929.

————. "Fifty Grand." *The Fifth Column and the First Forty-Nine Stories.* New York: Scribner's, 1938.

————. *In Our Time.* New York: Scribner's, 1930.

————. *Men at War.* New York: Crown, 1942.

————. *Men without Women.* New York: Scribner's, 1927.

————. *The Sun Also Rises.* New York: Scribner's, 1926.

McPherson, James A. "Indivisible Man." *Atlantic Monthly* 206 (December 1970): 45–60.

Murray, Albert. *South to a Very Old Place.* New York: McGraw-Hill, 1971.

———. "The Storyteller as Blues Singer." *American Journal* (April 10, 1973): 14.

Murray, Albert Lee. "*The Waste Land* and *The Sun Also Rises*: A Comparative Study." M.A. thesis, New York University, September 1948.

O'Meally, Robert G. *The Craft of Ralph Ellison.* Cambridge, Mass.: Harvard University Press, 1980.

Warren, Robert Penn. "Introduction." Hemingway, *A Farewell to Arms.* New York: Scribner's 1919, 1949.

White, William, ed, *By-Line: Ernest Hemingway.* New York: Scribner's, 1967.

Wright, Richard. "Bright and Morning Star." *The Negro Caravan*, ed. Sterling A. Brown et al. New York: Dryden, 1941.

The Meaning of Narration in
Invisible Man

VALERIE SMITH

◆　◆　◆

1

In Ralph Ellison's essays and interviews, the artist is a figure of
rebellion. Whether writing generally of the role and responsibilities of the contemporary American novelist or, more specifically,
of his own achievements, Ellison describes the artist always in
opposition to the restraints of received literary convention. In
"Brave Words for a Startling Occasion," his acceptance speech for
the 1953 National Book Award, he identifies some of the restric-
tions that limit modern American fiction. For him, neither the
"tight, well-made Jamesian novel" nor the "hard-boiled novel"
can contain the complexity of American life. He writes:

> There was also a problem of language, and even dialogue,
> which, with its hard-boiled stance and its monosyllabic utter-
> ance, is one of the shining achievements of twentieth-century
> American writing. For despite the notion that its rhythms were
> those of everyday speech; I found that when compared with
> the rich babel of idiomatic expression around me, a language

full of imagery and gesture and rhetorical canniness, it was embarrassingly austere.[1]

In response to these constraints, he suggests that the contemporary novelist assume an adversarial posture; he or she must "challenge the apparent forms of reality—that is, the fixed manners and values of the few, and . . . struggle with it until it reveals its mad, vari-implicated chaos, its false faces, and . . . until it surrenders its insight, its truth" (SA, 106).

Likewise, in his famous rebuttal to Irving Howe's "Black Boys and Native Sons," entitled "The World and the Jug" (1963–1964), Ellison describes his objections to the kind of protest fiction produced by Richard Wright and endorsed by Howe and other critics and reviewers. Finding such representations of black life inordinately bleak, more sociological than literary, he defends his right to create novels that "celebrate human life and therefore are ritualistic and ceremonial at their core. Thus they would preserve as they destroy, affirm as they reject" (SA, 114). Locating himself in the tradition of American literary craftsmen and moral writers like Twain, Faulkner, Hemingway, and T. S. Eliot, he denies his intellectual links with and debt to earlier black writers.

The assumptions behind Ellison's formulations have jeopardized his credibility with more ideological writers and scholars. Black aestheticians such as Addison Gayle, Jr., argue that by emphasizing the universality of his work and vision, Ellison eschews the specific political responsibilities of the black writer.[2] Offering a more subtle indictment, Donald B. Gibson demonstrates that although Ellison denies the political implications of his work, *Invisible Man* is nonetheless "a social document that supports certain values and disparages or discourages others, and as such it must take its place among other forces that seek to determine the character of social reality."[3] Perhaps most generously, Houston A. Baker, Jr., shows that although in his essays Ellison favors the tradition of Western literary art over folklore, his novel actually breaks down the distinction between the two modes of creative discourse and celebrates the black expressive tradition.[4]

The politics of Ellison's rhetoric of rebellion are obviously murky, too complicated to untangle here. His critical writing is replete with images of struggle, subversion, iconoclasm; yet he defends a dissociation of art from politics that is arguably reactionary. I share Baker's sense of the complex relation between the ideology of the essays and the novel. But I would suggest that in at least one way the essays may inform our reading of the fiction: The character of the artist in Ellison's nonfiction corresponds to the portrait of the protagonist of *Invisible Man.*

More than just a failed college student, factory worker, and public speaker, Ellison's Invisible Man is also an artist. His product: the novel that presents itself as a "simulated autobiography."[5] My analysis will show that like the artist figure in the essays, the fictional protagonist uses his literary talent to subvert his subordinate relation to figures of authority, to expand the overly restrictive conceptions of identity that others impose upon him. As Ellison himself has often remarked, the novel is in no way the story of his own life.[6] Yet, onto his protagonist he projects his own sense of the artist's power and responsibility. His characterization of the writer in his nonfiction can thus provide terms by means of which we may assess the power and development of the Invisible Man.

One might describe the story of Ellison's protagonist as the quest for an appropriate identity. Throughout his life he encounters figures of authority—Norton, Bledsoe, the Brotherhood—who impose false names or unsuitable identities upon him. His experiences teach him that the act of naming is linked inextricably to issues of power and control. When he attempts to live according to the dictates of others, he loses his autonomy and suffers repeated betrayals. He discovers the true meaning of his life only after he assumes responsibility for naming himself by telling his own story.

By linking the narrative act to the achievement of identity, Ellison places his protagonist in a tradition of Afro-American letters that originated with the slave narratives of the late eighteenth and nineteenth centuries. Although these earlier texts were written, at least in part, to generate funds for and interest in the abolitionist cause, they also enabled the writers to name themselves before a culture that had denied their full humanity. When the slave narrators wrote the stories of their lives, they seized symbolic authority over themselves from their masters in the South who considered them only partly human. The grandson of emancipated slaves, the Invisible Man enjoys privileges unavailable to his ancestors in bondage. His ostensible freedom notwithstanding, he is subject to subtler, more pernicious forms of injustice and oppression. He, too, then, employs the narrative process in his search for liberation.

2

The narrator's dying grandfather, a half-mad war veteran, and his college president all warn him in his youth that since the world deceives, he must learn to be deceptive. Speaking in elliptical paradoxes to express an ostensibly self-contradictory message, the grandfather advises his family to follow his example and undermine the system while pretending to uphold it:

> I want you to overcome 'em with yeses, undermine 'em with grins, agree 'em to death and destruction, let 'em swoller you till they vomit or bust wide open. . . . Learn it to the younguns. (16)

Dr. Bledsoe attributes his success to a similar ability to feign humility. Astonished by the young protagonist's ignorance of "the difference between the way things are and the way they're supposed to be" (139), Bledsoe shares the grandfather's belief in duplicity as a necessary precondition for achievement. Likewise, the veteran recognizes the world's deceptions. He, too, tells the protagonist that he must recognize pretense and learn to be duplicitous:

> . . . learn to look beneath the surface. . . . Come out of the fog, young man. And remember you don't have to be a complete fool in order to succeed. Play the game, but don't believe in

it—that much you owe yourself. . . . Learn how it operates,
learn how you operate. (151)

The Invisible Man trivializes this recurring lesson until he suffers repeatedly the consequences of trusting others too readily.
As early as the battle royal, he deludes himself into thinking that
he is shrewd enough to play whatever game is required of him
without believing in it. As if to belie his supposed worldliness,
however, his undertakings backfire and reveal him for the bump-
kin he is. When Emerson shows him Bledsoe's letter, the protagonist seems to realize that he must be skeptical about the way
things appear. This recognition proves to be short-lived, however,
because the Invisible Man soon becomes as devoted to the Brotherhood and its platform as he was to the American dream and
the myth of racial uplift as embodied by his college. Only after
Tod Clifton is murdered, and he recognizes the Brotherhood's
complicity in the Harlem riot, does he understand just how false
a face the world presents.

Feigning sophistication, the Invisible Man says, for example,
that he doesn't believe in the principles he articulates in his valedictory address, "that humility [is] the secret, indeed, the very
essence of progress" (17). He thinks he only believes that the
semblance of humility works. The embarrassments he suffers in
the battle royal, in college, and in New York show, however, that
he lacks sufficient irony about himself and about the nature of
authority to distinguish between what "is" and what "works."
Lacking any alternative values he may call his own, he invests
more of himself in the principles he espouses than he realizes.

The protagonist displays none of his avowed skepticism at the
time of the battle royal. To him, the opportunity to speak before
"a gathering of the town's leading white citizens" is unparal-
leled—"a triumph for [the whole black] community." He expects
that the occasion will be somber and dignified, and that once he
delivers his oration, the audience will "judge truly [his] ability"
(25) and reward him. The scenario the protagonist envisages reveals his sense that his speech, his polish, and his talent have

rendered him superior to his peers. But the actual episode resembles only in its basic outline the one that the protagonist anticipates.

The "gathering" turns out to be a bacchanalia. He finds that several black boys his age have been invited to the affair to fight each other; his oratorical skills notwithstanding, he is expected to fight with the others for the audience's entertainment. During the course of the evening the young men are made to watch a nude white woman dance, to fight each other blindfolded, and to dive for counterfeit gold coins on an electrified rug. Each ordeal is designed for their mockery. Yet the Invisible Man hardly recognizes the disparity between his expectations and the actual situation. He resents fighting in the battle royal not because the match itself is degrading, but because he is repelled by the notion of being lumped together with the other black boys. He fears that the association will "detract from the dignity of [his] speech" (17).

When the white guests ask him to speak at the end of the evening, the protagonist is as determined to impress them as he was when he first arrived at the hotel. Without a second thought, he resolves to recite every word and to observe each intonation as he had practiced them. His meticulous delivery and posture are at least out of place, if not entirely ludicrous, directed as they are at a noisy and disrespectful crowd. But the protagonist is so convinced of the "rightness of things" (30) that he does not even risk offending his audience by spitting out his bloody, salty saliva. The mere possibility of a reward justifies any insults and indignities to which he may be subjected.

The Invisible Man might have learned from the battle royal episode to mistrust appearances, since the riotous scene of which he was a part bears little relation to the ceremony he had expected. He might have begun to suspect the power elite at large because his audience treated him rudely. But the briefcase and scholarship he receives for delivering his speech eclipse all the earlier unpleasantness. They confirm his assumption that if he does what the world expects of him, he will be rewarded with respect and acceptance. This belief in a reliable relation between cause and effect proves that he is neither the artificer nor the skeptic he pretends to be. Were he at all skeptical of the face the world presents, he would have been somewhat dubious about the existence of causal connections. At this point in his life, however, he is fully confident that things are what they appear and that material rewards await the virtuous.

In college he becomes further committed to this version of the American dream. He and his fellow students virtually worship the administrators and trustees, embodiments of the material success that supposedly ensues from hard work and clean living:

> Here upon this stage the black rite of Horatio Alger was performed to God's own acting script, with millionaires come down to portray themselves; not merely acting out the myth of their goodness, and wealth and success and power and benevolence and authority in cardboard masks but themselves, these virtues concretely! Not the wafer and the wine, but the flesh and the blood, vibrant and alive, and vibrant even when stooped, ancient and withered. (109)

Dr. Bledsoe provides an even more consistently visible image of what the students' best efforts may yield. His story typifies the standard rags-to-riches formula: He arrived at the college barefoot, motivated by "a fervor for education," and distinguished himself initially by being "the best slop dispenser in the history of the school" (114).[7] After years of hard work he became not only president of the school, but a nationally prominent leader as well. In the following description, the protagonist betrays his own mythification of Bledsoe and his inability to distinguish between material reward and moral virtue. The passage, conspicuously lacking in irony, juxtaposes achievements with possessions. Political influence, leadership, and Cadillacs are functionally equivalent; moreover, a light-skinned wife ranks as an acquisition along with these other "possessions":

> [Bledsoe] was the example of everything I hoped to be: Influential with wealthy men all over the country; consulted in matters concerning the race; a leader of his people; the pos-

sessor of not one, but *two* Cadillacs, a good salary and a soft, good-looking and creamy-complexioned wife. (99)

When he first meets with Bledsoe after returning Norton to campus, the protagonist begins to see that the president's obsequious, meticulous demeanor is but a facade. In a gesture that emblematizes the disjunction between his veneer and his beliefs; Bledsoe instantaneously rearranges his facial expression, replacing rage with placidity, just before entering Norton's room. This quick, apparently effortless change confirms the protagonist's growing suspicion that Bledsoe's legendary humility is not genuine, but only a performance; at base, he is a manipulative, dishonest power monger.

During their second meeting, Bledsoe asks the protagonist why he did not lie to Norton to avoid showing him Trueblood's shack. The protagonist's response betrays his naiveté; he barely knows what the verb "to lie" means. Duplicity is so foreign to him that he cannot formulate a sentence of which he is the subject, "to lie" is the verb, and a white person is the direct object. "Lie, sir? Lie to him, lie to a trustee, sir? Me?" (137)

Upon realizing that Bledsoe intends to break his promise to Norton and punish him, the protagonist completely loses control of himself. He dimly perceives that if Bledsoe can break his promise to a trustee, and reprimand him although he was not at fault, then contradictions and accidents can happen and effects will not always follow from causes. The protagonist does not want to believe that inconsistencies are possible, however. In an almost surreal sequence, he makes himself reinterpret the meaning of his escapades with Norton, Trueblood, the veteran, and Bledsoe. He forces himself to recast the events in such a way that he is responsible for Norton's accident and that his punishment makes sense. He would rather misunderstand his own experience than see it as a lesson about the disjunction between the way things are and the way they are supposed to be.

Just after he learns of his suspension, the protagonist leaves Bledsoe's office and wanders back to his dormitory in a virtual delirium. Symptomatic of his inability to accept Bledsoe's sentence, he vomits outside the administration building and realizes to his horror that the world around him has literally gone out of focus. In order to restore his normal vision, he covers one of his eyes; by partially blinding himself, he is able to make his way back to his room.

This episode corresponds symbolically with the Invisible Man's response to what becomes his expulsion. His visual distortion provides an emblem of his brief recognition that his actual experiences with Norton and Bledsoe have disconfirmed his expectations. For a moment, he realizes that his expectations may be fulfilled predictably in his imagination, but that the real world operates according to rules that elude him, if indeed it follows any rules at all. But as he covers one eye to avoid seeing double images, so does he consciously deny the distinction between his expectations and reality. He convinces himself that he was at fault and deserves his suspension; he recasts the earlier sequence of events so that they will explain the outcome logically:

> Somehow, I convinced myself, I had violated the code and thus would have to submit to punishment. Dr. Bledsoe is right, I told myself, he's right; the school and what it stands for have to be protected. There was no other way, and no matter how much I suffered I would pay my debt as quickly as possible and return to building my career. (145)

When the protagonist says that he will "pay [his] debt as quickly as possible and return to building [his] career," he assumes that his future success will at least diminish by contrast, if not justify, his present suffering. To put it another way, he expects that the passage of time will convert his humiliation into a mere rite of passage. Such a progressive or linear vision of time is fundamental to both the American dream and the myth of racial uplift; moreover, it is the cornerstone upon which the college was founded. Norton tells the protagonist, for example, that the students are his fate. Their accomplishments in the future will validate and render meaningful his past and present efforts:

Through you and your fellow students I become, let us say,
three hundred teachers, seven hundred trained mechanics,
eight hundred skilled farmers, and so on. That way I can observe in terms of living personalities to what extent my money,
my time and my hopes have been fruitfully invested. (45)

As the protagonist exchanges single- for "double-consciousness,"[8]
however, he acknowledges the limitations of his temporal construct. It encourages an investment in the opportunities and possibilities of the future at the expense of the lessons of the past.
During the narrative he becomes increasingly able to consider his
past experience and learn its lessons.[9] Writing his "autobiography"
shows clearly that for him retrospection has acquired value. But
only after his second major disillusionment does this realization
take place.

During his early days in New York City, the protagonist remains deeply convinced of the rightness of linear vision, of following "the path placed before [him]" (144). The patterns of his
thinking display his eagerness to think ahead, his reluctance to
reflect. He fantasizes about the future, imagining circumstances
that will justify his disgrace. However, he avoids thinking about
his past. In his room in the Men's House, for instance, he puts
aside the Bible because it makes him homesick and he has no
time for nostalgia: "This was New York. [He] had to get a job and
earn money" (159). Similarly, when he inadvertently remembers
his anger at being expelled, he "hastily" (160) blocks it out. Instead
of acknowledging his resentment, he conjures up a future that
will redeem his humiliation, one in which he will be Bledsoe's
assistant:

In my mind's eye . . . [Bledsoe] was joined by another figure; a
younger figure, myself; become shrewd, suave and dressed not
in somber garments (like his old-fashioned ones) but in a dap-
per suit of rich material, cut fashionably, like those of the men
you saw in magazine ads, the junior executive types in *Esquire*.
(160–61)

The protagonist intends to find a job in New York by observing professional protocol conscientiously. Well-groomed, prompt, and articulate, he expects that he will easily find suitable employment. Ironically, despite his attempt to manipulate his own appearance, it is he, not the prospective employers, who is taken in by appearances. He trusts his letters because of superficial, inconclusive details: He knows that they are about him, and that they are addressed to "men with impressive names" (148). No doubt the watermark and college letterhead make the letters seem all the more trustworthy. But when Emerson shows him the text of the letters, the protagonist is forced to see that their content is radically different from their impressive exteriors.

After this revelation, the protagonist recognizes that the values upon which the school was founded, those that Bledsoe ostensibly tried to teach him, are a sham. His efforts to humble himself and find employment have backfired; he realizes that this version of the American dream will never work for him. Once he renounces the goals that betrayed him, the protagonist behaves in freer and more complex ways than he did previously. His behavior during his last visit to the Men's House, for example, symbolizes his newfound spontaneity and his thorough separation from his earlier goals. As he looks around the boardinghouse lobby, he feels alienated from the upwardly mobile men with whom he had so recently identified himself. He notes, "I now felt a contempt such as only a disillusioned dreamer feels for those still unaware that they dream" (250). By emptying the spittoon over the head of the Baptist preacher he thinks is Bledsoe, he overturns as well the embodiment of his former dreams.

His disillusionment also causes the protagonist to be less defensive about his past. He now tries to consider and learn from his humiliations, instead of running from them. On the way home from Emerson's office, he begins to hum the melody that someone near him whistles. The tune jars his memory and reminds him of the following lyric from his childhood:

O well they picked poor Robin clean
O well they picked poor Robin clean

Well they tied poor Robin to a stump
Lawd, they picked all the feathers round from Robin's rump
Well they picked poor Robin clean. (190)

After reconstructing the song, he is able to use its meaning to understand his own situation: He, like "poor Robin," has been "picked . . . clean." Previously he would have denied all knowledge of what he would consider trivialities such as folk rituals and childhood songs; now he admits that they contain lessons that apply to his present condition.

On the morning of his appointment with Emerson, the Invisible Man refuses to eat pork chops and grits for breakfast because he wants to avoid being identified with "country" tastes. After he reads Bledsoe's letter, however, he realizes that refined tastes will not necessarily get him anywhere; he therefore begins to accept and to follow his impulses more readily. A reversal of the restaurant episode, the scene in which he eats yams indicates his heightened self-acceptance. Buying the yams and eating them publicly illustrates his willingness to savor both the things he enjoys and the memories they conjure up:

> I stopped as though struck up by a shot, deeply inhaling, remembering, my mind surging back, back. At home we'd bake them in the hot coals of the fireplace, had carried them cold to school for lunch; munched them secretly, squeezing the sweet pulp from the soft peel as we hid from the teacher behind the largest book, the *World's Geography.* Yes, and we'd loved them candied, or baked in a cobbler, deep-fat fried in a pocket of dough, or roasted with pork and glazed with the well-browned fat; had chewed them raw—yams and years ago. More yams than years ago, though the time seemed endlessly expanded, stretched thin as the spiraling smoke beyond all recall. (256–57)

The narrator refers to his pre-Brotherhood, postcollege phase as a "period of quietness" (252). He would have done better to call it a "period of inactivity," for although he is unemployed, he does undergo a turbulent period of emotional upheaval during this time. When he could rely on a collectively shared set of values or ethics (like the American dream or the myth of racial uplift), his life was comparatively ordered, and he felt that he subscribed to a system of belief that bestowed upon him a meaningful identity. The intellectual maneuver he performs to make sense of Bledsoe's punishment shows the lengths to which he will go to fit his experiences into a logically explicable context. He appears resilient, if not placid, because he can contain or freeze his emotional responses, like "ice which [his] life had conditioned his brain to produce" (253). His disillusionment (the result of his conversation with Emerson) operates like a "hot red light"; it causes the "ice" to begin to melt and makes it impossible for him to continue to ignore his feelings. The pain of living at such an intense level of self-awareness makes the protagonist especially susceptible to the influence of an organization such as the Brotherhood. Despite his resolutions, the Brotherhood tempts him irresistibly by offering him a system of beliefs that both differs strikingly from the one that deceived him and promises to restore meaning and thus quiet to his life. Its superficial differences notwithstanding, the Brotherhood's ideals prove, of course, to be as unreliable as the American dream.

The Invisible Man begins to work for the Brotherhood with the same single-minded faith that he brought to his college and to New York. Predictably, his experience with the Brotherhood recapitulates his disaffection with the principles the college embodies. In the Brotherhood (as in college), the Invisible Man undergoes the ordeal of an undeserved punishment; in both cases he submits, and accommodates himself to the sentence. Both the Brotherhood and the college betray his faith a second time, however; in each case, the second betrayal occasions his final disillusionment.

In order to place his faith unconditionally in the Brotherhood's tenets, the protagonist thinks he will have to forget the sociology and economics he learned in college (297). In fact, he has to unlearn much more than that. To adhere to the Brotherhood's principles, he also has to deny virtually all of the lessons that his college and postcollege experiences have taught him. The Brotherhood's assumptions and tactics are sufficiently similar to those the protagonist rejected, that he might have recognized them and saved himself some of this despair. His need for place and for a system of belief is so profound, however, that it blinds him to these resemblances.

The Invisible Man becomes disaffected with the values Bledsoe represents at least in part because they sacrifice the individual for the system. Considering him utterly insignificant, the college president resolves to destroy the protagonist's career, despite his innocence, in order to save the image of the school. The protagonist finds Bledsoe's logic incomprehensible, if not nonexistent; he therefore distances himself from the traditional American values Bledsoe embodies in order to preserve or create his own identity.

The Brotherhood similarly considers the interests of the individual insignificant in relation to those of the organization, although unlike Bledsoe it admits this bias overtly. As Brother Jack tells the Invisible Man at their first meeting, "you mustn't waste your emotions on individuals, they don't count" (284). Tempted by the promise of material and intellectual comfort, the protagonist affiliates himself with the group, even though, for him, individuals (himself in particular) do count. Indeed, his subsequent problems with the Brotherhood arise from this difference of opinion. Although he considers it reasonable to follow his own judgment and try to articulate the concerns of the black community, the Brotherhood finds his behavior divisive and censures him.

The protagonist had learned earlier that his own past experiences, as well as folk traditions, could teach him about his present condition. He should therefore have suspected the Brotherhood when it tried to cut him off from his past by changing his name and offering him a "new beginning" (327). But he allows himself to be seduced into the Brotherhood because it provides him with a system of belief that makes individual and political action significant. He cannot resist the hope of finding some meaning in a life and in a world that appear to be chaotic. As he notes in a description of the early days of his Brotherhood career:

[For] one lone stretch of time I lived with the intensity dis-
played by those chronic numbers players who see clues to their
fortune in the most minute and insignificant phenomena: in
clouds; on passing trucks and subway cars, in dreams, comic
strips, the shape of dog-luck fouled on the pavements. I was
dominated by the all-embracing idea of Brotherhood. The organization had given the world a new shape, and me a vital
role. We recognized no loose ends, everything could be controlled by our science. (373)

The protagonist's eagerness to escape his past and begin his life
anew dooms him to repeat his earlier mistakes. Understandably,
he would like to forget his suffering, humiliation, and cynicism.
As he remarks before his first Brotherhood speech, "if I were
successful . . . I'd be on the road to something big. No more flying
apart at the seams, no more remembering forgotten pains" (327).
But when he forgets "his pains," he also loses his ironic perspective on figures of authority and makes himself vulnerable once
again to their mistreatment.

Indeed, he consciously stops himself from looking at the organization with any skepticism, as if being in the group but not
of it were only disloyal, and not self-protective as well:

I would have to take that part of myself that looked on with
remote eyes and keep it always at the distance of the campus,
the hospital machine, the battle royal—all now far behind.
Perhaps the part of me that observed listlessly but saw all,
missing nothing, was still the malicious arguing part; the dissenting voice, my grandfather part; the cynical, disbelieving
part—the traitor self that always threatened internal discord.
Whatever it was, I knew that I'd have to keep it pressed down.
(327).

As a result, he does not (or will not) recognize the Brotherhood's
mistreatment of him. He is as innocent of Brother Wrestrum's
accusations as he was of Bledsoe's. As he did in the president's
office, the protagonist initially explodes when he hears of his punishment. But he accommodates himself yet again to the will

of his superior so that he will not be forced to question the institution's ideology. He needs so desperately to trust the Brotherhood that he convinces himself that the reprimand and reassignment are signs of their faith in, not their displeasure with, him:

> [After] all, I told myself, the assignment was also proof of the committee's goodwill. For by selecting me to speak with its authority on a subject which elsewhere in our society I'd have found taboo, weren't they reaffirming their belief both in me and in the principles of Brotherhood, proving that they drew no lines even when it came to women? They had to investigate the charges against me, but the assignment was their unsentimental affirmation that their belief in me was unbroken. (398)

The sequence of events that culminates in Tod Clifton's murder precipitates the Invisible Man's thorough and lasting reexamination of himself and his relation to authority and ideology. When he sees Clifton selling Sambo dolls on the street corner, the protagonist assumes that he must have been mad to leave the Brotherhood (ostensible order and meaning) for such a degrading and meaningless endeavor: "Why should a man deliberately plunge out of history and peddle an obscenity?" he asks himself. "Why should he choose to disarm himself, give up his voice and leave the only organization offering him a chance to 'define' himself?" (428). As he considers the nature of Clifton's wares and the fact of his death, however, the protagonist begins to question this formulation. He considers what he and the Brotherhood mean by "history" and acknowledges that the record in which they jointly believe is selectively and arbitrarily preserved; the Brotherhood's ideology is, therefore, no more sacrosanct than any other. Moreover, he begins to question the significance of blacks as a race within the Brotherhood's historical construct, given that its spokesmen persistently deny the importance of race as a category of distinction. The sight of other young blacks causes him to realize that his devotion to the Brotherhood has alienated him from the needs of his people. He remarks that

Clifton "knew them better" (432) than he; presumably, his inability to reconcile the people's needs with the Brotherhood's forced him to abandon the organization. Once he perceives that the Brotherhood has ignored the interests of the race, it becomes clear (although it is not explicitly stated in the text) that Clifton's Sambo dolls are not randomly selected products to be hawked on the streets. The black caricatures dangled on a string are, instead, metaphors for the black members of the Brotherhood who are manipulated, unknowingly, by the white leadership.

The Invisible Man plans a public funeral for Clifton in hopes of organizing the black community in response to a particularly sensitive incident: the shooting of an unarmed black man by a policeman. The construction he puts on Clifton's murder differs markedly from the Brotherhood's because he places such a premium on the fact of race. For the protagonist, it is more politically significant that Clifton was black than it is that he was a defector. In addition, he is more concerned with organizing the black community than he is with preserving the integrity of the Brotherhood's reputation. The Brotherhood spokesmen, in contrast, see Clifton's death primarily as the murder of a traitor: an event that concerns them only minimally. They therefore rebuke the protagonist for organizing a hero's funeral. To their minds, faithfulness to the Brotherhood's cause outweighs race as a consideration.

The Brotherhood's response to Clifton's death and funeral confirms the Invisible Man's worst fears about the organization.[10] Within the Brotherhood, he is as invisible as he was in his hometown and at his college. He is significant to Brother Jack and the other leaders only to the extent that he effectively and obediently articulates the party line. Outside of his narrowly defined role within the organization, he does not exist for them. He had mistakenly thought that by upholding the Brotherhood's ideology, he would find purpose and meaning for his life. Clifton's death and his reprimand show him, however, that his life will derive meaning from the platform only if he renounces the prior claims of his own judgment, his own priorities, and, incidentally, his own race. To put it another way, he will have an identity in the

Brotherhood only if he concedes the possibility of creating the meaning of his life for himself.

The protagonist's mistrust of the Brotherhood precipitates a time of reflection for him. This betrayal reminds him of the other people who have betrayed him in similar ways. Like Norton and Bledsoe, Jack and others treat him as if he does not exist. Each man needs to think of him in a certain way, and thus sees only the image he projects:

> Here I had thought [the Brotherhood] accepted me because they felt that color made no difference, when in reality it made no difference because they didn't see either color or men.... [All the people who betrayed him] were very much the same, each attempting to force his picture of reality upon me and neither giving a hoot in hell for how things looked to me. I was simply a material, a natural resource to be used. (497)

His betrayal also prompts him to remember his grandfather's admonition; as he did at the beginning of the narrative, he resolves at the end as well to undercut the game (this time the Brotherhood's) even as he pretends to play it.

He reverts to his earlier attempt at duplicity, at least in part, because he discovers accidentally that he can manipulate his appearance to his own advantage. Afraid of being recognized and beaten by Ras the Exhorter's followers, the protagonist dons sunglasses and a hat, only to find that all of Harlem now thinks that he is Rinehart, the quintessential hustler. He realizes that if he changes his appearance just a bit, he is able to circumvent the problems of being himself and to enjoy the benefits of being someone else.

The Invisible Man's betrayals have caused him to believe that no institution, no ideology, is wholly reliable. Given his sense of a chimerical reality, the identity of Rinehart seems to suit him, for Rinehart is a consummate manipulator of surfaces: pimp, numbers runner, lover, and preacher, he is all things to all people. The protagonist finds the idea of a Rinehart appealing on two grounds. First, Rinehart provides him with an identity into which he can escape with ease. Second and more important, the Invisible Man is compelled by the hustler because he is able to change identities at will, thereby turning the ephemeral nature of the world to his advantage. In the following passage, he remarks on the place of a Rinehart figure in a chaotic society:

> What is real anyway? . . . The world in which we lived was without boundaries. A vast seething, hot world of fluidity, and Rine the rascal was at home. Perhaps *only* Rine the rascal was at home in it. It was unbelievable, but perhaps only the unbelievable could be believed. Perhaps the truth was always a lie. (487)

The protagonist thinks that by following the example of his grandfather (of which Rinehart is an extreme instance) and feigning compliance, he will protect himself from further deceptions and acquire some authority over his own life. This experiment works for a time; he reinstates himself in the Brotherhood's good graces by telling its leaders only those things about Harlem they wish to hear—that increased numbers of black people are joining the ranks, for example—and generally affecting a submissive demeanor. At the scene of the Harlem riot, however, he discovers that his false acquiescence has backfired. Because the leaders have withheld the full complexity of their platform, he has been implicated in a conspiracy of which he knew nothing. He had intended to organize the black community; instead, he has been involved unknowingly in the Brotherhood's effort to destroy it:

> It was not suicide, but murder. The committee had planned it. And I had helped, had been a tool. A tool just at the very moment I had thought myself free. By pretending to agree I had indeed agreed, had made myself responsible for that huddled form lighted by flame and gunfire in the street, and all the others whom now the night was making ripe for death. (541)

As this passage indicates, the Invisible Man realizes the implausibility of feigning compliance with the dominant ideology. Because he is necessarily subordinate to figures of authority, he will never know the full complexity of their program. Commitment to an ideology requires a leap of faith, a leap he has always been only too willing to make. Yet each time he commits himself, what he "leaps" over threatens to destroy him.

In other words, what he learns ultimately is that he will have no control over his own life if he tries to play the game but not believe in it. As he notes, "[he] had been used as a tool. [His] grandfather had been wrong about yessing them to death and destruction or else things had changed too much since his day" (552). Possibly his grandfather could feign compliance while undercutting the system, but he has repeatedly seen that for him, to comply in part is to comply altogether. He therefore resolves to sever his connections to society, to all of the organizations on which he had relied for self-definition, and accepts responsibility for creating his own identity. After his final conference with Brother Hambro he recognizes that if his life is to have any meaning, it must be the sum of all he had undergone: "I was my experiences and my experiences were me, and no blind men, no matter how powerful they became, even if they conquered the world, could take that or change . . . it" (496–97). When he retreats underground to write his own story, he commits himself to sifting through those experiences and attributing his own meaning to them.

3

By choosing to go underground and compose the story of his life, the Invisible Man shows that he has exchanged one group of mentors—his grandfather, Bledsoe, and the veteran—for another—Trueblood and Brother Tarp.[11] Both groups, whether explicitly or implicitly, warned him against being too trusting. But whereas the first emphasized the importance of learning to deceive as he is also deceived, the latter provides models for creating a sense of identity independent of what an organization or a collective set of assumptions requires. Throughout the course of his life, the Invisible Man learns that he can never quite learn to be deceptive enough. No matter how devious he thinks he is, those who control him always manage to trick and betray him. His efforts to create simultaneously an identity inside and outside of an institution therefore seem doomed to failure. When he decides to write his own story, he relinquishes the meaning generated by other ideologies in favor of one that is primarily self-generated. By designating a beginning and an end to his story, he converts events that threaten to be chaotic into ones that reveal form and significance. He creates for himself a persona that develops, indeed exists, in contradistinction to the images that others projected onto him. Moreover, he inverts his relation to the figures of authority who dominated him in "life." As author/narrator he is able to control the identities of such people as Norton, Bledsoe, and Brother Jack. By presenting them in uncomplimentary ways, he avenges the humiliations they inflicted upon him in life. The double consciousness of simultaneously playing and undermining the game proved implausible. But the solution to the problems of identity and authority can be found in the double consciousness of reliving one's story as both narrator and protagonist.

Brother Tarp and Trueblood both appear to realize that their identity is determined by the sum of the complex experiences they have undergone. Each man has a story that defines him over and against the identity that others try to impose or project. Tarp conceives of himself as the protagonist of the story of his prison experience. Because he "said no to a man who wanted to take something from [him]" (378), he spent nineteen years in jail and lost his family and his property. He remained in prison until he was able to break free, at which time he determined that he could make it. The story he tells the Invisible Man, his inescapable memories, his limp, and the link from his leg iron are all ways in which Tarp keeps his past with him in the present. They remind him that he is still looking for freedom, and they remind

him of "what [they're] really fighting against" (379). In other
words, they keep ever before him those values that he holds most
dear and that give his life meaning.

Jim Trueblood also tells a story about a critical experience that
reveals his sense of identity. Although the protagonist meets him
at a point in the narrative when he can in no way appreciate
what the farmer represents, his decision to write his story harks
back to Trueblood's tale.[12] Like the protagonist, Trueblood is invisible: No one sees him as he is. Because he has slept with his
own daughter, blacks consider him a disgrace and whites think
of him as a sort of dirty joke. Although others ostracize and
ridicule him, Trueblood asserts his own sense of identity by telling
and retelling a tale of his own creation. He acknowledges the
complexity and ambiguity of his situation: being both guilty and
not guilty of incest. As Selma Fraiberg notes, however, instead of
allowing myth (or convention) to determine the meaning of his
action, Trueblood refuses "to hide behind the cowardly deceptions
that cloak sin; he faces the truth within himself."[13] He understands, as the protagonist comes to learn, that he can control the
meaning of his life if he converts his own experiences into a
narrative and therefore determines what construction should be
placed on them. His well-crafted tale prefigures the protagonist's
autobiography, a text that endows with meaning events that
seemed random as they were "lived" by imposing artistic form
on them.[14]

Before beginning his story, Trueblood assumes the stance of
the narrator par excellence: "He cleared his throat, his eyes
gleaming and his voice taking on a deep incantatory quality, as
though he had told the story many, many times" (53). He sets
the stage for a complex and subtle story. In order to create the
atmosphere of the evening he slept with Matty Lou, he evokes
visual, olfactory, and aural images. On that tranquil, critical night,
past and present merged for him; he lay in bed with his wife and
daughter, remembering another peaceful time in his life when he
lived with an earlier lover in a house on the Mississippi. He recalls
hearing the river boats approach and conjures up the scene with
fluid, sophisticated imagery. Human and animal worlds all the

senses, dream and waking life, merge. He analogizes the sound of the distant river boats to the "boss bird" calling the covey together during quail season:

> I'd be layin' there and it would be quiet and I could hear it comin' from way, way off. Like when you quail huntin' and it's getting dark and you can hear the boss bird whistlin' tryin' to get the covey together again, and he's coming toward you slow and whistlin' soft, cause he knows you somewhere around with your gun. Still he got to round them up, so he keeps on comin'. Them boss quails is like a good man, what he got to do he *do!* (55)

He captures the sound of the boat nearing the house in terms of a visual image that becomes, in turn, aural, gustatory, and then visual again:

> [It] sounded like somebody hittin' at you slow with a big shiny pick. You see the pick-point comin' straight at you, comin' slow too, and you can't dodge; only when it goes to hit you it ain't no pick a'tall but somebody far away breakin' little bottles of all kindsa colored glass. . . . Then you hear it close up, like when you up in the second-story window and look down on a wagonful of watermelons, and you see one of them young and juicy melons split open a-layin' all spread out and cool and sweet on top of all the striped green ones like it's waitin' just for you, so you can see how red and ripe and juicy it is and all the shiny black seeds it's got and all. And you could hear the sidewheels splashin' like they don't want to wake nobody up; and us, me and the gal, would lay there feelin' like we was rich folks and them boys on the boats would be playin' sweet as good peach brandy wine. (55)

His use of synesthesia reveals the heightened sensuality of his reminiscences on the night he slept with his daughter. Furthermore, the artistry of his story displays the extent to which he has shaped the experience linguistically. By following the associative patterns of his thoughts, he seems to relive the situation as he first experienced it. However, his tale is anything but spontaneous: His use of imagery indicates that he is self-consciously creating the impression (whether true or not) that the atmosphere of the evening was largely responsible for the act of incest.

Given the sensuality of his ruminations while he lies in bed awake, it seems logical that he would have an erotic dream once he falls asleep. As his dream opens, he has just violated custom and entered a white man's house through the front door. Unintentionally, he proceeds to a large white bedroom and discovers there a white woman dressed in a negligee. Although he tries to escape, she holds him back. The tension of the situation is heightened by the grandfather clock, which strikes faster and faster. When he throws the woman on the bed "to break her holt," the two of them begin to sink into her bed:

> It's sinkin' down so far I think it's going to smother both of us. Then swoosh! all of a sudden a flock of little white geese flies out of the bed like they say you see when you go to dig for buried money. Lawd! they hadn't no more'n disappeared than I heard a door open and Mr. Broadnax's voice said, "They just nigguhs leave 'em do it." (58)

In the next phase of the dream, he runs toward the clock and describes his entry into it in terms suggestive of the sexual act and climax.

In the first phase of the dream, Trueblood transgresses a series of social taboos: He enters the white man's home by the front door and has sexual contact with a white woman. Then the dream landscape changes from the representational to the phantasmagoric. When he awakens, he realizes that his actual situation parallels his dream. In life he has just violated a sexual taboo, albeit incest instead of miscegenation. The presence of his wife in the same bed compounds his horror, just as the ticking of the clock exacerbates the tension in the dream. Furthermore, he acknowledges in life, as well as in the dream, the sexual pleasure he derives from the forbidden act.

As Trueblood narrates the sequence of events that took place after he had relations with his daughter, he heightens the reader's sympathy for him by demonstrating both his willingness to accept responsibility for his sin and his attempt to endure his wife's rage. He describes Kate's fury and his readiness to submit to physical punishment by her hand. He even agrees to leave his family for a while. Eventually, however, he insists on returning to them and facing the consequences of his actions. Moreover, he refuses to allow either his wife or his daughter to abort his child and chases away everyone who tries to stand between him and his family.

During the time Trueblood is away from his family, he tries and fails to explain himself to his minister. But religion cannot accommodate or justify his sin and thus cannot help him make sense of his behavior. He tries to determine on his own the extent of his guilt, turning the incident over in his mind. Eventually he sings the blues; like his narrative itself, the music he creates allows him, finally, to come to terms with what he has done.

The subtly complex narrative Trueblood constructs replaces the reductive, derogatory version that the townspeople tell. According to his story, the ambience of the evening and the dreams it triggered prompted him to initiate intercourse before he was fully awake. He was therefore not entirely conscious when the encounter began. However, he has sufficient self-respect to assume responsibility for his actions, whether intentional or not. Thus he transforms himself from villain or buffoon to hero by proving simultaneously his innocence and his willingness to accept blame.

Like Trueblood, the Invisible Man chooses and designs his own identity with great care. He rejects the assumption that his past experiences are meaningless and merely sequential in favor of the belief that, taken together, they make up who he is. In his youth he thought that the past was best put at a distance, that identity could be changed at will, and that it could be defined by one's affiliations. By the time he writes the narrative, however, he realizes that all other-imposed identities are false. One's true identity is the sum of one's experiences; therefore, to deny one's past is to deny oneself:

It was as though I'd learned suddenly to look around corners; images of past humiliations flickered through my head and I saw that they were more than separate experiences. They were me; they defined me. I was my experiences and my experiences were me, and no blind men, no matter how powerful they became, even if they conquered the world, could take that, or change one single itch, taunt, laugh, cry, scar, ache, rage or pain of it. (496–97)

Telling his story allows him to arrange and recount his experiences in such a way as to display the meaning of his life. The beginning and end he chooses, the recurrent patterns he discloses, refute the prevailing opinion that his life lacks significance and is therefore expendable. He shows through his narrative that there is coherence to his life and method to his humiliations. As he learns the value of increased self-reliance, he develops from naiveté and powerlessness to wisdom and authority.

The Invisible Man might have selected any incident from his life to open the narrative action of his autobiography. If he had wanted immediately to call his reader's attention to his talents, for example, he might have begun by describing at length the first occasion on which he delivered his valedictory address, his high school graduation. Because he intended the first chapter to create quite a different effect, however, he selected for the first memorable event of the novel one that highlights his naive and overly trusting persona. By essentially beginning the narrative with the juxtaposition of the battle royal against the valedictory address, he calls the reader's attention to his own myopia and his overdependence on others' values. This beginning guarantees the reader's awareness that these shortcomings also cause his subsequent humiliations.

The narrator focuses on his own limitations, at least in part, to justify his susceptibility to betrayal. By revealing certain motifs that attend his humiliations, he further shows that some order infuses his experiences even though he was unable to see it when he "lived" them. For example, as I noted earlier, his betrayal by the Brotherhood recapitulates his betrayal by Bledsoe. The Invisible Man might have avoided his second deception if he had recognized the techniques of deception and his own credulity from his earlier betrayal. Had he wanted to call the reader's attention to the arbitrariness of his humiliations, he could have presented the story in such a way as to emphasize the differences between the two betrayals. The protagonist would then have appeared to be the powerless victim of random, inexplicable circumstances. He highlights both the predictability of organizations and his own culpability, however, by underscoring the similarities between the college and the Brotherhood.

Recounting his story also allows the protagonist to redress the abuses he suffered and overturn the authority of those who misled him in college and in the Brotherhood.[15] Although he was unable to confront them in life, as author of the narrative he can deflate the images of those who ridiculed or deceived him by characterizing them as buffoons and villains. He presents Norton and Homer Barbee, for example, with no small degree of irony in order to undercut the beliefs they profess.

When he is a student, the Invisible Man clearly reveres Norton and all that he represents. Rich, shrewd, elegantly attired, and exceedingly well-mannered, Norton embodies everything to which the protagonist aspires. Flattered at having been asked to drive for the trustee, the young man is eager to please, fearful of offending. Characteristically, he expects that if he drives and converses well, he will receive some reward: "Perhaps he'd give me a large tip, or a suit, or a scholarship next year" (38). Indeed, even after the protagonist is suspended, he thinks that Norton will be able to help him if only he can find him. By the time he writes the narrative, of course, he has ceased to believe either that wealthy white benefactors are necessarily virtuous or that institutions like the school can uplift the race.

As if to retaliate against Norton for having misled him, the Invisible Man subtly but unmistakably impugns the motives behind his philanthropy. Norton thinks that he is primarily impelled to support the school by his wish to commemorate his late daughter's memory. The words the narrator attributes to Norton betray his incestuous attraction to her, however, and imply strongly that his generosity may well be an act of atonement for a sin he fails to recognize. When Norton speaks of his daughter, his tone is more that of a bereaved lover than of a father. In addition, he says that he was never able to believe that she was his own, and he expresses an undefined sense of guilt about her. Taken together, these features of his description disclose his problematic relation to her:

> [My daughter] was a being more rare, more beautiful, purer, more perfect and more delicate than the wildest dream of a poet. I could never believe her to be my own flesh and blood. Her beauty was a well-spring of purest water-of-life and to look upon her was to drink and drink and drink again . . . She was rare, a perfect creation, a work of purest art . . . I found it difficult to believe her my own . . .
> "She was too pure for life," he said sadly, "too pure and too good and too beautiful. . . . I have never forgiven myself." (42)

Norton's response to Trueblood further indicates that his daughter may well have some sexual appeal for him. He overreacts wildly when he learns that the man has slept with his own daughter and has gone unpunished: " 'You did and are unharmed!' he shouted, his blue eyes blazing into the black face with something like envy and indignation" (51). Trueblood's powerful narrative devastates Norton because it forces him to confront his own deeply concealed desires. By juxtaposing Norton's and Trueblood's responses to incest, the narrator reveals the extent of both the trustee's misguidance and the farmer's self-awareness. When the event occurred, the protagonist was so overwhelmed by the white man's image and so worried about his own that he totally misread the situation. He not only overestimated Norton, he also treated Trueblood dismissively. In the narrative he corrects this error in judgment. He deposes Norton as a mentor, and by telling his own tale follows Trueblood's example instead.

The protagonist is likewise overly impressed by the Reverend Homer Barbee, who preaches a sermon on the evening of the

Trueblood–Golden Day episode. Having jeopardized his college career, the protagonist is moved to guilty tears by Barbee's address, for it celebrates all that the school represents. The minister reminds the students of the legacy of the Founder: Like the school itself, he sprang up from nothing and dedicated himself to the progress of the race. Moreover, Barbee praises Bledsoe's benevolence and leadership:

> Your leader has kept his promise a thousandfold. I commend him in his own right, for he is the co-architect of a great and noble experiment. He is a worthy successor to his great friend and it is no accident that his great and intelligent leadership has made him our leading statesman. His is a form of greatness worthy of your imitation. I say to you, pattern yourselves upon him. Aspire, each of you, to some day follow in his footsteps. Great deeds are yet to be performed. (30–31)

At the time he hears the speech, the protagonist feels so ashamed of himself that he is unable to stay for the entire service. The speech has convinced him, for at least a short while, that his error has threatened the entire institution. "I could not look at Dr. Bledsoe now, because old Barbee had me both feel my guilt and accept it. For although I had not intended it, any act that endangered the continuity of the dream was an act of treason" (132).

But looking back at the episode from the end of the narrative, he realizes that the values Barbee articulates are corrupt. The very way in which he notes the minister's blindness mocks his faith in these principles. Given that the narrator knows at the time he recounts the episode that Barbee is blind, he might have acknowledged that fact when he describes the minister's approach to the lectern. If he had wanted to preserve Barbee's image, he might have introduced his speech with a statement like "His blindness did not detract from the insightfulness of his sermon." Instead, he conceals the fact of his blindness until Barbee has completed his stirring message. He describes his sudden fall to his face and then explains in two abrupt sentences why the minister fell: "For a swift instant, between the gesture and the opaque glitter of his glasses, I saw the blinking of sightless eyes. Homer A. Barbee was blind" (131). One might argue that he narrates the episode as he does to recapture the sequence of his perceptions. But his motives are more complex than such a reading would suggest. He intends the fall and the disclosure of Barbee's blindness to reflect back on the sermon itself. Although he did not realize it when he heard the speech, he now thinks that Barbee must have been intellectually imperceptive (that is, blind) if he believed what he professes.

Like any autobiographer, the Invisible Man chooses an ending for his narrative that is logically consistent with the meaning of the story as a whole. As Frank Kermode writes, "The provision of an end [makes] possible a satisfying consonance with the origins and with the middle."[16] He has constructed the tale of his development from ignorance to knowledge both of the meaning of identity and of the proper relation to the power elite. It is therefore to his advantage to end at a point where he is palpably wiser than he was before. However, the Invisible Man has given his narrative a cyclical structure. Repeatedly he thinks he has figured out how best to maneuver his way around figures of authority, only to find that his strategy has failed him. The decision to remove himself from society and write his own story thus might represent only one of an interminable list of strategies. However, this last one seems to differ from the earlier attempts, for it appears to require him to depend upon himself for the construction of his identity more than his earlier ventures did. But since the story ends before he reenters society, the reader never knows the degree to which he conforms to institutional expectations once he reenters the world.

By ending where he does, then, the Invisible Man loads the dice in his own favor—one final advantage to telling his own story. He leaves the reader with his conviction that the double consciousness of being both narrator of and participant in his own story empowers him in a way that his earlier duplicity did not. Had he ended his story later, however, this solution might have proven as unfeasible as his previous attempts at compliance or deceit. The persona of the narrative present (the voice of the prologue and the epilogue) may well seem more sophisticated than the protagonist only because he knows where to stop.

Notes

1. "Brave Words for a Startling Occasion," in Ralph Ellison, *Shadow and Act* (New York, Random House, 1972), p. 103. This volume will hereafter be cited as *SA*.

2. See Gayle, *The Way of the World: The Black Novel in America* (Garden City, N.Y.: Doubleday, 1976), pp. 246–58.

3. Gibson, *The Politics of Literary Expression: A Study of Major Black Writers* (Westport, Conn.: Greenwood Press, 1981), p. 93.

4. Baker, "To Move without Moving: Creativity and Commerce in Ralph Ellison's Trueblood Episode," in *Black Literature and Literary Theory*, ed. Henry Louis Gates, Jr. (New York: Methuen, 1984), pp. 221–48.

5. Richard Bjornson's term. See his essay "The Picaresque Identity Crisis," in *The Novel and Its Changing Form*, ed. R. G. Collins (Winnipeg, Canada: University of Manitoba Press, 1972), p. 16.

6. See, for instance, "The Art of Fiction: An Interview," in *Shadow and Act*, p. 167.

7. This incident in Bledsoe's past may well be a parody of Booker T. Washington's "entrance examination" for Hampton Institute, when he swept out a recitation room. See *Up from Slavery* in *Three Negro Classics*, ed. John Hope Franklin (New York: Avon Books, 1965), pp. 56–57.

8. The phrase comes, of course, from W. E. B. Du Bois's landmark work, *The Souls of Black Folk*, in *Three Negro Classics*, p. 215.

9. In Robert O'Meally's words, the invisible man learns that "history moves . . . like a boomerang: swiftly, cyclically, and dangerously. . . . when he is not conscious of the past, he is liable to be slammed in the head with it when it circles back." See his book *The Craft of Ralph Ellison* (Cambridge, Mass.: Harvard University Press, 1980), p. 103.

10. O'Meally also sees this scene as a turning point in the Invisible Man's development. See *The Craft*, p. 97.

11. Robert Stepto divides up these mentors rather differently than I. See his *From behind the Veil* (Urbana: University of Illinois Press, 1979), p. 177.

12. Trueblood's function in the novel has been the subject of critical debate. E. M. Kist argues that he is an opportunist, "a comic bumbler who cashes in on his pitiful situation by recounting it with broad irony

and folk humor." See "A Langian Analysis of Blackness in Ralph Ellison's *Invisible Man,*" *Studies in Black Literature* 7 (1976): 23. For studies that evaluate Trueblood as a blues artist, see Raymond Olderman, "Ralph Ellison's Blues and *Invisible Man,*" *Wisconsin Studies in Contemporary Literature* 7 (1966): 146; George E. Kent, "Ralph Ellison and the Afro-American Folk and Cultural Tradition," in *Ralph Ellison: A Collection of Critical Essays,* ed. John Hersey (Englewood Cliffs, N.J.: Prentice-Hall, 1974), pp. 45–46; and Robert O'Meally, *The Craft,* pp. 86–87.

13. Selma Fraiberg, "Two Modern Incest Heroes," *Partisan Review* 5–6 (1961): 659.

14. O'Meally also notes that Trueblood's tale redeems his "absurd situation." See *The Craft,* pp. 36–37.

15. Stepto also discusses Ellison's demystification of mentor figures in the novel. See *Veil,* pp. 178–83.

16. Frank Kermode, *The Sense of an Ending: Studies in the Theory of Fiction* (New York: Oxford University Press, 1967), p. 17.

The Conscious Hero and the Rites of Man

Ellison's War

JOHN S. WRIGHT

◆　◆　◆

T HE PSYCHOGENESIS OF *Invisible Man*, Ralph Ellison has reiterated periodically, lies in a World War II furlough's tonic state of "hyperreceptivity": Sent home from the Merchant Marines in the winter of 1944 to recuperate from wartime stress, Ellison had "floundered" into a powerful intuition. With the aesthetic conviction that "war could, with art, be transformed into something more meaningful than its surface violence" (*IM*, xiv), he had begun work on a recalcitrant war novel. That work was subverted, he says, by a punning inner voice that brooded over the perennial conundrum of black soldiers fighting for the right to fight for freedom in a war designed to return them home unfree. The voice announced irrepressibly, "I am an invisible man." Its words rebutted sharply the sociological truism that most Afro-American troubles sprang from the group's "high visibility," and spurred Ellison to abandon his planned war novel for a highly experimental, panoramic, and picaresque fictional "memoir." The new work concerned itself more broadly "with the nature of leadership, and thus with the nature of the hero ... [and]

with the question of just why our Negro leadership was never able to enforce its will. Just what was there about American society that kept Negroes from throwing up effective leaders?"[1] Absorbed at the same moment with Lord Raglan's *The Hero: A Study in Tradition, Myth, and Drama* (1936), Ellison turned his explorations into modern myth, mores, and caste codes to the specific subject of American "race rituals." His probings subsequently yielded, as a narrative embryo, the grotesque high school graduation rites undergone by a young, would-be leader of his people in the tale "Battle Royal," which Ellison published in 1947, five years before the novel for which it would serve as the opening chapter.

With riffs on Lord Raglan's myth of heroic biography guiding the ritual understructure, and with "Battle Royal" as a reverberating point of entry, Ellison devised a carefully articulated skeleton for the body of the narrative he then encircled with prologue and epilogue:

> I began with a chart of the three-part division. It was a conceptual frame with most of the ideas and some incidents indicated. The three parts represent the narrator's movement from, using Kenneth Burke's terms, purpose to passion to perception. These three major sections are built up of smaller units of three which mark the course of the action.... The maximum insight on the hero's part isn't reached until the final section. After all, it's a novel about innocence and human error, a struggle through illusion to reality. Each section begins with a sheet of paper; each piece of paper is exchanged for another and contains a definition of his identity, or the social role he is to play as defined for him by others. But all say essentially the same thing, "Keep this nigger boy running." Before he could have some voice in his own destiny he had to discard these old identities and illusions: his enlightenment couldn't come until then.[2]

The "blues-toned laughter-at-wounds" Ellison created to narrate the tale serves as the controlling consciousness of the underground memoir. But his "identity" is only nominally its subject: The functional subject is the proper conduct of his battle royal for freedom and full consciousness in a modern picaresque world. This world of flux and contradiction is one where identity itself is strategy more than entity and where selfhood is a synonym for improvisation. As if in illustration of Clausewitz's psychology of guerrilla war (the first American translations of Clausewitz's *On War* appeared during World War II and selectively infiltrated the warborn novels of the era), the narrator's wounding movement toward enlightenment reveals progressively the psychic need for the materially weak to be morally strong in the face of an adversary and to subordinate potentially suicidal military conflict to social, political, and economic engagements. Ultimately, the Invisible Man is locked in a war of wills, and his attempt to master society's meanings and patterns, to acquire a conscious philosophy and a pragmatic code of living in it—and to lead—become an inadvertent Clausewitzian study in the conduct of war by other means. His is a struggle to keep the will to struggle from being destroyed by an ambiguous enemy's insidious psychological warfare.

In this connection, the legacy of the Civil War is one of the great understated themes of *Invisible Man*. The dramatic historical reversals, from Civil War battlefields to Reconstruction politics to Reconstruction's subversion in turn by armed terrorism and political compromise, are reconstituted here in the riddling "orders" the hero's dying grandfather bequeaths him. And they are evoked in the old man's fierce divulgence to all of his heirs that "our life is a war and I have been a traitor all my born days, a spy in the enemy's country ever since I give up my gun back in the Reconstruction" (16).

These words announce the novel's partisan premise that, with giving up the gun, politics necessarily becomes the substitute for war—and potentially its antidote. And that premise shapes how Ellison adapts the conventions of the picaresque and of heroic myth. The world of *Invisible Man* recreates the familiar warring society of the picaresque—only nominally civilized, a scene where life, death, incest, fornication, treachery, insanity, prostitution, labor strife, scatology, mutilation, political violence, and riot are all inescapably intermingled. And in a society so construed, the true rogue/picaro—the con man Rinehart—is the ultimate warrior and predator. It is he who rules as subversive antitype to Lord Raglan's hero of tradition, originally a royal warrior on an epic quest and an unquestioned embodiment of his future kingdom's deepest religious and political values. Historically, the unpredatory picaresque alternative to the destructive rogue from the social underground has been a rational, upwardly mobile potential bourgeois, one whose roguery is less criminality than pragmatism: more a maneuvering around obstacles to his full assimilation into society than an attempt to destroy society itself.

In neither incarnation was the modern picaro necessarily a conscious rebel; and even when most subversive, he or she was never politically oriented. Moreover, the picaresque hero had little sense of community or family and was too engrossed in the arduous struggle to survive and win the social war to seek any satisfactions in heterosexual love beyond the merely biological or honorific. Caught up in the pressures of the present, he lacked any abstract sense of the macrocosmic workings of society and any historical consciousness.[3] In American fiction, Mark Twain's moralized use of picaresque conventions in *Huckleberry Finn* incorporated the picaro as an obstreperous contrabourgeois white-trash scamp who remains "preideological" as well as ultimately unamenable to life within society. In *Invisible Man*, by contrast, Ellison's commitment is to a formally educated black protagonist, politically impassioned and struggling toward philosophical awareness. He is a rising bourgeois hero, closer to Quixote, Candide, Gulliver, or Melville's Ishmael than to a rogue—though he is ultimately impelled to roguery by circumstance. For this hero, even temporary life outside society finally becomes untenable; indeed, for him the animating goal is that of public leadership—the preeminently bourgeois aspiration that appears most typically in picaresque narrative as an object of ridicule.

What indeed is programmatically ridiculous about the situation of Ellison's Invisible Man derives from his being, functionally, the bourgeois hero of a bildungsroman displaced, incongruously, into the realm of the picaresque. His apprenticeship to life and leadership, in the lenient logic of the bildungsroman, would have allowed him numerous mistakes of judgment and repeated chances to right himself without experiencing undue suffering. Instead, his "education" is hyperbolized, by the brutal logic of the picaresque, into a chronicle of comic catastrophe; and he is caught in a labyrinth where his errors unerringly cause him pain and where only a true picaro, who is *born* knowing and needs no education, would not err. The heroic expectation of overcoming and the comic hope of not being overcome collide at nearly every point of crisis in Ellison's black-and-blue tragicomedy; crises determined here neither by episodic happenstance nor naturalistic law but by the alternate and no less rigid determinism of the ritual process. The narrative patterns of heroic myth and of the picaresque converge in this context. For the picaresque, even without the schematic mythology Ellison employs, characteristically retains elements of ritual, especially rites of passage, which test, often mock-heroically, its protagonist's "mother wit" and wisdom.[4]

Ellison's protagonist, more pointedly than other laughers-at-wounds with whom he is compared all along his road of trials, is, from his rude southern beginnings to his rising fame and fall up north, a thoroughgoing mock-heroic counterpart to Lord Raglan's hero of tradition. With a slave's genealogy of shame to mark and mock him, and with no dynastic family traditions save his ex-slave grandfather's secret roles as traitor and spy and agent provocateur, he enters the world "no freak of nature or of history" but born of parents who are, if not unknown, then unnamed and otherwise unnecessary to his ritual progress. His preinvisible childhood days are a blank spent miming his grandfather's steely meekness until vague promptings to leadership propel him, as initiate, into the nightmarish battle royal of life. With his grandfather's riddling counsel still to be deciphered along the way, and the word magic of his native oratorical powers to sustain him, he moves away from the seemingly stable and naturalistic world of the rural South and Negro miseducation (really a semi-feudal "flower-studded wasteland" seething with disorder). Fortuitously deceived, he embarks on a journey *up north* geographically but *down* existentially into a netherworld of human and mechanical monsters and misleaders who preside over surreal forms of establishment and antiestablishment chaos. In his search for a place in the world, he finds himself unceasingly embattled, alone, and *dis*placed. Outside the maze of *mis*namings that his treacherous allies lay before him, he remains nameless. His own self-chosen moniker—a mock *title*, not simply a name—links him to a mock kingdom by way of a salient greeting-response ritual common in 1930s and 1940s black communities: "How are you?" The response: "Like Jack-the-Bear: just ain't nowhere" (*SA*, 297).

He is, however, succored at crucial junctures by symbolic foster parents and by the survival wisdom of the maternal folk community he at first foolishly repudiates but ultimately reaffirms. He wins all of his victories through such self-affirming eloquence as he commands, and all of his reverses spring from self-negating acquiescence. He rises to a brief reign as orator-king over an uptown realm of restive Harlem subjects. In turn, he is deposed suddenly by his treacherous "brothers," exiled downtown to what the Brotherhood considers to be the ideological backwaters of the "woman question," and finally he vanishes, first, metaphysically, into the urban wonderland behind a pair of magical sunglasses and then literally, when driven underground by his rebellious subjects and into sepulchral hibernation. Ultimately, he resurrects himself from the ashes of his political failures and personal dissimulations by inscribing a "code of laws" in the form of his codified life—the memoir of a ranter turned writer.

If Ellison has given his narrator all of these ritual trappings of the mock-mythical hero, the context enforces riffing variations on Raglan's biographical pattern. The hero's potentially Oedipal antagonism toward the father-king and his desire for the surrogate mother-queen are inverted sexually, for the king to be deposed and his potential deposer are crossed in Jack-the-Bear's world by racial as well as incest taboo. The same antagonism is deflected politically, because Ellison's rising hero *misleads himself* repeatedly not to rule but to be ruled. A rabble-rouser, not a warrior, he makes speeches instead of making war; and he fails his many trials comically more than tragically because all of his re-

verses are self-generated "boomerangs"—bruising but inconse-
quential pratfalls. A creature of the age of mass ideology and
modern technology, he models a comedy at the brink of tragedy
that is less akin to Odysseus's heroic saga of comic wiliness and
adaptability, or to Aristotle's comic "species of the ugly which is
not painful," than to the image Ellison found in Henri Bergson's
Laughter of human behavior become mechanized, rigid, life-
denying, robotic, and hence comically maladjusted.

If Jack-the-Bear is not the martial hero fated to found king-
doms, destroy his enemies, kill his father, or dispel plagues, neither is he the rutting picaresque hero of play and waggish sensuality, prone to the pleasures of the senses and the lure of bawd
and belle alike. *Politics* is his passion, ritualized and romanticized.
And he disciplines himself against dissipation, averring in youth
his college roommate's more natural passion when "the grass is
green" to seek out "broad-butt gals with ball-bearing hips" (*IM*,
104); and weakening in later years only before the pandering al-
lure of enemy sibyls or to the "political" necessity for fornica-
tional reconnaissance. Through it all, the narrator dimly suspects
conspiracy, betrayal, and persecution; but he nearly always dis-
regards all warnings. His unfaced fears are confirmed at the
novel's end and reach a crescendo in the castration dream that
punctuates his ritual progress.

Ellison's awareness of the suppressed psychic and symbolic
"power of blackness"[5] attuned him more than Raglan had been
to the dark side of heroic myth, to its demonic and demiurgic
possibilities. Accordingly, he found a major role in his conception
for what in Raglan's ritual drama had been a minor character:
the *Spielman*, a figure half-trickster, half-devil, who, like the Norse
god Loki, is the sacred plotter and wily father of artifice who sets
the conflict in motion and drags the demons and giants toward
their ultimate defeat. And in Mephistophelian fashion, though he
plays no part in the drama, the *Spielman* is the motive power
behind key characters, inspiring them to tabooed acts and leading
them to ruin. As ritual prompter and stage manager appearing
in different guises throughout, Ellison's *Spielman*—speaking in the
voices of the prologue's "singer of spirituals," or the Golden Day's

mad veteran, or the cartman "Peter Wheatstraw-the-devil's-son-in-law," or Tod Clifton after his plunge outside history, or the omnipresent mocker-mentor figure of the narrator's grandfather—persistently utters the magic words that goad the hero to act.

The Invisible Man's acts of attempted leadership mark the stages of his ritual progress "from purpose to passion to perception"; they also chronicle his relationships with a procession of post-Reconstruction black leadership archetypes. The narrator's ongoing meditations on the methods and mysteries of leadership, the complex patterns of animal and mechanical and aesthetic imagery, and the periodic eruptions of unofficial leadership that counterpoint the parade of official power brokers—all expand his narrative's range of political commentary. *Invisible Man* probes the character of leadership strategies as well as the relationships between the leaders and the led; identifies the spectrum of tactical constraints within which political maneuvers must be devised; and makes utopian as well as pragmatic leadership the object of satiric dissection. A trio of heroic images from the black past—Frederick Douglass, Booker T. Washington, and Marcus Garvey—provide a genealogy of authentic political leaders; and a pantheon of nonpolitical heroes—Louis Armstrong, Paul Robeson, Joe Louis, John Henry—suggest, if only as names or cameo images, certain attitudes, techniques, and attributes proper to the movers and shakers of humanity.

Quite naturally, the nameless narrator's problem of identity, which is bound up at one level with his progress in reintegrating into his life the traditions of his repressed folk past, on another level must be resolved concretely in the personal drama of his leadership ambitions. One lesson implicit in his boomeranging movement across the social landscape is that the identity he seeks, like the leadership to which he aspires, is not a fixed entity but a pattern of transactions with other people. At its most lifegiving, leadership entails a creatively improvised assertion of the leader's whole self within and against the group will; and at its most eviscerating, it merely camouflages the self's public retreat into sanctioned dissimulation.

As he turns his talent for public oratory into his tool for leading, his attempts to harness the power of words record his slow progress in consciously unifying the elements of his developing will, wisdom, and technique. The bizarre world he inhabits and the role he blunderingly seeks keep these facets of the whole man and the true leader fragmented and at odds. At the town smoker after the humiliating rites of the battle royal, the Invisible Man "automatically" mouths Booker T. Washington's Atlanta Compromise Address for the unhearing throng of his abusers. His parrotry is a parody of leadership as are his self-avowed "powers of endurance" and naive "belief in the rightness of things." He is, as the Golden Day's mad vet later incisively proclaims, a "walking zombie" who has learned "to repress not only his emotions but his humanity" (92). As willing heir to that "great false wisdom taught slaves and pragmatists alike, that white is right," he is ready to do the bidding of such false gods as the white millionaire philanthropist, Mr. Norton, and his self-anointed appeaser, the black college president, A. Hebert Bledsoe. And it is Bledsoe's mode of leadership as well-heeled sycophancy that claims the neophyte leader's attention in his college years:

> He was the example of everything I hoped to be: Influential with wealthy men all over the country; consulted in matters concerning the race; a leader of his people; the possessor of not one but *two* Cadillacs, a good salary and a soft, good-looking and creamy-complexioned wife. (99)

The mastery of oratorical magic that the narrator associates with such leadership is demonstrated most tangibly for him on Founder's Day in the orotund homiletics of the Reverend Homer Barbee. Barbee's sermon is a praise song to the ex-slave-cum-demigod who rose from oppression and obscurity to found a citadel of learning in a hostile wilderness. Barbee has mastered the myth of heroic biography (Ellison vivified Raglan's ritual pattern here in unerring detail) and its officious power in the college's annual "black rites of Horatio Alger." Ellison allows Barbee's oratorical prowess to wax unmocked until the speaker stumbles from the rostrum, revealing his blindness. The author thereby allows the reader to feel with the narrator the full powers of Barbee's eloquence, powers that, though yoked here to a finally delusive vision of the race's history as "a saga of mounting triumphs," nonetheless hold the promise of leadership for whoever might possess them.

Cast out by Bledsoe from that saga's sacred ground, which the Invisible Man identifies (echoing Candide) as "the best of all possible worlds," he treks north with his confidence and optimism reviving. Not yet aware of how thoroughly he has been betrayed and "kept running," he preserves undimmed his enthusiasm for oratory and the art of leadership. Being a leader is still, he thinks, a matter of "playing a leading role," of learning "the platform tricks of the leading speakers," of affecting an image of sophistication and hygienic respectability, of stage-managing contacts with "big men," and of mastering such Bledsoe-like "secrets of leadership" as cultivating an aura of mysterious profundity to keep oneself omnipresent in the minds of one's inferiors. Nor, he thinks, could a prospective leader give much thought to love, for "in order to travel far, you had to be detached."

But he is driven to a higher level of consciousness by a cumulation of experiences. The first is his workingman's fiasco at Liberty Paints with Lucius Brockaway and at the factory hospital. The next is his deep alienation from the black fantasy world of upwardly mobile posturing and narcotic self-aggrandizement that he encounters among the roomers at the Men's House. Last is his resentment toward Bledsoe, which erupts after the narrator sloughs off repressive bourgeois prohibitions against yam eating and in so doing releases the submerged well of feeling that spurs his virtuoso streetcorner exhortation against the eviction of an elderly black couple. The speech marks his transition from a phase of egocentric leadership "for" society to a phase of self-effacing leadership "against" the social order. And his extemporaneous rhetorical pyrotechnics signal his regenerated political will to freedom and his new mastery of oratorical "technique." At last he unites his own unconstrained psychic experience with the complex symbols of his people's emotional history—which he has now perceptively deciphered in the tangled heap of mementos piled before the dispossessed couple. Consequently, he is able to articulate a transforming vision and move a mass of men and women to action that, for a moment at least, breaks the chain of injustice.

On the basis of this effective fusion of controlled anger, abstract principle, and vernacular style, he is ushered immediately into the politics of the Brotherhood (whose glorification of archcapitalist Booker T. Washington and whose leader's symbolic Fourth of July birthdate warn against any such easy identification with the Communist party as readers in search of political scapegoats might wish). Renamed, relocated, reclothed, and initiated into the doctrinal mysteries of "scientific" political theory, the narrator now adopts a new professional leadership role. Ellison dramatizes its successes and tensions in the narrator's subsequent rabble-rousing Brotherhood speeches; in such promotional innovations as his People's Hot Foot Squad and the symbolic posters of a future "rainbow" coalition of America's races; and ultimately in his funeral oration for his martyred Brotherhood comrade, Tod Clifton. Jack-the-Bear's changing conceptions of leadership mirror his shift of allegiance from the example of the Founder (which he secretly adopts in opposition to the Brotherhood's desire to make him another Washington) to that of Frederick Douglass, whose portrait becomes his personal totem. As he becomes ambitious to rise in the Brotherhood hierarchy—he thinks it the one organization in the country in which he faces "no limits"—such changes in role model signal his growing clashes with the group's depersonalizing rigidity and thinly veiled racism.

The Brotherhood veteran Tod Clifton, symbolically "black-marble"-skinned to the narrator's "ginger" color, and a man of action more than words—handsome, sensual, and with the air of "a hipster, a zoot suiter, a sharpie"—is the "possible rival" who becomes the narrator's true brother and leaderly alter ego. Clifton's tragic plunge outside what the Brotherhood calls "history" sets in motion a chain of events that leads the narrator into self-proclaimed guerrilla war against the Brotherhood and leads the Harlem community into the apocalyptic riots that are triggered,

like Clifton's death, by a murderous political logic that betrays
the weak and then singles them out to be sacrificed in the name
of leadership's "higher law." Swept along in these riots that ter-
minate his tale, cornered and about to be killed by Ras the Destroyer's followers, the narrator finds his apprenticeship in leading
finally at an end. And now finally wordless, he faces an angry
group of the Harlemites he had hoped to lead as instead

> no hero, but short and dark with only a certain eloquence
> and a bottomless capacity for being a fool to mark me from
> the rest; [I] saw them, recognized them at last as those whom
> I had failed and of whom I was now, just now, a leader, though
> leading them, running ahead of them, only in the stripping
> away of my illusionment. (546)

The narrative logic behind his final political failure, however,
is not, as so many of Ellison's commentators have somehow concluded, a cumulative determinism that despairingly dooms all of
this world's political possibilities to defeat. The logic is rather that
of a rigorous Ellisonian phenomenology of consciousness and
strategic style, which posits unequivocally a genuine autonomy
in the ways individuals and groups *conceive* their experience and
choose (or fail to choose) ideas, techniques, and attitudes that defy
whatever or whoever limits their possibilities.

The limits imposed on black leaders and political action are
hyperbolic realities in the world of *Invisible Man*, experienced directly as the powers of persons and contexts to dominate consciousness first of all. In the narrative's southern context, power
polarizes between the local black-baiters who orchestrate the battle royal and the northern millionaire impresarios who bankroll
black miseducation in the name of manifest destiny. The logic of
such limitation drives the conventional black leadership class—
the ex-soldiers, lawyers, politicians, preachers, doctors, teachers,
and artists that the narrator encounters at the Golden Day—
either into straitjackets and the insane asylum or into the self-
humiliating, Janus-faced machinations of a Bledsoe. In the North,
the same class, nominally freer and with access to wider strategic

alternatives, falls prey to urban alienation and anonymity. They become dissociated from their communities and are forced, by organizational default, to fall in line "like prisoners" to the dictates of outside political directorates like the Brotherhood.

Nor are the prospects for combating these nightmare conditions any less dreary in a broad national context that seems to offer the narrator

> no possibility of organizing a splinter movement, for what would be the next step? Where would we go? There were no allies with whom we could join as equals; nor were there time or theorists available to work out an over-all program of our own. . . . We had no money, no intelligence apparatus, either in government, business or labor unions; and no communications with our own people except through unsympathetic newspapers, a few Pullman porters who brought provincial news from distant cities, and a group of domestics who reported the fairly uninteresting private lives of their employers. (499–500)

Moreover, the masses, for obscure reasons, but with consequences not obscure at all, seem to *tolerate* the versions of Bledsoe, Ras, Jack, and Rinehart who cynically or romantically exploit them. In dramatizing this perverse mental landscape, Ellison's narrative yields the psychic and material forces of political disintegration a commanding sway—and yields the narrator full consciousness and the ability to articulate it only in retrospect.

Implicit in Jack-the-Bear's growth of perception, however, is a restabilizing calculus that measures each of the leaders or misleaders in the narrative in terms of a complex phenomenological equation that, like a gestalt, treats leadership as an organized whole whose parts belong together and that cannot function otherwise. As a reaction to the specific realities the novel proposes, in other words, true leadership in *Invisible Man* is finally not a matter of political will or technical mastery or ethical values or inspiration or ideology or analytical accuracy or shared sensibilities, but the whole and creative integration of all of these ele-

ments into an effective organic response. No stranger to psychological theory, Ellison put Freudian and Jungian concepts and the
role psychology of Harry Stack Sullivan to eclectic rhetorical use
in his fiction. And for Ellison, the theory of gestalt—unlike the
others a psychology of *perception*, and thus directly relevant to his
concept of invisibility and his Burkean view of the ritual process—cogently suggested symbolic techniques for showing his
characters in harmonious or unharmonious relationship to their
immediate private and political situations. Jack-the-Bear's accounts of his jangling experiences and his political speechmaking
accordingly dramatize richly detailed holistic gestalts of physio-
logical, perceptual, syntactic, emotional, and ideological interaction that measure the unity he is able to achieve, as a leader, in
the course of persistently *dis*unified events.

The specific import of such a calculus is that it conceives the
problem of leadership and the problem of identity as related aspects of the human organism's struggle for creative unification.
The parade of misleaders we encounter in *Invisible Man* is not one
of fixed types representing unambiguously defective philosophies
and completely discardable strategies. They are, rather, types of
ambiguity, Empsonian in the ways they personify how warring
contraries might either be bound up schizophrenically in a single
psyche or fused in "antagonistic cooperation" to clarify a com-
plexly unified sensibility. They represent, also, older vernacular
or allegorical types of ambiguity that suggest human dispositions
strangely distorted, unbalanced, fragmented by some fixed obses-
sion or constitutional disproportion of humors. In Bledsoe, Barbee, Norton, Emerson Jr., Brockway, Ras, and Jack, vision and
impaired vision coexist, as do reality and unreality, plausible pragmatism and the perversely irrational. Accordingly Bledsoe's high-
handed tricksterism evokes the rich history of folk-fable wisdom
to lend it credence. Barbee's grandiloquent eulogy of redemptive
progress roots itself in faiths indispensable to group and individual
effort. And the strategy with which Lucius Brockway has made
John Henry's martyrdom obsolete and himself indispensable to
the Machine is a pragmatic though precarious and inevitably paranoid adjustment to life as a black workingman on the horns of

the white man's capitalist-unionist dilemma. Similarly, Ras's fervid pan-Africanism yields accurate assessments of white men's treachery, even though it is blended with a violently quixotic atavism whose results are "not funny, or not only funny, but dangerous as well, wrong but justified, crazy and yet coldly sane" (552). Even Brother Jack's mechanistic theory of life as all pattern and discipline and science, though fascistically brutal, conveys truths without which organized political action is inconceivable.

Yet measured against Ellison's paradigmatic leadership gestalt, all of these misleaders and their dispositions are absurdly neurotic and politically inadequate representatives of a fractured humanity. Worshipers of control and manipulation, all are rigid, robotized, automatic types, unadaptive and painfully comic in the Bergsonian sense; partisans of some merely provisional tactic or ideology unsuited to endure change or to ensure dignity, incapable of conceiving the world in all of its fluid reality, much less of transforming it creatively.

In the South, Trueblood's dream-driven act of incest provides a point of gestaltic convergence triangulated by the competing imperatives of the three misleaders who control the sharecropper's peasant existence: first, the land-owning southern whites who, led by the "boss man" and the sheriff, intercede for Trueblood and make his "unnatural act" of incest a cause for celebration; second, the moneyed northerners who, in the person of Mr. Norton, atone for betraying Trueblood's ancestral Reconstruction dream of forty acres and a mule by converting the reprobate farmer's sexual misfortune into a hundred-dollar scapegoat ritual; and third, the black college people on the hill who, as the narrator confesses, "hated the blackbelt people, the 'peasants,' " for returning the college's efforts to uplift them by doing, "like Trueblood, . . . everything, it seemed, to pull us down" (47).

Trueblood's relationships with each side of this triumvirate reveal the political truths behind his metaphorical self-identification with the powerless but still perceiving jaybird he describes, who is paralyzed by yellow-jacket stings "but still alive in his eyes and . . . watchin' 'em sting his body to death" (62). The southern whites regularly confirm their power to rule with such rites as the battle royal and with such bestowals of feudal largesse as sending the scholarship-winning narrator to his miseducation. More crucially, they confirm their delusory right to rule with the kind of symbolic magic Trueblood has "accidentally" ceded them by dreaming into being the perversity of his life. And as Trueblood's perverse mishap confirms the power of the southerners to reenslave him, it confirms the impotence, conversely, of northern liberalism to free him. For the first fruit Mr. Norton will see of his investments in the Founder's effort to transform "barren clay to fertile soil" is Trueblood's harvest of sexual sin. That harvest, at the sharecropper's cabin initially and later at the Golden Day, is shown to be, for Norton and his Emersonian ministry no less than for Trueblood and his star-crossed family, a "black 'bomination . . . birthed to bawl [his] wicked sin befo' the eyes of God" (66).

Concomitantly, the black college "power house" on the hill, which closes the third side of the triangle around Trueblood's emblematic life, sustains *its* power with rites of leadership that, again, expropriate and alienate Trueblood's peasant community rather than serve and empower it. Ellison's narrative carefully distinguishes the historical personage of Booker T. Washington from that of the fictional Founder and the Founder's protégé, Bledsoe. But all three are representatives of the same overarching philosophy of racial uplift that historically dominated southern black education during the age of Booker T. Washington. And Jim Trueblood, in the rhetoric Washington so assiduously cultivated, is the novel's primary embodiment of that "man farthest down" for whom the buckets of racial uplift ostensibly are to be lowered. Yet as Trueblood relates, he once had gone to the Founder's college for book learning and for help with his crops. But instead of leadership, he had received contempt and ridicule, subsequently losing his land and his independence in the course of the college's rise to nominal power—and so ironically being lowered into disgrace instead of being lifted to liberty.

The deified Founder in whose name the sharecropper has quite literally been sacrificed—Trueblood's "primitive spirituals" are appropriated to sanctify the "black rites of Horatio Alger" and his public shame extirpated from the college's official consciousness—is no mere apostle of wealth or prestige. He is an energetic cult's supreme oracle and avatar, wielding "the power of a king, or in a sense, a god," one who presumably rules benevolently, through faith, not fear. His "living agent," Bledsoe, however, has converted the Founder's utopian vision into a cynical power game engineered with sleight-of-hand, with pandemic fear, and, where black pawns like Trueblood are concerned, with undisguised threats and intimidation. If Bledsoe is "a leader, a 'statesman' " more than just the president of a college, he is also the "coal black daddy" whose "magic" patriarchal leadership is a reign of terror capable, he informs the narrator, of having "every Negro in the country hanging on tree limbs" to sustain itself. Again, it is through Trueblood, who is forced to checkmate Bledsoe's machinations against him with the equally treacherous power of the white bosses, that Bledsoe is first unveiled as Norton's counterpart and accomplice—a shape-shifting, mask-wearing "lyncher of souls."

As Trueblood focuses Ellison's leadership calculus in the southern context, so the zoot-suited trio in New York's subway underground provides a focal image for unmasking the character of leadership in the urban North. There, in symbolic tableau, Ellison's meditations on Raglan's heroic mythology and the problem of black leadership converge explicitly in a riddle of cultural creativity that his 1942–1943 *Negro Quarterly* editorials had proposed as a functional test in political decipherment for those who would be masters of social movements.[6] Ellison's assertion then that the zoot suit, or the symmetrical frenzy of the Lindy-hop, might conceal "profound political meaning" crucial to black leaders expands here, in the wake of the genuinely tragic death of Tod Clifton (the novel's most idealized figure of political possibility), into a metaphysical consolidation of all of those notions of history, culture, consciousness, art, war, and dominion that the ritual progress of the hero-narrator has cumulatively brought to the surface.

Looming suddenly before the narrator as silent, ambiguous figures with hard conked hair and bodies reshaped by costume into the semblance of "African sculptures, distorted in the interest of a design," the trio move before the narrator's finally unfettered vision "like dancers in some kind of funeral ceremony" (430). They score their movements unself-consciously with the rhythmic streetcorner staccato of tap dance, and share a puzzling and complete absorption in, significantly enough, comic books. The narrator's jolting perception here is one of the book's true epiphanies. He realizes that, though "outside history" like Clifton after his plunge from the Brotherhood, the zoot-suiters might actually be "saviors, the true leaders" of an unfathomably irrational counterhistory. This revelation is succeeded by his seeing too that they are not anomalies but part of a whole uptown populace of "surreal variations" on downtown styles. The narrator now no longer sees that populace as a fixed mass to be led, but as a mysteriously fluid configuration of personalities and motives in terms of which his own capacities for leading must be recalculated and his ideal of leadership and its genesis reexamined. At this moment before his belief in the Brotherhood has been completely blasted, that ideal is still represented by the talismanic image of Frederick Douglass. But "what was I in relation to the boys," he now must ask himself, and replies, "Perhaps an accident, like Douglass"— glimpsing here that the presumably "scientific" linkage between a leader and the led might, like the boys themselves, instead be outside science and the "groove of history" (432–33).

Douglass is the book's only undiminished historical image of knowledge and power humanely united. (Marcus Garvey, who is fleetingly praised by Clifton for his apparent ability to move a people who "are hell to move," is diminished implicitly by his association with Ras the Exhorter, just as Washington is diminished by explicit connection with the Founder, the Brotherhood, and the battle royal.) And Douglass is joined here in the narrator's mind with himself and Clifton, each of them gauged against the cryptic political possibilities of the comic-book-reading, zoot-suited boys. Until his experience of Rinehart and then Dupre and Scofield and their cadre of "rational" rioters completes this initial vision, the narrator will have no fuller revelation of leadership's inverse points of reference.

Rinehart, the "confidencing sonofabitch" who is a darker brother of Melville's Confidence Man, becomes Ellison's "personification of chaos." Rinehart pushes the calculus of leadership to its logical extreme and the narrator's political consciousness past thinking it *his* job somehow to get the zoot-suiters and their surreal brethren back inside the groove of history. In his grasp of the "vast seething, hot world of fluidity" beneath official history, and in his adjustment to modern life's fullest possibilities, Rinehart is the narrative's ultimate image of social mastery. A connoisseur of techniques and machines and a consummate decoder of the dark recesses of the human soul, he is, as he advertises, a "spiritual technologist" whose ability to manipulate private dreams, public myth, and symbolic structures like the zoot suit, the Lindy-hop, storefront revivals, or sexual fantasy makes him potentially a more powerful leader than a man of principle such as Tod Clifton. Clifton is acknowledged even by his rival, Ras, as a natural leader, a "black prince." And Clifton, like Rinehart, understands the zoot-suiters better than the narrator ever will. But Clifton is fatally *misled* by his fervent belief in the Brotherhood to *misread* the ulterior motives of his comrades. By contrast, Rinehart's "smooth tongue and heartless heart" and his willingness to do *anything* bespeak an utter lack of sentimentality about human vices and values and a cynicism that runs deeper and purer even than that of Ras. Ras "works on the inside" as effectively as Rinehart, and Ras is better able than Clifton or the narrator to penetrate the fog of Brotherhood ideology and to identify his natural enemies and allies. But his atavistic impulses distance him from the hypermodern world of the zoot-suiters and keep him from mastering the pragmatic techniques of empowerment.

If in the narrative's agrarian zone Bledsoe and Norton have proven themselves incapable of accommodating Trueblood's sensibility and its implications for genuine leadership, in the urban context Brother Jack, Ras, and Clifton as well, all prove inadequate to the task of leading zoot-suited Harlem. Only Rinehart is technically and metaphysically equipped to lead, but he is the most demonic misleader of all. Not surprisingly, the narrator's decision to take Rinehart as his model, and Rinehartism as his political instrument for undermining the Brotherhood's confidence, boomerangs—as have all of his preceding instrumentalities. First of all, he lacks the ruthlessness necessary to carry out the sexual intrigue he plans as a reversal of the Brotherhood's earlier efforts to neutralize him through the agency of a white woman. Then, after discovering a certain horrific sameness between the Brotherhood's real attitudes toward its Harlem constituents and Rinehart's—the Brotherhood's admitted "trick" of leadership is "to take advantage of them in their own best interest"—he finds that his counterapplication of Rinehart's cynical tactics leads not to the destruction of the Brotherhood, as he intends, but to the apocalyptic riots that the Brotherhood has helped engineer with his and Ras's unwitting complicity, making Harlem a dark sacrifice to political expediency.

The moment at which Jack-the-Bear commits himself to political Rinehartism, though, is another moment of epiphany, building on the perceptions that the trio in zoot suits had triggered. Here the reader witnesses the Invisible Man's first full acceptance of his personal past and its humiliations, his sense now of suddenly being able "to look around corners," his subsequent look around such a psychic corner to see Jack and Norton and Emerson "merge into one single white figure" of bat-blind absurdity. Here at last comes the narrator's first full recognition of his invisibility and his admission that, though he still didn't know what his grandfather's riddling strategy meant, he "was ready to test his advice." That the moment structures an even more comprehensive synthesis, one not yet fully known to the now very knowing narrator, is signaled in the punning metaphor he culls to link the contradictions of invisibility with the political exigencies of the moment: "I *was* and yet I was invisible. . . . I was and yet I was unseen. . . . Now I saw that I could agree with Jack without agreeing. And I could tell Harlem to have hope when there was no hope. . . . *I would have to move them without myself being moved.* . . . I'd have to do a Rinehart" (496).

The Invisible Man's role of inspiring emotion and action in others while remaining detached from the Rhetoric of inspiration, the task of having to "move without . . . being moved," is one that the narrator now links to Rinehart's confidencing maneuvers. It also is a provocative echo and revision of the precise terms in which Jim Trueblood had recounted his incestuous somnambulistic "tight spot" astride his daughter and alongside his wife. Trueblood comes to see the phallic dilemma he had awakened to as a metaphor for his life in general: Having to move without moving had been his predicament on the socioeconomic and political ladder, as it had then become his sole salvation from sexual sin. At authorial behest, Trueblood expresses here a psychological sense of context akin to the seventh and most ambiguous of William Empson's seven types of ambiguity: that involving absolute opposites that define a center of conflict and that, like dreams in Freudian analysis, place in stereoscopic contradiction what one wants but has not got with what one has but cannot avoid, a conflict unresolvable save in another dimension beyond syntax and logic—in feeling rather than thought, in poetry rather than philosophy.

Short of some such resolving power in another dimension, the only material escape for Trueblood lay in the unmanning possibilities of a gelding knife, a mode of escape from context whose price, for as manly a "daddy quail" as Trueblood feels himself to be, is "too much to pay to keep from sinnin' " (59). In his full awareness, then, of the irredeemable cost of freedom from sin and the attendant consequences of freely sinning, Trueblood gives eloquent testimony to his own tragic sense of life and to that need for transcendence he finally satisfies only in the resolving poetry of the blues. Thus he is marked off in his own mind, as he later will be in the narrator's mind as well, from that world of mastery without limits, beyond ethics and love and art—beyond flesh-and-blood humanity—that the narrator discovers in the disembodied traces of Bliss Proteus Rinehart.[7] A matter of potent political import for the novel, Rinehart and Trueblood are ultimately the *non*political poles of sensibility between which the narrator must mediate his own ambiguous sense of freedom as necessity *and* as possibility. Despite Rinehart's unmediated freedom and Trueblood's subjection to psychic and social necessity, what Rinehart and Trueblood share is their existential awareness that to be free one must be able to move without moving, a problem that Rinehart *masters* but Trueblood transcends.[8]

In this oblique contrast rests the staunchest fusing power of the narrator's prologue and epilogue to his tale, though Rinehart appears there only fleetingly and Trueblood not at all. Here, the narrator declares that both his underground hibernation and his prosecution of his grandfather's guerrilla war are at an end: Political action and love and responsibility are still possible, he decides. And he realizes that he wants neither Rinehart's freedom nor Jack's power. In so resolving, he recapitulates consciously Trueblood's ultimate rededication to his family, to seeing his "black 'bomination" birthed and not aborted, and to accepting his life's agonizing limits as perhaps inescapable but nevertheless endurable. If Trueblood's phallic dream has led him unconsciously to the brink of abysmal sexual sin and he has refused to unman himself to keep from sinning, so the narrator's political tactics—which finally implicate him in Clifton's death and the bloody Harlem riots—lead him unconsciously to the brink of a social abyss. And *his* phallic dream there of being unmanned girds his final refusal to substitute Rinehart's mode of moving without moving for Trueblood's.

In the epilogue, Jack-the-Bear's will to so refuse is no desperate leap of faith denying the cumulative truth of his bruising, boomeranging experiences. Nor is it simply an expression of the bourgeois qualm that Rinehart's nihilism is criminally antisocial. Rather, the narrator's reborn will consolidates the patterned affirmations in his tale, which all along the way have counterpointed the chaotic reversals and explosions of negativity that otherwise dominate his movement through life. These affirmations constitute nothing so formidable as to subdue the forces of negation he has come to know: Though recurring throughout, they are momentary at best, isolated from the centers of pragmatic power, and often ambiguous in their own right. Most characteristically, they surface in the stream of resurgent folkloric figures and images from childhood that give his ritual experiences much of their emotional texture and hold him back from cultural deracination.

At their highest pitch, they form a rhythm of epiphany and gestaltic unification that forcefully defies the rule of chaos and destruction and dehumanization. The first and most resounding of these affirmations comes, again, in Jim Trueblood's cathartically sacred and profane riff, his church song–spawned blues. This creative will to transcendence asserts itself repeatedly in the narrative, often in reaction to, or anticipation of, the most dispiriting circumstances. The narrator, waiting for the hypocritically stage-managed "black rites of Horatio Alger" to begin in his college chapel, drifts into a countervailing reverie of himself, "the bungling bugler of words, imitating the trumpet and the trombone's timbre," that sweeps him away from Bledsoe's officious exercise in cynicism into a loving, lyrical paean to the silent, gray-haired campus matron, Miss Susie Gresham, an old "relic of slavery" who is beyond being "fooled with the mere content of words" and who bears "something warm and vital and all-enduring, of which in that island of shame we were not ashamed" (111–12). There also, at vespers, counterpointing the sterility and meaninglessness of official ritual, he witnesses a sequence of a capella song and spontaneous prayer that simultaneously possesses the unnamed singer——her "voice seemed to become a disembodied force that sought to enter her, to violate her, shaking her rocking her rhythmically, as though it had become the source of her being." And witnessing her reduces the audience to "profound silence" (114–15).

Similarly, up north and alone, caught emotionally between his lingering country ways and his citified aspirations, the narrator encounters a loquacious yam vendor, yields to temptation and nostalgia, and then, on devouring the hot buttered yam, experiences an "intense feeling of freedom" and exhilaration. That feeling blossoms into a triumphantly comic fantasy confrontation with Bledsoe and prepares the narrator, unwittingly, for his succeeding eruption of indignation at a streetcorner eviction scene, which propels him into a new life as a professional rabble-rouser. Here as elsewhere in the narrative, the moment of affirmation is a moment also of self-unification——of mind, feelings, and physiology harmonized and expressively eloquent. The subsequent progress of his career as a Brotherhood orator is marked by a tension between his self-consciously controlled techniques or ideology and his spontaneous eruptions of compelling emotion. The ideological taboos that Jack imposes and the subject-object separation that Rinehart's smooth-tongued rhetoric requires are overruled in the moments of true union with his hearers and with his deepest understandings. He is most moving when moved himself.

At Tod Clifton's funeral, the Invisible Man's driving eulogy for his fallen brother is preceded by a moment of transcendent affirmation in which the funeral procession, ambiguously poised between love and "politicized hate," is transformed by the unprompted rise of a single plaintive, anonymous voice and the euphonium horn that rises to accompany it on "There's Many a Thousand Gone" (440ff.). The funeral procession becomes, in spirit, a march. The young marchers join the old; the white marchers blend with the black. Singing "with his whole body, phrasing each verse as naturally as he walked," the first singer, an old man, becomes leader and follower simultaneously, unselfconsciously voicing "the old longing, resigned transcendent emotion" beneath the words. And by moving the crowd with "something deeper than protest, or religion," the anonymous elder unifies them into a powerful "singing mass"—and moves the narrator to wet-eyed wonder, and to envy also, as he confronts in the otherwise unleaderly, knife-scarred old man the resplendent powers and art of leadership he has struggled so long to master.

In this dramatic image of art and leadership conjoined, the undergirding logic of the narrator's epilogue optimism reveals itself. For the problems of heroic leadership in *Invisible Man* through which Ellison focused his extrapolations from myth, folk tradition, history, and political philosophy ultimately move toward resolution through an assimilation of the myth of the birth of the hero to the myth of the birth of the artist. Though rarely read in such terms, the novel is, as Ellison has quietly insisted, a "portrait of the *artist* as rabble-rouser" (*SA,* 179).

That the novel has few of the aesthetic signposts of conventional *Kunstlerroman* creates part of the confusion. Save for a brief punning allusion to the prototypic Joycean portrait of the artist, only in the framing prologue and epilogue is the theme of aesthetic idealism explicitly joined in the narrator's mind to his ritual struggle with politics and invisibility. And there it is not *his* oratorical art but the music of Louis Armstrong that functions as an index of cultivated sensibility and creative conflict. Ellison was clearly aware that narratives of artistic evolution frequently have a ritual substructure paralleling that of the mythic hero-king. The genealogy of talent admits the same dramatic dislocations and confusions as the genealogy of hereditary power. As a zone of adventure and contest, the world of artistic means and motives offers its own endemic monsters, mazes, and underworld terrain. And the patterns of quest and conquest inhere in the struggle for technique, style, and aesthetic vision no less than in the world that the heroes of myth inhabit. But in *Invisible Man* the psychological drama of the narrator's undesigned, unself-conscious evolution as an artist is veiled by his conscious, designing passion for political heroism. His explicit struggle to master the techniques of oratory, for example, registers only subliminally as an artist's labor to fashion a personal style. He focuses not on creating and expressing his own sensibility but on affecting and directing others. And the object of his artful pragmatism is not to communicate a vision of beauty or unalloyed truth as a subject for contemplation, but to spur the acquisition of practical power by moving men and women to action.

In such a context, he becomes conscious of himself as an artist only when his failure as a hero seems complete. In the prologue and epilogue, as ranter turned writer, he has supplanted his original quest for Washingtonian leadership with a quest for yet-to-be-discovered forms of overt action intimated musically in the heroic lyricism of Louis Armstrong's blues. If here it seems uncertain that he has anything more than revived illusion to sustain a hinted future return to rabble-rousing or to "playing a role"—if Armstrong might be only an ambiguous new mirage to "keep this nigger boy running"—nevertheless Ellison's theory and concept-toting "thinker-tinker" does repudiate his former illusions. And he does draw a cautionary veil of consciousness be-tween Armstrong and himself: Louis has made "poetry out of invisibility" because he is *unaware* that he is invisible. The inference is that being unaware may give Armstrong a creative edge, at least provisionally. For awareness, Jack-the-Bear has learned, in its initial stages, insofar as it illuminates the awesome forces of chaos and unfreedom without vouchsafing countervailing strategies, need be no boon at all; it may rather be a burden, a burden from which Armstrong apparently is free. Jack-the-Bear's own com-pulsion to "put invisibility down in black and white," he rumi-nates, may be an analogous urge to make *music* of invisibility—to annex the musician's powers of synesthetic perception to the more limited ones available to a man who has chosen to be "an orator, a rabble-rouser . . . and perhaps shall be again" (14).

Jack-the-Bear has been a man of words; but because words cannot contain all of reality, his dependence on them prescribes failures and confusions from which the maker of music is com-paratively freer. The Word's entanglement with scientific and his-torical rationality and denotative constraints bars the penetration into time and space that music's relative elusiveness and freedom from official intelligibility make possible. And his memoir's rid-dling problem of freedom is, he discovers, unresolvable apart from a decipherment of the culture's and his own consciousness of time. He enunciates time's strategic possibilities in his recollection of a prizefighter boxing a yokel and his seeing the former's vastly superior science, speed, and footwork knocked "cold as a well digger's posterior" when the yokel simply steps inside his oppo-nent's sense of time to deliver a single felling blow. What the narrator discovers vaguely in the "nodes" and "breaks" of Arm-strong's music is such a sense of time.

Music—bound more than any of the other arts to time and timing—was for Ellison, even more than for his music-minded novelistic exemplar, Malraux, that expressive penetration into ul-timate reality whose forms, patterns of evolution, traditions, and metamorphoses supplied the clues not only to the souls of black folk but to the rhythms and style and soul of modern civilization. For such inquisitors of modern life as Hegel, Nietzsche, Spengler,

and Yeats, the cycles and spirals and gyres hypothetically circum-
scribing the course of human events were mimed and ofttimes
mocked by the shifting forms of art, literature, and especially
music. For these thinkers, the old romanticist ethos and its expressive theory of art were raised to cosmic significance. In Malraux's view, it was the drama of art confronting the world and
refusing to follow the "natural" order that the visual arts especially, and music more than literature, recorded in their own
autonomous history.[9] And that history, a history of "style" and
the mysterious logic through which style unfolds and imposes
itself on the world, is the history whose structured principles in
blues and jazz and vernacular signification and folk fable Ellison's
narrator ultimately wields against the structure of lies and illusions that have dominated and diminished the sense of possibility
he had discovered as an invisible man:

> My God, what possibilities existed! And that spiral business, that
> progress goo. . . . And that lie that success was a rising *upward*.
> What a crummy lie they kept us dominated by. Not only could
> you travel upward toward success but you could travel down-
> ward as well; up *and* down, in retreat as well as in advance,
> crabways and crossways and around in a circle, meeting your
> old selves coming and going and perhaps all at the same time.
> (498–99)

Such multidimensional possibilities are visible to the musician
more than the man of words because, as the irresistible "club" of
reality has impressed on Jack-the-Bear, there is "an area in which
a man's feelings are more rational than his mind." And music,
freed from the constraints of ordinary linguistic thought, maps it
more completely than communicative rhetoric, which, however
much it strives to expand its symbolic powers, replicates only a
fragment of the vast repertoire of human expressive possibilities
manifest in grins, growls, and gestures on to the masterpieces of
high art and the wizardry of machines. The liberating possibilities
of music, however, remain untapped because music, he admits,
is perceived one-dimensionally—"is heard and seldom *seen* except

by musicians" (13). Conversely, as his hallucinogenic hyperper-ceptivity teaches him, when music's full synesthetic possibilities *are* grasped by the perceiver, its explorations into time and space may be so overwhelming as to actually "inhibit action" and defy the political will expressed in the narrator's own undaunted belief "in *nothing* if not in action" (13).

If the "laws" of history impose a tyranny of time, circumstance, and conceptual limitation on humanity, Armstrong's art, Trueblood's, the singer of spirituals, and the psychic geometries of the zoot suit offer escape from the bondage of history, not through any evasion of circumstance but through the evocation and consolidation of styles and attitudes for confronting it. In Malraux's psychology of art, which Ellison converted enthusiastically to his own ends in the late forties, this "deflection" of history is rooted in a resurrection of the conventional romantic elevation of creative genius and of the artist as hero: Living in time, but also in the presence of the timeless world where art's collective testimony prevails regardless of the change and mortality outside, the artist "escapes" ordinary history—and historical fatalism—in those isolated moments of unique creativity when the expressive gesture liberates him or her from inherited traditions and reveals a style entirely his or her own.[10] In making such creative gestures, the artist participates in a "history" of creative events, in moments of creative heroism that constitute their own continuity, deflected from, if sometimes parallel to, conventional history.

For Ellison, the danger of trying to escape into this antihistory by way of either the creative or the religious imagination was manifest in the Afro-American past, where, as he decried in his 1945 review of Wright's *Black Boy*, the special conditions of black life and its consequently "defensive character" had regularly transformed the "will toward organization" into a "will to camouflage, to dissimulate" (*SA*, 93). Creative heroism, for Malraux and Wright and Ellison, could be energized only by a will to confront both the world of circumstance and the world of creative gesture. Creative power manifested itself in the capacity to *transcend* circumstance—by experiencing it directly, exploring it exhaustively, and then reintegrating it by acts of willed imagination in such a way as to remake potentially the culture of which it is a part. The attraction of the blues, their manifest power, lay in their discovery of a style for expressing simultaneously the agony of life and the possibility of conquering it. Rather than a flight into aestheticism or a passive cultivation of sensibility, they were a codified assertion of will—if not overtly political, then nonetheless allied with the political will to convert, through action, conscious experience into felt power.

To unify the political will and the creative will against the backdrop of sweeping historical change and of human values confronting such change was Ralph Ellison's most ambitious intention as a novelist. That his tragicomic judgment of the characters he places under such pressure veers finally toward aesthetic norms and away from the narrowly political links him, of course, to such acknowledged literary ancestors and relatives as Malraux, again, and to Hemingway, Miguel de Unamuno, and, more obliquely, Richard Wright. For the former three, the interpenetration into extreme human situations of such aesthetic norms as grace, balance, contemplative detachment, and élan was central to the drama of the heroic. In *Invisible Man*, Louis Armstrong's projective sense of style—which culminates the novel's long series of creative gestures and affirmations in extremity—is Ellison's clearest corollary: It is Armstrong who personifies the narrator's consummatory maxim that "humanity is won by continuing to play in the face of certain defeat" (564); and it is Armstrong who, as he "bends" his military instrument into a beam of lyrical sound, carries Jim Trueblood's country blues standard, by phonograph, into the narrative's urban fray.

But Ellison's Invisible Man knows that for all of Trueblood's and Armstrong's flesh-and-bone wisdom and their lyric aplomb, the bluesmen have styled preliminary attitudes and transcendental resolutions of conflicts whose possible solution through material means he, not they, is better suited by proximity to power, by technique, and by consciousness to undertake. That Trueblood and Armstrong are unaware of their invisibility—as the narrator's grandfather also had been—is both their advantage and their limitation. Unlike Rinehart, whose freedom is a destructive freedom that feeds on illusion and breeds chaos and death, and whose victory over the material world is won at the cost of absolute self-effacement, Armstrong does not trade on invisibility and is not self-diminished by it. He has transcended defeat by imposing his own personality on his horn and converting its "Bad Air" to communal poetry. In so doing, he has asserted his own undefeated will and defies death itself with an indestructible artistry. Without the strategically crucial sense of space and time that conscious invisibility provides, however, extending his conquest of the world of art into the world of material circumstances remains a hope limited by the ability of his auditors to hear truly.

In Malraux's world, the problem of art's pragmatic relation to the pattern of material existence remains characteristically unresolved. The hero-revolutionaries of his political novels and the artist-heroes of his aesthetic essays are spiritually related but kept consistently apart. The humorless political heroes, inevitably defeated by the failure or betrayal of social revolution, choose consciously to act out doomed commitments they can no longer see as anything but absurd and to martyr themselves, as in *Man's Fate*, to their transcendent passion for the ideal. The hero-artists, by contrast, escape the world of men, in which freedom is finally impossible, steal creative fire from the gods, and in their own self-constructed world of art win the freedom that the hero-revolutionaries can only imagine. Ellison's impulse in *Invisible Man* was to reject forms of transcendence limited either to final political martyrdom or to a hermetic world of aesthetics, and instead to unify the dissevered possibilities in the figure of a political man of words and action redeemed and reborn through art. If Richard Wright, like Malraux and Hemingway, cleaved to a secular vision of heroic, or antiheroic, martyrdom in *Native Son*, Ellison in *Invisible Man* found it possible, indeed necessary, both to reject the cult of death and to affirm the hope of spiritual rebirth by recording symbolically his group's true pangenerational transcendence of material defeat through the agencies of art.

As his own immersion in his people's and his nation's history had taught him, and as he would later remark, "the art—the blues, the spiritual, the jazz, the dance—was what we had in place of freedom" (*SA*, 254–55). Rather than proposing any substitutional or merely compensatory role for art, *Invisible Man* makes artistic transcendence the one unsuppressible means through which human freedom is imagined and achieved and human beings made whole. Its narrator's torturing himself to put down in black and white the chronicle of his abysmal pain, and the progress through illusion to perception that enables him to see the pattern in its chaos, carry to a higher level that articulate probing of a grievous wound that Jim Trueblood modeled for him with his tale and defeat-defying blues. The telling of his own tale—his "buggy jiving"—is the hibernating narrator's initial reengagement with a world that still conspires to defeat him. It is a cathartic release of anger and angst that, through the power of words, converts what begins as an act of war into what he finally knows has become an act of disarmament. And it is, on the terms its author proposes, an act of conscious leadership in which one man's will to selfhood brings to comic and tragic clarity his and his reader-followers' common property in the buggy, jiving, blue-black rites of man.

Notes

1. Ralph Ellison, "On Initiation Rites and Power: Ralph Ellison Speaks at West Point," ed. Robert H. Moore, *Contemporary Literature* 15 (1974): 170–71.

2. Ralph Ellison, *Shadow and Act* (New York: Random House, 1964), p. 177. This volume will be cited hereafter as *SA*.

3. Frederick Karl, *The Adversary Literature: The English Novel in the Eighteenth Century* (republished as *A Reader's Guide to the Eighteenth-Century English Novel*) (New York: Farrar, Straus and Giroux, 1974), pp. 14–18.

4. Ibid., p. 17.

5. See Harry Levin, *The Power of Blackness: Hawthorne, Poe, Melville* (New York: Knopf, 1958).

6. Ralph Ellison, "Editorial Comment," *Negro Quarterly* 1 (Winter–Spring 1943): 295–302.

7. Ellison states the character's full name in *Shadow and Act*, p. 56.

8. For an aptly focused explication of this recurring motif in its

initial setting in *Invisible Man*, see Houston Baker, "To Move without Moving: An Analysis of Creativity and Commerce in Ralph Ellison's Trueblood Episode," *PMLA* 98 (October 1983): 828–45.

9. William Righter, *The Rhetorical Hero: An Essay on the Aesthetics of André Malraux* (London: Routledge & Kegan Paul, 1964), pp. 21–25.

10. Ibid., p. 41; and Avriel Goldberger, *Visions of a New Hero: The Heroic Life according to André Malraux and Earlier Advocates of Human Grandeur* (Paris: M. J. Minard, 1965), pp. 234–43.

Notes on the Invisible Women in Ralph Ellison's *Invisible Man*

CLAUDIA TATE

◆ ◆ ◆

QUESTIONS ABOUT THE FEMALE CHARACTERS in Ralph Ellison's *Invisible Man* seem to elicit two types of response: The initial one is "What women?" since women clearly occupy peripheral roles in the novel. And then after Mary Rambo and the other female characters—that is, the old slave woman, the magnificent blonde, the rich sophisticate Emma, the anonymous seductress, and finally the prophetic and pathetic Sybil— are recalled, the second response is something like "Oh, those stereotypes" (Sylvander, 77–79). Both replies are virtually automatic and both are legitimate, given the factual details of the narrative. But we must not be misled by what can be seen with a quick glance; we must not neglect what lies hidden behind the mask and proclaim that the mask is the face. Instead, we must remember Ellison's own witty admonition that the rind is not the heart[1] and look for the concealed truth which lies beneath the stereotyped exteriors of his female characters.

IN HIS ESSAY "Twentieth-Century Fiction,"[2] Ellison contends that stereotypes, though indisputably one-dimensional and therefore oversimplified, frequently hide complex aspects of human character. Moreover, he adds that "the Negro has been more willing perhaps than any other artist to start with the stereotype, accept it as true, and then seek out the human truth which it hides" (*S&A*, 43). Perhaps this is also an appropriate procedure to follow when examining the female characters in *Invisible Man*; that is, "start with the [female] stereotype[s], accept [them] as true, and then seek out the human truth which [they] hide." Perhaps by following this example, we will not be attempting merely to define female humanity but to recognize, as Ellison suggests, broader aspects of the humanity of all of us.

THAT A MALE character dominates the novel is certainly without question. The entire story centers on an anonymous, young black man's painful acceptance of his social alienation, which is so extreme that he has virtually no control over the sequence of events that directs the course of his life. He receives so little recognition for his efforts to define a meaningful identity for himself that he assumes a new name, which characterizes his feelings of acute marginality: the Invisible Man. At first he believes that being black is responsible for his plight, but he soon learns that everyone, black and white alike, lives in a lawless, amoral, chaotic world, where honorable intentions and high moral standards have little absolute value. Painfully disillusioned by this knowledge, the young man retreats from human contact and takes up residence in an abandoned basement. There he must live in almost total isolation until he is able to discover some order, some meaning from the chaos he has unwittingly discovered.

Deriving meaning from his experiences and measuring their impact on his life are processes that the hero must complete before he can escape from the underground. At this point in the young man's development, the female characters become important beyond their obvious roles in the narrative.[3] Like the underground station masters of the American slave era, these female characters assist the Invisible Man along his course to freedom. Their associations with him force him to recognize their common plight. Through his contact with them, he comes to understand that he is the means to another's end; he is a victim, growing ever more conscious of his victimization.

At the end of the novel, we are left to ponder whether he will be successful in his attempt to escape the underground. But since Ellison has him say that he is merely hibernating and that hibernation is a covert preparation for overt action (*IM*, 16), we are inclined to believe that his retreat underground marks only a temporary period of intensive, preliminary reflection. During this time, he comes to understand that his fear and desire, guilt and innocence, the ambiguity of his experiences in general, and his resulting ambivalent feelings have propelled him along a seemingly chaotic course over which he has had so little control that he feels as though he has been boomeranged. But before he can leave the underground, he must understand the appropriateness of this analogy. He probably already knows that the course of the boomerang is, in fact, predictable, although the time of its arrival seems unexpected to those who do not witness its launching or understand the principles governing its movement. But he must apply these principles to his experiences in order to predict and understand their outcome. In so doing he will learn not to grope through his life in blind naiveté, expecting others to give him credit for his good intentions. He must nurture them to fruition, himself, with a mature strategy, based on discerning a person's genuine character without being distracted by color or gender. In this manner, he will be able to control, to some degree, the course of his future and not only map out the way to the upper world but also arrive at the method for participating, in meaningful ways, with those who inhabit the aboveground region.

But despite the optimism Ellison incites, we are not fully convinced. Doubt lurks, as we face the possibility that the young protagonist may not be successful in securing the necessary knowledge for staging his escape. Ellison does not resolve our dilemma, but I suggest the narrative does provide a method for measuring the likelihood of the young man's success. The possibility for his escape is directly related to his ability to distill meaning from his encounters with the women I have mentioned.

They embody the knowledge he needs to stage his escape. If he can discern the impact that his relationships with them has on the direction and quality of his life, he will be able to abandon his polarized, black-or-white version of the world, as well as his outdated ambition to be an accommodationist race leader. Instead, he will know that power exploits color merely as a means to an end and that there is strength in manipulating one's powerlessness and in not allowing oneself always to be seen. What is most important, he will have learned that there are order and, ultimately, utility arising from accepting the ambivalence and contradictions of life. If he cannot assess the significance of his relationships with these women, he will not have learned the essential lessons, and his every effort to leave his hiding place will be aborted in fear, time and time again.

"Old woman, what is this freedom you love so well?" I asked around a corner of my mind.

"I done forgot, son. It's all mixed up. First I think it's one thing, then I think it's another. It gits my head to spinning. I guess now it ain't nothing but knowing how to say what I got up in my head." (*IM*, 14)

The old slave woman in the prologue provides the young protagonist with the motivation for recalling his experiences which form the sequence of events for the story. She tells him about her slave master-lover, who repeatedly promised to free her but never kept-his word. She also tells him that she loved her master dearly, but that she loved freedom more. She further explains her decision to assist their sons in a scheme to murder their father and secure their precious freedom. The Invisible Man responds to her story by asking that she define her understanding of freedom, which appears to have been the force that propelled her into action. Her endeavor to respond to his request incites her recollection of powerfully conflicting feelings, hence the ambiguity of her reply. As she continues her response, her head begins to ache, and she cries out in pain. Her sons come to her rescue and insist that the next time the Invisible Man has a question like that, he should ask himself, instead. His effort to heed their command results in his attempting to answer this question, and he follows her example by recalling what's in his head. His recollection results in his reconstructing the events of his life, and they in turn constitute the plot of the novel.

The hero's encounter with the slave woman provides a lesson about the nature and acquisition of freedom. As we have seen, the old woman's desire to obtain her freedom was so urgent that it demanded action. The hero must learn by her example. He must learn that it is not enough for him to choose to leave the underground and articulate that choice. He must commit himself to action and thereby realize adult heroic potential. His initial steps follow her course, but whether he can exercise his determination and leave the underground remains to be seen. In any event, Ellison has the young man follow her example, and in so doing the author provides structure for the novel and gives it purpose as well.

> . . . and in the center, facing us, stood a magnificent blonde—
> stark naked. . . . I felt a wave of irrational guilt and fear. . . . I
> felt a desire to spit upon her as my eyes brushed slowly over
> her body. . . . I wanted at one and the same time to run from
> the room, to sink through the floor, or to go to her and cover
> her from my eyes and the eyes of the others with my own
> body . . . to caress her and destroy her, to love her and murder
> her, to hide from her, and yet to stroke her. (*IM*, 22)

The hero's encounter with the magnificent blonde marks his first direct encounter with ambivalence. On seeing the naked woman, he becomes keenly aware of his chaotic sexual responses which cannot be tempered by any social code. His every effort to control his reactions results in emotional conflict and an intense sensation of bewilderment. But she is not just any woman; she represents the forbidden white woman. Centuries of prohibition forbid his even looking upon her, but his gaze is so willfully direct that he virtually consummates their sexual union with his eyes. As a result he feels guilty, and yet he is innocent; he is bold, and yet he is afraid.

This encounter with ambivalence is not without its lesson for the young protagonist, although we cannot be certain when he learns it, if at all. When he sees the magnificent blonde, he knows immediately that he longs to possess her, but he must not touch or even look upon the forbidden white woman. Not only is she a sexual taboo; but more significantly she is the means by which the possibility of freedom is withheld from the nameless young man. In fact, she is the means by which black people in general were penalized for exercising the freedom of choice, in that the penalty was translated into the accusation of rape and the sentence was death. The symbolic linkage between the white woman and freedom, therefore, finds its origin in hundreds of years of southern race relations. And Ellison employs her as a potent vehicle for dramatizing the young protagonist's psychological journey to the region of consciousness where he can assert his newfound freedom, but only after he confronts this taboo in her various symbolic forms.

The magnificent blonde foreshadows the succession of white women who provide the circumstances for the young protagonist to realize that freedom is nothing less than the active exercise of his willful, independent choice. Emma, the anonymous seductress, and Sybil arouse his feelings of prohibited sexuality, but, more important, they are also the means by which he realizes that freedom is first a state of mind. In order to secure it for himself, he must move beyond the need merely to conquer them sexually or to outwit the Jacks and the Rineharts of the world. He must acknowledge the humanity of these women and release them as well as himself from the sexual taboos and stereotypes that deny their acquisition of freedom. His encounters with these women provide him with opportunities to perform these tasks.

Returning to the battle royal, which is the first stage of the young protagonist's development of consciousness, we see that the magnificent blonde is elevated to such a degree that he does not realize that they share a common plight. Both are exploited

objects for sensual entertainment. The blonde has learned, however, to conceal her human character behind the mask of a Kewpie doll, therefore rendering her innermost thoughts and emotions incomprehensible to the "big shots who watched her with
fascination" (*IM*, 23). She has learned to use this method of concealment to her advantage. In essence, she is invisible, and she
provides the young protagonist with his first lesson in invisibility.

The young protagonist manages to put on a good show at the
battle royal, win the scholarship, and go off to college with the
hope of becoming another Booker T. Washington. Despite his
humiliation, he continues to believe that he can overcome virtually all obstacles with good intentions, conscientious effort, and
self-control. At college he again encounters the intense feeling of
ambivalence, which is of such proportions this time that it is
entirely beyond his comprehension. He does not know how to
respond to his dilemma and therefore faces peril.

The circumstances giving rise to this encounter result from
his escorting one of his college's founders, Mr. Norton, around
the campus. The young man is entrusted with this task precisely
because he is an exemplary student. But while he is exercising his
good faith and honorable intentions, he encroaches upon the
unexpected and is engulfed in chaos. Rather than control the
route for Norton's tour and show him evidence of racial progress,
our overly zealous protagonist allows Norton to stumble upon
Trueblood and his family, who are the personifications of disgrace
for the local black community. Trueblood tells Norton of his
incestuous relationship with his daughter. As a result Norton
becomes faint and is in need of a strong stimulus to revive him.
The young man eagerly takes him to the nearest tavern, the
Golden Day, which is besieged by lunatics from the local state
mental hospital, who both physically abuse and ridicule Norton.
Upon their return to campus, the young man repeatedly says he
is innocent of wrongdoing, but despite his claims of innocence,
he is held responsible for his poor judgment, and the punishment
is expulsion from school.

Still holding onto his dream to become a race leader, he goes
to work for a paint factory in the North, deluding himself with

the notion that he will earn enough money and be permitted to return to school in the fall. His continued effort in this regard results in his being seriously injured in an accident, and Ellison uses his extraordinary recovery to suggest the young man's symbolic rebirth and acquisition of a new identity. Upon regaining his consciousness, the young man finds that he must qualify his new identity and determine a course for his new life. His character is like a blank page on which some words must be written, and it is Mary Rambo who writes his new name and nurtures his new awareness of himself.

> Her eyes swept the machine and as she soothed her smashed fingers she snickered, "You must be awful strong for them to have to put you under all this pile of junk. Awful strong. Who they think you is, Jack the Bear or John Henry or somebody like that. . . . Say something, fool!"[4]

Mary Rambo's character is not fully delineated in the 1952 edition of *Invisible Man*, where she is portrayed more as a force than as an actual person (225). But by referring to a section of the original manuscript that was deleted from the 1952 edition, published in *Soon One Morning* and titled "Out of the Hospital and under the Bar" (247), we can see that Mary achieves complexity of character, whereas she is only briefly sketched in the novel.[5] In this short story, from which the foregoing excerpt is taken, Mary provides the young protagonist with her tried and true folk wisdom as a means of protecting him against the irrational, unknown world. She is also the vehicle by which he departs from the world of "Keep this nigger-boy running" and arrives at the threshold of a new region of consciousness where he moves toward realizing his adult, heroic potential. Moreover, Mary Rambo gives him the folk vernacular and perspective to articulate the impact of his experiences on his evolving identity. Whereas the old slave woman motivates the telling of his story, Mary provides him with the words and the narrative voice. She teaches him the folk vernacular, and it sets the tone as well as determines the idiomatic language for the novel.

Mary's physical appearance and her folksy manner may resemble the "mammy" of plantation lore, but she is not bound by this stereotype. She is the nurturer of a *black* child, not the master's white child. She is the young protagonist's surrogate mother who bears this son to fulfill a similar destiny, outlined in the old slave woman's story. He, too, is destined to grasp at freedom, and Mary is a means toward this end. She literally feeds and comforts the young protagonist, as a mother comforts her child. She nurtures his faltering vision of himself, by renaming him Jack the Bear and, thereby, announces his potential to achieve great strength but only after enduring a temporary period of hibernation. By naming him John Henry, she also announces his potential to acquire full confidence and power as a leader of his people ("Hospital," 247).

While living with Mary, the young man is called into action by witnessing an eviction of an old couple, but rather than rely on the identity and wisdom Mary has given him, he accepts a new name and a new program and subsequently loses his way on the course to asserting his own freedom. He becomes a pattern in Brother Jack's design and finds himself destined to repeat the lessons of the past and fight another battle royal.

The Brotherhood promotes the ultimate battle royal, but unlike the contest of his youth, this one has three preliminary dances, where the hero is not permitted simply to observe but is compelled to dance literally with one white woman, Emma, and figuratively with two others, the anonymous nude and Sybil.

> Just then Emma came up and challenged me to dance and I led her toward the floor as the piano played, thinking of the vet's prediction and drawing her to me as though I danced with such as her every evening. (*IM*, 273)

Dance number one is with Emma. Unlike her predecessor, the magnificent blonde, she provides the young protagonist with his first opportunity to approach the white woman, the sexual taboo, on presumably equal footing. She therefore represents stage two of his development, which is apparent when he tries to convince himself that he is not intimidated by her, but the fact that he overcompensates for his past feelings of racial anxiety makes us believe the contrary. Even though he witnesses Jack's act of defining Emma as the financial means for the Brotherhood's activities, the young protagonist does not realize that he shares Emma's fate. Both are instruments for the exercise of another's control and assertion of power, but he must finish the next two dances before he can recognize his own as well as another's exploitation.

> She was a small, delicately plump woman with raven hair in which a thin streak of white had begun almost imperceptibly to show, and when she reappeared in the rich red of a hostess gown she was so striking that I had to avert my somewhat startled eyes. (*IM*, 355)

Dance number two is with the anonymous, rich white woman who seems to be a real-life replica of the pink Renoir nude hanging on the wall in her penthouse apartment. She coaxes the young protagonist to her home under the pretext of discussing the woman question. His initial response to her is one of prohibition and desire (359), like his response in the earlier incidents with her symbolic predecessors—the magnificent blonde and Emma. But in this case his anxiety subsides, and he succumbs to the desire of the flesh, not as a black man who is trying to prove his equality but as a man who has been sexually aroused by a woman.

His encounter with this woman represents stage three of his development. Through his relationship with her he recognizes that, like her, he is an instrument operating in a plan not of his own design. As he realizes that a third party controls and debases both himself and this woman, his perception of their common exploitation moves into focus. But before he can clearly see his relationship with the magnificent blonde, Emma, and the anonymous seductress and acknowledge their respective marginality, alienation, and ultimately their respective invisibility, he must dance his third and final dance, in which his partner is Sybil.

"Oh, I know that I can trust you. I just knew you'd understand; you're not like other men. We're kind of alike." (450)

Sybil is not the magnificent blonde Kewpie doll of the battle royal; neither is she the "gay and responsive Emma . . . with the hard, handsome face" (446); nor is she "the small, delicately plump woman" (355) who "glows as though consciously acting out a symbolic role of life and feminine fertility" (354). To the contrary, Sybil is a "leathery old girl with chestnut hair" (448), who "would soon be a biddy, stout, with a little double chin in a three-ply girdle" (449). Sybil is a virtual parody on the magnificent blonde of the battle royal; Sybil is a pathetic buffoon who is, nevertheless, humanly vulnerable and intensely sensitive to those who share her plight of invisibility.

Sybil, like Mary, is another surrogate mother who comes to deliver the young protagonist from the deception of his false identity with the Brotherhood. She is also another symbolic blonde, who ushers him to the threshold of the final battle royal. In addition, she is his last teacher, who propels him along the course to freedom by making him aware that invisibility is not necessarily a liability but possibly a valuable asset.

"Come to mama, beautiful" (447), she chides the young man, as she sexually entices him. Although she is a consenting adult, she regards the desired consummation as rape, fantasizing that rape by a black male is some type of ultimate sexual "high" that can release her from years of sexual frustration. She believes that the young protagonist possesses some sexual magic that can restore her vitality. And although he only "rapes" her in symbolic fashion, her request forces him to confront the taboo that has meant fear, death, and destruction for generations of black people. By confronting her, he realizes that possessing her sexually is not identical to possessing some vague sense of freedom. His confrontation also forces him to acknowledge his complicity with his exploiters, in that he has willingly allowed them to reorder his priorities and to force him to lose sight of his original ambitions. He sees that he has imitated the Brotherhood's tactics and interpreted freedom as the exercise of power over another. As a result he refuses to exploit Sybil sexually but instead reveals his genuine concern for her well-being. Once she realizes that his is not the conventional reaction, she responds by telling him that he is "not like other men" (450), that he is beautiful, and that he is capable of genuine compassion and understanding. Like the magnificent blonde, Sybil enables him to approach the threshold of the final battle royal, but not before she has had the opportunity to dispel his misplaced ambition and revive his faltering sense of responsibility, first to himself and then to others.

In each instance stereotype confronts stereotype, as the young protagonist confronts the succession of minor female characters. Each of the four white women represents the other's prohibition, and by confronting the taboo, the young man is slowly and painfully liberated from illusion until he reaches the story's climax. At this point he realizes that he is responsible for his own spiritual death as well as the senseless murder of countless black people. He realizes that by saying yes to the Brotherhood, he has, in effect, been saying no to his own survival as well as to that of black people in general. He is responsible for mobilizing the forces of death and destruction that exploded into the Harlem battle royal. He is guilty, and the knowledge of his guilt is so devastating that he is compelled to seek refuge at Mary's.

I was trying to get to Mary's. (484)

I was going for Mary's but I was moving downtown through the dripping street rather than up. (485)

To Mary, I thought, to Mary. (485)

But I was never to reach Mary's. (490)

The young protagonist desperately seeks Mary—he needs her once again to provide a nurturing refuge from the pain of his disillusionment. He needs her once again to deliver him from the world of "Keep this nigger-boy running" and to foster his folk identities as Jack the Bear and John Henry. He needs her to name him, but his need is unfulfilled, and he remains nameless. Instead of finding Mary, he finds himself "whirling on in the blackness, knocking against the rough walls of a narrow passage, banging [his] head and cursing... coughing and sneezing, into another dimensionless room" (492). He is lost in the inanimate womb of the underground.

So we end where we began, which is not surprising, inasmuch as Ellison told us in the prologue that "the end is in the beginning and lies far ahead" (*IM*, 9). The central question that motivated this essay, therefore, confronts us again: Will the Invisible Man be successful in his attempt to escape the underground? I admit that Ellison supplies no easy answer; he gives us only the riddle of the text. But I offer my answer nevertheless. I predict that the Invisible Man's efforts to leave the underground, though valiant, will be aborted time and time again, since he has no mother to give him birth. The womb that encases him cannot deliver him to the aboveground region. As a result, not only is he without recognizable substance and, thus, invisible; he is, as Ellison says in the epilogue, "a disembodied voice" (503) without a face. He is an idea, an abstraction, a painful memory of a wasted life full of disillusionment. He is knowledge without matter; he is a child unborn, suspended between the fact of his conception and the impossibility of his birth. And he haunts us with the truth that the fate of utter and devastating disillusionment is not reserved for him alone. "Who knows," Ellison admonishes, "but that, on the lower frequencies, [the Invisible Man] speak[s] for [us all]" (503).

Notes

1. A twist on a phrase Ellison repeatedly uses throughout the narrative of *Invisible Man*. Citations from this work appear in text as *IM*.

2. Ralph Ellison, "Twentieth-Century Fiction and the Black Mask of Humanity," *Shadow and Act* (New York: Vintage Books, 1972), 24–44. Further references appear in text as *S&A*.

3. See Sylvander, 77–79; Overmeyer, 13–15; and Waniek, 7–13.

4. Ellison, "Out of the Hospital and under the Bar," 247.

5. Also see Melvin Dixon, "O, Mary Rambo, Don't You Weep."

Works Cited

Dixon, Melvin. "O, Mary Rambo, Don't You Weep." *Carleton Miscellany* 18, no. 3 (1980): 98–104.

Ellison, Ralph. *Invisible Man.* New York: New American Library, 1952.

————. "Out of the Hospital and under the Bar." *Soon One Morning: New Writing by American Negroes 1940–1962,* ed. Herbert Hill. New York: Alfred A. Knopf, 1963.

————. *Shadow and Act.* New York: Vintage Books, 1972.

Overmeyer, Janet. "*The Invisible Man* and White Women." *Notes on Contemporary Literature* 6, no. 3 (1976).

Sylvander, Carolyn W. "Ralph Ellison's *Invisible Man* and Female Stereotypes." *Black American Literature Forum* 9, no. 3 (1975).

Waniek, Marilyn Nelson. "The Space Where Sex Should Be: Toward a Definition of the Black American Literary Tradition." *Studies in Black Literature* 6, no. 3 (1975).

Luminosity from the Lower Frequencies

LEON FORREST

◆ ◆ ◆

I SHOULD LIKE TO DISCUSS certain intellectual, cultural, and historical influences upon Ralph Ellison's sense of the hero's character in process and the structure of the major chapters throughout his monumental novel, *Invisible Man*. Several influences come to mind: Kenneth Burke, Lord Raglan, Dostoevski, and Faulkner, as well as the artistic and jazzlike rendering of folkloric sources.

From the literary critic Burke, Ellison came to see the possibility of using a formula to structure a chapter. Burke held that a pattern could be employed to achieve character-in-process progression through the formula of *purpose, passion,* and *perception:* each chapter begins with a *purpose* for the hero, but then much of the action of the middle section involves a struggle, or *passion,* over this *purpose,* or quest. Out of this mix or confrontation with others and the self, the hero comes away with a heightened *perception,* a keener awareness about his life, so that a metamorphosis, or rebirth, is implied. But these moments are stages of his processing into life, and the cycle, once completed, unleashes new problems and struggles.

Another literary influence on *Invisible Man* came from Lord Raglan, whose seminal book *The Hero* argues that a constant pattern of biographical data defines the lives of the heroes of tradition. The heroes Raglan calls forth run a gamut from Oedipus Rex to Elijah, Zeus, Orpheus, and Robin Hood. The pattern traces some twenty-two steps from birth to death. But the central constant in Raglan's pattern of heroic dimension is this: the hero dies, goes through a life underground, and is reborn. Raglan's concept meshes neatly with Burke's formula of purpose, passion, and perception. For instance, the passion, or conflict, is quite similar to the turmoil in the mental underground and all of the attendant agonies. The idea of a heightened perception can be linked to Raglan's concept of rebirth, or even redemption in the Christian sense, and to discovery and self-recognition in the Aristotelian sense.

In the major chapters of his novel, Ellison—a jazz trumpeter who studied musical composition—orchestrates and improvises upon an introductory theme raised through a character at the beginning of a chapter. And he ends the chapter on an upbeat thematic moment (sometimes with an enriching, elusive literary statement that speaks for the chapter and the intelligence of the novel as a whole "at the lower frequencies") which stands in opposition to the opening thematic idea. Our sense of luminosity is heightened with the hero's, because of the sweeping poles or polar distances traversed from the beginning to the end. These are mini-odysseys of purpose, passion, and perception, we might say.

Ellison's arrangement of characters and themes standing in during confrontational moments forms a constant source of instruction, as we see the hero's character in process evolve and the novel evolve; and it helps the reader to see how these apparently oppositional forces are really quite closely connected. This device recalls anthropologist Claude Lévi-Strauss's concept of *thesis, counterthesis, synthesis*. And it is related to Dostoevski's uses of *doubling* and of character. One way of looking at doubling is to see it as a blending of opposites—characters who stand in sharp opposition to each other and yet have much in common.

The novel abounds with instances of this Dostoevskian doubling. There is for example the Norton/Trueblood pairing—a one-to-one confrontation, with the Oedipal desire/act forging a linkage between the rich, white, blue-blood philanthropist, Norton, and the poor, black, uneducated peasant farmer, Jim Trueblood. In Trueblood's dream, we discover an abundance of underground images indicating that Trueblood lusts for power in the real world as much as the powerful Norton lusts for the body of his own daughter—behind the monument of money he has donated in her honor to the school. Another form of Dostoevskian doubling occurs in the reverberating manner in which characters in apparent oppositional quest, status, or station are paired by a theme at completely different stages and times.

For instance, the theme of *eloquence*, its manipulation, uses, and misuses, links the tall, Lincoln-like Hambro, mouthpiece for the Communist-like Brotherhood, with the spokesman-versifier for the Negro college and the American white way, the blind, Founder-celebrating minister, Homer Barbee. Short and ugly like Homer, Barbee gives a high-priest choral arrangement and tribal eulogy for the Founder that sounds like Whitman praising Abe Lincoln (note Ellison's parody on the great Whitman's grand blindness to Abe's angularity, his blemishes, his body-and-soul torment over slavery, his complexity of motives). Now these two high-powered word-artists-cum-magicians, in turn, represent two power-mad, master tricksters. For Hambro illuminates the enslaving dogma espoused by the one-eyed Cyclops, Brother Jack, Head White Man in Charge (HWMC) of the Brotherhood. And as Hambro attempts to drop the illuminating (but really enshrouding, and blinding) veil of "understanding" over the student-hero's eyes, he also blinds himself to the pranks of public policy that enslave the individual for the public good of this most private, elite of American parties. Thus he is veiled by his own public pronouncements.

And that high priest of bamboozlement, Odyssey-echoing Homer Barbee, eloquently drops the enslaving veil of intellectual blindness across the students' eyes, to please that manipulator of polished slave chains, the college president, Hebert Bledsoe, and his captive audience of white trustees, that is, overseers. For in this situation, at least, Bledsoe is not only the Head Nigger in Charge (HNIC), but he has actually reversed the plantation system so that he is slavemaster on this plantation, with Barbee as slave driver of history. And Barbee, in turn, is blinded like the statue of the Founder, as he drops the veil honoring institutional power, which is manifested in the body and soul of the Founder's epic story (not in the students' learning and intellectual development). Barbee participates in his own self-impaling ceremony: he dims the light of his own intellectual and moral vision of history, preferring the luxurious delusion of "sweet harmonies" over the reality of the chaos of African-American life. And as he extinguishes his vision with his words, Barbee recalls Oedipus, who, having seen too much, tears out his eyes with the clasps of Jocasta's gown. Barbee's physical blindness seems a fitful banishment from the lost North Star light of daring freedom and progress, or as he himself says at one point, as he recalls the declining luminosity in the Founder's life on the train:

> I remember how I looked out of the frosted pane and saw the looming great North Star and lost it, as though the sky had shut its eye.[1]

In this sense, too, the phrase-polishing Barbee becomes a kind of scapegoat for Bledsoe, as minister Homer leads the lamb-innocent Negro students to a slaughtered rendering of their history. Yet their only hope for escape is the Underground Railroad, as it were, and that too on an individual basis. For each must read his or her own way through Barbee's fabulous spiel, and the only hope for escape from reenslavement is to hold fast to the undersides of their history, beneath Barbee's words and memories, and hope that probing questions will ignite a liberating response from their fellow blacks. Indeed they must be ready to commit a kind of "treason" like that "snowy-headed man" at one of the

Founder's ceremonial lectures who demands that the Founder cut the accommodationist spiel and

"Tell us what is to be done, sir! For God's sake, tell us! Tell us in the name of the son they snatched from me last week!" And all through the room the voices arising, imploring, "Tell us, tell us!" And the Founder is suddenly mute with tears. (97)

Like Ulysses escaping the Cyclops in the cave, the students must approach Barbee's story with cunning to match the blinding light of his language and, like Ulysses, must catch hold of the sacred and the profane aspects of their history under-the-belly, and hold on for dear life—as Ulysses says, "so I caught hold of the ram by the back, ensconced myself in the thick wool under his belly and hung on patiently to his fleece, face upwards keeping a firm hold on it all of the time." For the students would need to reverse so much of Barbee's speech and to reveal the truths from oral history handed along by the great storytellers, truths that he constantly subordinates and countermands. This is a central problem for a young Negro confronted by all of the distortions of that peasant, underground history—a fact that the Klan-beset snowy-headed man in Homer Barbee's saga-spiel knows only too well.

Ellison is concerned there in the Barbee-Founder-Bledsoe trinity, as it were, with the unquestioned reverence for leadership that still seems to haunt certain groups within the race vulnerable to the cult of the personality, especially when touched by the fires of political-religious enterprise. But there is a yeasty truth in Barbee's saga. Barbee knows the language of power, and he manipulates it as it manipulates him—and in that sense he's masking the wisdom of his peasant tongue. Similarly, it is not so much what Brother Jack says about the party but the fact that he lost his eye which keeps him from facing his underground history. When his false eye drops out into the glass of water in a moment of confrontation with the hero late in the novel (over the Invisible Man's unauthorized speech for Tod Clifton), he must drop the party line that covers his vision and babble back into his peasant tongue or into the obscuring language of power. The dropping out of Jack's eye recalls the revelation of Barbee's blindness at the end of his spiel, as he trips in his darkness after having maintained his verbal high-wire act with such deftness, symmetry of line, and balance of power. It recalls chaos-loving Rinehart's manipulative spiel of eloquence that extracts handouts from the blinded, lamb-innocent church ladies. Rinehart's spiel is tied to the profane eloquence of chaos-destroyed hypersensitive Tod Clifton, whose streetcorner spiel about the Sambo doll—that it will be whatever you want it to be—reflects the gist of what the streetcorner hustler tells all slum dwellers hungry to be recognized or loved.

Even in small segments of the novel we see how these clusters, formulas, and influences operate with Ellison's materials. Chapter 9 starts off soon after the hero gets to Harlem on his way to Mr. Emerson to check out the job reference letter given to him by the powerful black president. The hero was booted out, you will recall, because quite by accident he showed the white trustee, Norton, the underground of Negro life and the black madness manifested at the riotous Golden Day, and showed him, as well, the base human passions (and by indirection Norton's own purposeful passion) revealed by Jim Trueblood's eloquent saga of incest.

Now our hero starts off with the purpose of finding a job, but early on he runs into a bluesman whose song celebrates the powerful, sexually fulfilling catharsis he achieves from his love-making lady, whose praises he sings as follows:

> She's got feet like a monkey
> Legs like a frog—Lawd, Lawd!
> But when she starts to loving me
> I holler Whoooo, God-dog!
> Cause I loves my baabay,
> Better than I do myself. (131)

Now this blues song celebrates the fulfilling sex life of a poor bluesman at the bottom, whose woman's beauty is questionable according to standards of beauty in the upper world. Yet their sex life is an affirming glory of life at the bottom, and it leads him to swear that he loves her better than he does himself. The second point is this: the blues singer is certain about his identity, about who he is sexually; and as it turns out, he is a fierce individualist who tries to tell the hero to be what he is, not to masquerade himself, not to deny the bluesman.

Now toward the end of the chapter the hero comes to discover and recognize his new fate, when he finds out that the masquerading trickster, Dr. Bledsoe, indeed has written the hero out of history and driven him toward the unattainable horizon, not with a job reference letter, as the hero assumed, but rather with a prank piece of paper that says, in effect—"To Whom It May Concern, Keep This Nigger-Boy Running." But now at this agony-filled, perception-sharpening junction, another kind of song comes bubbling up to the surface of the hero's consciousness, rescuing him from self-pity—a mock dirge, played traditionally in the Oklahoma area. After a burial, Negro jazz musicians would light up into this dirge once they hit the Negro business section of town. It expresses the attitudes central to the black man's memory of his history, that if he is to survive he must not allow himself to wallow in self-pity over death, or over the constant dream-shattering, death-dealing experience that is his fate, his mocked fate. The dirge goes:

> O well they picked poor Robin clean
> O well they picked poor Robin clean
> Well they tied poor Robin to a stump
> Lawd, they picked all the feathers round
>   from Robin's rump
> Well they picked poor Robin clean. (147)

The bluesman's song is filled with life, possibility, and the affirmation of love and identity through fundamental sexual confrontation and confirmation. The dirge stands in apparent opposition, since it comes at the time of a death; yet it is life giving and intelligence heightening, even as it is innocence destroying—

mocking our hero's false pride and his naive hero worship of Bledsoe. The song mocks and thereby instructs him that each person must constantly die, or shed the skin of his innocence, in order to grow. The mock dirge comes after a moment of the hero's mock murder, through the pen of bloody Bledsoe. Finally, the song says that savage experience picks us clean of the plumagelike illusions round our baby-soft rounded rumps and leaves us picked clean to the bone of our innocence—but then, perhaps, that is indeed the necessary price of eating of the forbidden fruit of experience and knowledge. Unlike the blues, "which allows no scapegoat but the self," the dirge allows us to "lighten our load by becoming one with the bird, as he symbolically takes over our bone-picked sorrow."

This pattern of death, agony, and mocking affirmation or momentary rebirth informs the entire novel, but is pointedly suggested in that marvelous skeleton of a call-and-response sermon by the black minister in the prologue. There, in the cellar of the hero's racial consciousness where Ellison's version of Underground Man is dwelling, the preacher says, "I said black is . . . an' black ain't . . . Black will git you . . . an' black won't . . . It do, Lawd . . . an' it don't—Black will make you . . . or black will unmake you" (8). Bledsoe, the black president of the college, has undone the hero. And minister Barbee looks through a glass darkly, never face to face. But it is a black dirge that sourly surges forth from the underground racial past and it helps rescue, school, and repair the hero at the junction in chapter 9. Here again the movement from affirmation through denial to affirmation, or from thesis to counterthesis to synthesis, is treated dialectically as it was by the man at the bottom, the bluesman Peter Wheatstraw.

The bluesman is doubled with the hero in the Dostoevskian sense. The streetwise bluesman knows everything about northern idiom and what it takes to get along in this here man's town and on the lower frequencies; and yet Peter Wheatstraw is lost and homeless in the world of power, unable at the higher frequencies to manipulate its symbols or to manifest his vision, and he's uneducated in the school sense. At the other end, the Invisible Man is lost in the streets of Harlem and is also homeless in the world of power; indeed, the most powerful man in his world has just kicked him out of this world (upstairs, you might say, to the North) to Harlem, which is, of course, *nowhere*. And the Invisible Man is undereducated in the street sense. Still, there is synthesis possible for the hero if he but trusts his underground peasant intelligence and memory. For as the hero reflects upon one riff in Peter Wheatstraw's spiel, he thinks:

> I liked his words though I didn't know the answer. I'd known the stuff from childhood, but had forgotten it; had learned it back of school . . . (ellipsis in original; 134)

But at this junction, too, the hero and the bluesman are tied together again because it is very important to him that this "new boy" in town not deny him. Peter Wheatstraw's concern is almost prophetic because, at the end of the chapter, the hero is to be denied by his *Peter*, Hebert Bledsoe. Bledsoe is glad to see him at first and then denies him privately. The fear of being denied by race brother, by public power, and by father figures sets the stage for the hero's next confrontation.

In the middle of chapter 9, the hero undergoes the passion phase of Burke's law via a confrontation with young Emerson, a man of shattered dreams, denied personal fulfillment, at the top of the economic spectrum. His sexuality is confused and so is his identity about a host of subjects, ranging from the way he really feels about blacks to the ambivalence about his powerful father, who has figuratively devoured his son, as Cronus did unto Zeus. Young Emerson, a homosexual undergoing a form of psycho-analysis which apparently brings him no affirmation, stands, then, in direct opposition to the solidly based, blues-singing, dirt-poor, black man of the streets at the beginning of the chapter, who knows who he is. Yet this pairing also recalls the Norton-Trueblood pairing and doubling.

And this pairing also recalls the old American story of the man who has everything and nothing: young Emerson is rich, white, free, and twenty-one, yet he really has nothing but a world of confusion; and the bluesman has nothing but a batch of blueprints showing his dreams of powerful towns and country clubs that he will never erect. He has everything, though, in a real woman who loves him with a great sexual power, even though her beauty, at the lower frequencies, is invisible to all with the naked eye. It is young Emerson, the homosexual, who unfolds the truth of the letter to the hero, just as it is the remarkable-looking lady of the bluesman who gives him the sexual, naked truth and renders him a celebrant of her naked powers, body and soul. One recalls how it is the blind hermaphrodite, Tiresias, who bears to Oedipus the truth below the king's self-righteous existence. But the homosexual at the top and the bluesman at the bottom are also linked; for both are existential outlaws in our society, yet at the same time both are high priests from the peripheral underground, warning the hero of hidden reality. Tangentially, we might reflect here that so many of our current musical dance patterns have their genesis in black bars, on the one hand, and gay bars, on the other, long before we all began to dance, dance to the music. Indeed, one recalls that young Emerson tells the hero about a kind of peripheral bar, the Club Calamus:

You haven't? It's very well known. Many of my Harlem friends go there. It's a rendezvous for writers, artists and all kinds of celebrities. There's nothing like it in the city, and by some strange twist it has a truly continental flavor. (141)

At this point the hero has undergone a mini-motif of Lord Raglan's pattern in this chapter—he has figuratively died, undergone an underground agony, and been reborn tougher and more perceptive and able to laugh at himself. Finally the wonderful spiel delivered by the bluesman as he is advising our hero has provided the first confrontation the southern-born hero has with a northern black, and it is significant that, although they are speaking the same language, he hardly understands the bluesman's transformed tongue, at first. Migrate from one part of America to another and you are often lost in terms of idiomatic meaning. Yet in the case of the black man the genesis of language has an ancestral underground root in the old country of the Southland. To show Ellison's many-dimensioned use of idiom, let me now attempt to unravel one of his bluesman's riffs:

> "All it takes to get along in this here man's town is a little shit, grit and motherwit. And man, I was bawn with all three. In fact I'maseventhsonofaseventhson bawnwithacauloverboth-eyesandraisedonblackcatboneshighjohntheconquerorandgreasy-greens—" he spieled with twinkling eyes, his lips working rapidly. "You dig me daddy?" (134)

Let me suggest that here Ellison is rendering up the fusion of myth and lore which is the genesis of Negro/Black/White/Afro-American idiomatic versification. "The seventh son of a seventh son" comes from the Scottish-English influence upon the former slaves and suggests how myth-bound and haunted the slaveholders were and refers to one who is born lucky. "Bawn with a caul over both eyes" suggests one who is born with the gift of clairvoyance and has an Ashanti linkage from the African aspect of the heritage. "Raised on black cat bones" is from the Afro-*American* version of voodoo and the context is this: in voodoo, which always reverses meaning (as does so much of Negro idiom), you throw a live black cat into a boiling pot of hot water; after the flesh has fallen away you pick out its bones and gnaw away; and if you are lucky, and gnaw down upon the right bone, you will become *invisible*. High John the Conqueror is a mythical hero from slavery, an invisible hero who sided with the slaves, during bad times, with good advice. And "greasygreens," of course, refers to African-American cuisine, in the old country Southland.

The hero's presence in the North at this time in the novel recalls the migration from the South to the North of blacks who came, often on the run, pursuing the dream of a peaceful kingdom, jobs, and personal fulfillment. But the hero's dream becomes a nightmare through a mocking note that, unknown to him, reads: "To Whom It May Concern: Keep This Nigger-Boy Running." It is significant, and one of the ironies of the meshing of race and class, that (while looking for employment) the hero discovers this dimension of his representative fate in the North from a rich white entrepreneur's son whose mock employment has brought him no fulfillment.

But it is even more significant that the hero first recalls the "nigger-boy running" joke via a recalled dream that he has of his grandfather, at the end of chapter 1, just after he wins his scholarship to the Negro college. For in the dream, through his grandfather, the hero is ritually warned and instructed:

> He told me to open my brief case and read what was inside— and I did, finding an official envelope stamped with the state seal; and inside the envelope I found another and another, endlessly, and I thought I would fall of weariness. "Them's years," he said. "Now open that one." And I did and in it I found an engraved document containing a short message in letters of gold. "Read it," my grandfather said. "Out loud!"
>
> "To Whom It May Concern," I intoned, "Keep This Nigger-Boy Running." (26)

And there is an underground story beneath this memory. For in the old South, a form of black baiting which had its genesis in slavery would proceed as follows: A Negro newcomer would arrive upon the scene, looking for gainful employment; he would go to a prospective white employer. This ordinary small-town white businessman would immediately spot the fact that this was not one of the local blacks and would tell the black outsider that he did not have work at this time but that he did know of someone who might have jobs available down the road, perhaps.

The white businessman would then give the horizon-seeking black a sealed letter to take to the next prospective employer. Upon reaching the next white man, the letter would be presented, opened by the white man, read and mused over, and then the Negro would hear the same old story—"no jobs" here but perhaps "up the road," and then the white merchant would scribble something on the note, reseal the communiqué (like the Negro's fate), and hand the letter back to the outreaching dark hand. This would happen again and again, until the black finally opened the letter and read the message, or got the message, and read out his symbolic fate (or some variation upon the theme): "To Whom It May Concern: Keep This Nigger-Boy Running." This brutal joke of course had its antecedents in slavery, when many or most slaves couldn't read or write, and could only go from plantation to plantation with a note signed by the master, or his earthly representative. The slave didn't in fact know what might or might not be written down on that note. And although this tortuous ritual or bad-faith convenant came from the pastoral scenes of the gallant South, actually the jobs search and its attendant mocking ceremony were often played out in the industrial North. Or more to the point, the duplicity operative at the paint factory in *Invisible Man*, which in fact did hire our nameless hero, but only as a scab (union strike buster), signified the way industrial bosses pitted the racial and ethnic groupings of the underclasses against each other. And when the Invisible Man's day labor was used up, he was discarded and put on tentative welfare after signing some papers which freed him from work— new slave papers meant to quiet his aggressive appetite for employment.

It is structurally salient that Ellison establishes early the ancestral tie with the grandfather's folk voice, via the underground avenue of the dream. For the grandfather's appearance and intelligence in the dream is the deeper Underground Railroad reality beneath the American Dream for the Negro. And the grandfather is the oldest ancestor within the hero's family memory. And who is the *grandfather's* authority? No doubt the oldest member of the tribe in his memory, perhaps *his* grandfather—and then we are back into slavery; so that in a highly oral culture the grandfather is the proper high priest to pass on mythical reality and survival wisdom from the battle zone. Throughout the novel, a warning or extolling voice issues forth from underground (often coming to the hero's aid, like Tarp's voice at the bottom of the Brotherhood) during moments of agony, conflict, trial, public and private passion. And (like the rescuing dirge, or High John the Conqueror) this intelligence informs his hard-won experience, thereby constantly presenting the reader with a hero's awareness or perception that is heightened. Not all of the underground warning voices confer benefits upon the hero as they warn him, however, as Lucius Brockway, in the underground of the paint factory, demonstrates. Brockway becomes a most trying combination of Tar Baby and Proteus for the Invisible Man.

Now in some cases the ancestral voice comes directly out of the remembering hero's own past, as did the rescuing dirge. The second kind of ancestral voice issues from the hero's consciousness when he recalls moments from his own personal history, which then leads him to racial memory, as did the dream of the grandfather. The third kind of historical-ancestral linkage comes from symbols or specific items which don't touch the hero's own past but which form a lucid part of his racial memory and the consciousness of the race, in the Joycean sense, suggesting then a duty and a task and a covenant or responsibility to the ancestral community.

Now these symbolic objects surge forth at moments of passion or trial. For instance, when the hero, late in the novel, discovers another kind of "keep this nigger-boy running" note on his desk at the Brotherhood's office, Brother Tarp, the man at the bottom of the organization, gives the hero a picture of Frederick Douglass, our man at the top of Negro leadership in the nineteenth century. Later Tarp gives the hero his own leg irons, retained from a chain gang. The hero must learn to trust those symbolic ancestral tokens, voices, or manifestations—yet he must sort out the consulting surge of past and present counselors. Indeed one of the hero's many agonies is to learn not to accept the advice from authority figures without question and to wrestle with advice until he's made it his own and understood it, or spurned it, or accepted it and by accepting it, made certain he's reshaped the advice to fit his own experience. For the other side of the most profane or the healthiest advice is that it renders the hero somebody's "running boy" and does not allow him to be his own man.

So, motifs involving power, sex, women, images of light and dark, broken taboos, Afro-American folklore, papers of importance, quests for identity and responsibility, individualism, music, violence, and uses of eloquence all come in clusters and order the improvisations of Ellison's orchestrated novel. Here we can see the influence of William Faulkner's *Light in August*, in which the major scenes are ordered by the presence of sex, women, food, and money, and are in turn connected with images of light and dark, religion and slavery, as integrating forces which undergird the associative patterns of each narrative section. In terms of power Ellison is constantly improvising upon the whole plantation system as a metaphor for understanding American institutions. This improvisation on the plantationlike hierarchy can be seen in the "descent" section of the prologue, in the pecking order at the paint factory, in life at Mary Rambo's rooming house, in the Brotherhood, at the college, at the battle-royal smoker, and at the Golden Day.

Connected with this imagery of the plantation is another, deeper dimension of Ellison's metaphoric patterning in which he projects a symbolic model of American history—thereby joining the very select company of Melville, Hawthorne, and especially Faulkner in this recombining of metaphorical vision with history. All of Faulkner's major works involving the black presence, it seems to me, possess this epic design. For instance, in *Absalom, Absalom!* the design of metaphor can be read in the following manner: Let the French architect stand for America's "borrowed" French principles of refinement, creativity, artistry, ideals of culture, freedom, and liberty (indeed our fitful intellectual indebtedness to the French Revolution); and let Sutpen stand for American know-how, cunning, outlandish daring, bigotry, savage frontiersmanship-hustle, furious energy and industry, and white-ethnic class hatred; and let the Negro slaves of Sutpen's Hundreds stand as the enslaved bases of the American economic order.

Sutpen must reduce all others to "niggers" (blacks, women, his family, outside family, poor whites, his son) as he hacks his insanely ambitious way to the top. The new American Adam must reduce the French architect, at the other end of the social spectrum, to a subhuman, to a nigger, once he has used up the architect's expertise. And he then attempts to free his body from Sutpen's clutches. Sutpen, in turn, reenacts a mock French Revolution by bringing down the French aristocrat-artist. But the

French architect only flees when he discovers that he too is en-slaved—thus the synthesis between slave and aristocrat is forged by *slavery's* chains. And the French architect's flight and Sutpen's pursuit of him with hound dogs recalls that of a runaway slave and the ritual pursuit by hound dogs.

Dostoevski's hero in *Notes from Underground*, and the illumined Invisible Man of the Ellison prologue and epilogue, are manifestations of hyperawareness and terror concerning the inner meanness of the outer world: they observe it as a treacherous terrain. Structurally, the prologue contains within it all of the materials needed for Ellison's invention; and the core of the work then goes on to illustrate and orchestrate these materials. In Underground Man's world, part 1 is a presentation of the arguments, and in part 2 we have the illustrations. *Notes from Underground* can be seen as a monologue rich with personal and political commentary. The grand sweep of the many monologues in *Invisible Man* carries a similar personal, political doubleness. But Ellison's monologues have a kind of epic grandness that goes beyond Dostoevski. Witness, for example, Trueblood's saga and Barbee's sermon.

At every turn in *Notes*, Underground Man is out to shock the reader, to shock reason itself. The Invisible Man is out to shake the reader into an awareness that is streaked with a soured humor and a great gift for hyperbole. Both novels are within the tradition of the memoir, and, like *Notes*, *Invisible Man* is seasoned in the tradition of the confessional literature of the seductive underground diary.

The Russia of Underground Man's day was highly repressive, and so for Ellison's hyperaware man there is ever the feeling of alienation and dispossession. (And you will recall that the Invisible Man's second public address treats the theme of dispossession, and he uses it in his third address at the stadium.) In Dostoevski's Russia you either accepted your socioeconomic status as your fate or you dropped out. No mobility. Faced with the fitful combination of power, race, and wrenching leadership, the Invisible Man faces a comparable terrain, cut off in the cellar from upward movement. Perhaps even more in keeping with the vaulting, scorning attitude of Underground Man are the men in the Golden Day, who remain as Afro-American examples of broken men, though madness has consumed their soured brilliance.

Both narrators appear to be onto something concerning the way the normal world of power operates in a system of deceit—especially if you are highly aware, you are apt to be driven to treason. For example, after seeing too much, in an ancestral dream of the shattering past in the prologue, the Invisible Man recalls:

> And at that point a voice of trombone timbre screamed at me, "Git out of here, you fool! Is you ready to commit treason?" (8)

Both narrators suggest that the mind of highly aware man contains much spite and even vengeance. Underground Man seeks revenge, not justice. But the Invisible Man would seek both. There is a sense in both works—particularly in *Notes*—that hyperconsciousness leads to paralysis. Therefore the only action issues out of a sense of willfulness and spitefulness. The Invisible Man, though, is obsessed with responsibility, and cultural enterprise, and the rage for freedom that remains a viable ancestral imperative. The Invisible Man, however, frets about overstaying his time of contemplation in the underground and knows he is bound to come up; he seeks love, and spite can only lead to disintegration of personality, as in those memorable figures in the Golden Day. Ultimately, of course, going underground is a kind of psychological going within oneself for both narrators.

Ralph Ellison starts out wanting to reverse the idea, current at the time he conceived *Invisible Man*, that the Negro was invisible. The narrator says, "I am invisible simply because you refuse to see me." But having committed himself to assaulting the current sociological metaphor of the day, Ellison turns the metaphor into a dialectic vision of modern America as a brier patch. The metaphor of invisibility is doubly enriched by his constant allusions to the plantation system. The logic is as follows: *Thesis*: You (society) say I'm a slave. *Counterthesis*: But I'm not a slave in my soul, or in my mind. *Synthesis:* I'll admit that slavery is the system in which I dwell, but I see myself as slave in that system only if you'll accept the metaphor of how the system enslaves us all, Master. . . . And because I've lived with this knowledge longer, I've learned how to make the plantation my brier patch; though it enslaves my body I have learned how to keep my mind and spirit free from its damnation of the spirit. And Master, economically your survival depends upon my body's productivity in the slave system that obsesses your mind and spirit.

Alternatively, the Invisible Man asks himself, and us, as he weaves through the possible meanings of the grandfather's advice in the epilogue:

> Was it that we of all, we, most of all, had to affirm the principle, the plan in whose name we had been brutalized and sacrificed—not because we would always be weak nor because we were afraid or opportunistic, but because we were older than they, in the sense of what it took to live in the world with others and because they had exhausted in us, some—not much, but some—of the human greed and smallness, yes, and the fear and superstition that had kept them running. (433–34)

Like Dostoevski's Underground Man, the Invisible Man puts down the idea of racial invisibility; he embraces the metaphor, assaults it, then reverses it. He discovers at the height of the race riots in Harlem that he cannot return to Mary's either, that he is invisible to Mrs. Rambo as he is to Jack, Ras, and Bledsoe. For like Underground Man, he discovers that statistical computations for the collective good, or institutional asylums for the individual's good, or visions of the individual's good by powerful figures and forces constantly leave out one important impulse: man's urge and capacity to conceptualize his humanity beyond statistics and regimentation; his willfulness to do what he wants, in the underground economy of his imagination, to turn a plantation into an underground brier patch or a hostile terrain into the sources and resource points of escape via the mind's Underground Railroad.

For finally the Invisible Man is underground indeed; but he has decided that it is time to end his hibernation and come up to meet a new level of experience. And it is plain to me that at the end of the novel, our hero, reborn, is about to emerge from his womb of safety in the underground; yet it is also clear that he is trapped in a personal way between two voices. For as he acknowledges:

> Thus, having tried to give pattern to the chaos which lives within the pattern of your certainties, I must come out. I must emerge. And there's still a conflict within me: With Louis Armstrong one half of me says, "Open the window and let the foul air out," while the other says, "It was good green corn before the harvest." (438)

Now the "green corn" motif comes from a Leadbelly song and refers to a state of innocence before the harvest of experience. Innocence is beautiful but it carries dangerous naiveté with it— a naive skin that our hero sheds.

But first of all the hero hears a lyrical line from the man who makes poetry out of invisibility, Louis Armstrong, a song which suggests the sophisticated, toughened shape the hero's perception of reality has taken on out of the furnacelike bad air of passion and conflict which has been his experience throughout the life of the novel. The line refers to a song by Buddy Bolden which Louis Armstrong—also known as Dipper Mouth and Bad Air— used to sing:

> I thought I heard Buddy Bolden say,
> Funky-Butt, Funky-Butt, take it away,
> I thought I heard somebody shout,
> Open up the window and let the foul air out.

The Funky-Butt was a powerhouse jazz nightclub in New Orleans, where the solos on the horns were as furious and glorious as the sex act itself, filled with bad air and ecstatic charges, savage thrusts and stellar flourishes. Armstrong, as a kid of ten, used to stand outside the door of the Funky-Butt and listen to Bolden, the great jazz trumpeter who ended up in a madhouse, blowing and singing and wailing. Bolden would sing the song in tribute to the funkiness and the foul air in the dance hall, caused by the jelly-tight dancing.

Without the liberating bad air that riffs through the chamber of the good-bad horn of plenty (which also resembles the chamber from whence all life emerges), you can't have the real music of life, or the dance. For as the hero comments:

> Of course Louis was kidding, *he* wouldn't have thrown old Bad Air out, because it would have broken up the music and the dance, when it was the good music that came from the bell of old Bad Air's horn that counted. (438)

Note

1. Ralph Ellison, *Invisible Man* (New York: Random House, 1952), 99. All subsequent citations are to this edition.

Ellison's *Invisible Man*

JOHN F. CALLAHAN

◆ ◆ ◆

R ALPH WALDO ELLISON was no stranger to what he called "our national library,"[1] the Library of Congress. In 1964, more than a decade after publication of *Invisible Man*, he brought his middle name out of hibernation at the library's Jefferson Building, where an elegant room, looking out on the Capitol, now bears his name and houses his most cherished books. His talk that evening was called "Hidden Name and Complex Fate." In my mind's eye I see him then, almost fifteen years before I knew him, speaking in a confident, steady voice that would rise a little at first, as it did when he was nervous or impatient, and, after he relaxed, settle into a southwestern drawl. I can see him— dreamy, boyish, wistful, intense, and stubborn, by turns—as his warm, defiant, brown eyes flashed up from his manuscript to individual faces in the hall. . . .

"[Ralph Waldo] Emerson's name was quite familiar to Negroes in Oklahoma during those days when World War I was brewing," Ellison remembered on that evening thirty-five years ago, "and adults, eager to show off their knowledge of literary figures, and

obviously amused by the joke implicit in such a small brown
nubbin of a boy carrying around such a heavy moniker, would
invariably repeat my first two names and then, to my great an-
noyance, they'd add 'Emerson'." Unlike the invisible protagonist
of his eponymous novel, who allows his name to be changed by
others, Ellison merely "reduced the 'Waldo' to a simple and," he
hoped, "mysterious 'W'." Trying to have it both ways, Ellison told
his audience at the Library of Congress that he "did not destroy
that troublesome middle name of mine; I only suppressed it."[2]
But not entirely, as it turned out. Going through his papers before
their transfer from the Ellison apartment to the Library of Congress in 1995, I discovered a clutch of letters from 1933 written
by a young lady in Oklahoma City and addressed to Waldo Ellison, c/o Tuskegee Institute. Doubtless Ellison knew whereof his
narrator, Invisible Man, spoke, when the latter said, "I too have
become acquainted with ambivalence."[3] And, of course, ambivalence, not least toward names and naming, became a touchstone
in Ellison's great novel of identity, *Invisible Man*.

But first, who was this man named Ralph Waldo Ellison whose
one and only finished novel electrified the nation in 1952, when
the "separate but equal" doctrine of racial segregation was still in
force as the law of the land? (When the American Rubicon of
integration was crossed two years later in the *Brown v. Board of
Education* decision, Ellison paid a tithe to his crossbred identities as
an American, a Negro, a writer, and, not least, a native of a
frontier state on the border of the Old Confederacy: "Why did I
have to be a writer during a time when events sneer openly at
your efforts, defying consciousness and form?" he wrote his old
teacher Morteza Sprague, librarian at Tuskegee. "Well, so now the
judges have found and Negroes must be individuals and that is
hopeful and good.")[4]

Ellison, it should always be remembered, was born in
Oklahoma in 1914, a mere seven years after the former Indian
Territory had become a state. "Geography is fate,"[5] he liked to
say, and the Heraclitean epigram inevitably led him to recount
his parents' migration from the deep South of South Carolina
and Georgia, after a brief stop in Chattanooga, to the new state

of Oklahoma. As Mrs. Weaver, a character inspired by Ellison's widowed mother, Ida, tells her son James in "Boy on a Train," one of the earliest short stories, a generation of Negroes came west "because we had heard that colored people had a chance out here."[6] For Ellison, Oklahoma, despite its regression to Jim Crow laws and customs—"Some white folks are out to turn this state into a part of the South" (*Essays*, 823), Ellison's mother told him (he also remembered her being arrested more than once for demonstrating against segregated housing in Oklahoma City)— stood for the territory, a metaphor for the diversity, complexity, possibility, and above all, fluidity of American life.

The logic of his life's ambition drew him first to Tuskegee Institute in Alabama, where he won a state scholarship to study trumpet and composition under the renowned conductor and composer William L. Dawson. In those days it was more expedient and inexpensive for the state of Oklahoma to award gifted Negroes scholarships out of state than to integrate its colleges or build separate-but-equal ones. Even though he lit out for New York, Oklahoma remained "a dream world."[7] Its geography, history, and human diversity embodied the actual and potential, if oft-denied richness, of the country. From Ellison's boyhood all the way to old age, "the territory" remained, in words he inscribed in a friend's copy of his second book of essays, *Going to the Territory,* "an ideal place, ever to be sought, ever to be missed, but always there."[8]

"You have to leave home to find home," Ellison once scribbled in a notebook, and it was during his unexpected, grief-stricken, penurious sojourn in Dayton, Ohio, from October 1937 to April 1938 that he began the writer's apprenticeship that led to *Invisible Man*. Although intrigued by connections between the techniques of T. S. Eliot and Louis Armstrong, James Joyce and the riffing vernacular improvisations of African-American speech that boiled up from the underground of consciousness at Tuskegee, Ellison still pursued his artistic star through music. In New York, however, where he had gone in the summer of 1936 to earn money for his senior year, and stayed, he would be forced to hock his trumpet to raise train fare for Dayton, where in the fall of 1937 his mother's misdiagnosed tuberculosis of the hip suddenly worsened.

Arriving, Ellison rushed to the hospital to find his mother's pain so intense that she did not recognize him, and the "next day she was gone."[9] Ten days later Ellison, whose father, Lewis, had died when he was three, wrote Richard Wright back in New York that his mother's death marked the true end of childhood. Unlike the simulacrum of change he associated with coming to New York City, the loss of his mother was "the most final thing I've encountered."[10] Yet in the blues tradition, her unexpected death became a painful, wrenching catalyst. Exiled in Dayton, where he felt the full force of what he would later call "our orphan's loneliness" (*Essays*, 35), Ellison began his passage to the writer's vocation. It was during this period, he recalled in *Shadow and Act*, that he "started trying seriously to write and that was the breaking point" (*Essays*, 73).

Ellison's intriguing reference to "the breaking point" suggests fractures of self akin to those revolutionary poetic and musical breaks he was so startled by earlier at Tuskegee in Eliot's *Waste Land* and Armstrong's "Chinatown." In his secret heart Ellison continued to regard himself as a musician, indeed as an aspiring symphonic composer, another clue, perhaps, to the form and technique that would emerge years later in *Invisible Man*. But during those six months in Dayton, he untied the Gordian knot of what he would later call his "complicated, semiconscious strategy of self-deception, a refusal by my right hand [the musician's] to recognize where my left hand [the writer's] was headed" (*Essays*, 49). Reading Ellison's retrospective account of his wavering artistic allegiances, one can't help thinking ahead to what he made of such psychological fissures while writing *Invisible Man*. For in his first novel he dared turn the narrative over to a character who would go from being unemployed and down-and-out (as Ellison had been in Dayton and New York) to up-and-coming Brotherhood spokesman for the Harlem District; aware, against his will, that

there were two of me: the old self that slept a few hours a night and dreamed sometimes of my grandfather and Bledsoe and Brockway and Mary, the self that flew without wings and plunged from great heights; and the new public self that spoke for the Brotherhood and was becoming so much more important than the other that I seemed to run a foot race against myself. (180)

Here is Ellison's (and belatedly, Invisible Man's) uncompromising, painful awareness of the fact that not only were others responsible for "Keep[ing] This Nigger Boy Running" (33), but that, "on the lower frequencies" (581), Invisible Man, too, was responsible for keeping himself running, and for refusing "to run the risk of his own humanity" (*Essays*, 221).

In Dayton, and later in New York, the musician and the writer in Ellison stayed in close enough cahoots for his artistic identity to emerge in an advantageous, ambidextrous equilibrium between music and literature. The young man who had dreamed of composing a symphony by the time he was twenty-six pledged allegiance to the novelists' tribe. He wound up writing *Invisible Man*, a novel whose orchestration shows symphonic traces as well as tragicomic blues tones and the beat and breaks of jazz.

Though a first novel, *Invisible Man* was an artistic culmination. In "Flying Home" and other short stories written between 1937 and the mid-1940s when, unbeknownst to him, Ellison was about to conceive *Invisible Man*, and in essays like "Richard Wright's Blues" (1945) and "Twentieth-Century Fiction and the Black Mask of Humanity" (1946), he seized and held fast to his theme of American identity. He began to imagine in sketchy, preliminary guises the *"uncreated features of his* [invisible character's] *face"* (354)—a character who, because of the irreducible individuality of his mind as well as his experience, would become an archetypal representative of the black American, and, *no less*, the modern American.

Certainly three of Ellison's stories from 1944, "King of the Bingo Game," "In a Strange Country," and "Flying Home," foreshadow *Invisible Man*. "King of the Bingo Game" owes something to the violence and surreal urban chaos of two Harlems—the actual city within a city and the internal, Eliotic "Unreal city"[11]—agitating Ellison's imagination. At the climax of "In a Strange

Country," set in Wales during World War II, the members of a Welsh singing club recognize the protagonist, Parker, whose eye has been blackened by his fellow Yank servicemen, as the true American. Seeing this "black Yank" as his white countrymen do not, they recognize that, as Ellison was to write years later, there is "something indisputably American about Negroes" (*Essays*, 583). Moreover, Parker's struggle for self-definition foreshadows Ellison's fully realized intention, expressed in his 1981 introduction to the thirtieth anniversary edition of *Invisible Man*, "to create a narrator who could think as well as act" and whose "capacity for conscious self-assertion" was "basic to his blundering quest for freedom" (xxi–xxii). Like Todd, the protagonist of "Flying Home," Parker anticipates Ellison's creation, in *Invisible Man*, of "a blues-toned laugher at wounds who included himself in his indictment of the human condition" (xviii), and who was therefore better able to resist conformity in all of its guises, and see and embrace the world in all its cockeyed diversity.

In that same 1981 introduction Ellison describes the pilot of "Flying Home" as a "man of two worlds," who "felt himself to be misperceived in both and thus was at ease in neither." Looking back at *Invisible Man* from a vantage point thirty years later, Ellison confesses that "I by no means was aware of his relationship to the invisible man, but clearly he possessed some of the symptoms" (xiv). The articulation of consciousness and character in these stories along with Ellison's conviction, expressed in 1946, that "[p]erhaps the most insidious and least understood form of segregation is that of the word" (*Essays*, 81), anticipates *Invisible Man*, with its freighted, frightening, fraternal "lower frequencies" of American democracy.

BEGUN serendipitously in a barn in Waitsfield, Vermont, in the summer of 1945, *Invisible Man* was seven hard years in the making. Unsurprisingly, considering "the desperate gamble involved in [his] becoming a novelist" (xi), Ellison was tense about its reception. "Good things are being said and publishers' hopes are high," he wrote his friend and fellow Tuskegean Albert Murray in February 1952, "but I'm playing it cool with my stomach pitching a bitch and my dream life most embarrassing." Perhaps alluding to experience he had mined and tried to transform into something precious in the novel, Ellison confessed that "I keep dreaming about Tuskegee and high school, all the scenes of test and judgment."[12] Thirty years later, he would write retrospectively (and more sedately) that "[m]y highest hope for the novel was that it would sell enough copies to prevent my publishers from losing on their investment and my editor from having wasted his time" (xxiii).

As it turned out, Fanny Ellison, her husband's alter ego on more than one occasion, had more prescient expectations. Writing Langston Hughes a couple of weeks before publication to thank him for his "very special generosity" during Ellison's seven years of struggle with *Invisible Man*, she speaks of feeling "these days as if we are about to be catapulted into something unknown—of which we are both hopeful and afraid." Prophetically, she spoke of being on "the threshold of this new and looming thing which awaits (whether only in our minds or really outside our closed door)."[13]

Fanny Ellison's intuition was on the mark. In April 1952 *Invisible Man* burst upon the American scene with the combustion of a prairie fire accelerating across the open country of Oklahoma and the Great Plains. The novel was reviewed everywhere that mattered by some of America's most formidable literary lions.[14] In *Commentary*, Saul Bellow, whose subsequent *The Adventures of Augie March* (1953) also was fired by a picaresque American vernacular idiom and energy, called *Invisible Man* "a brilliant individual victory" that mocked premature pronouncements of the novel's demise, "proving that a truly heroic quality can exist among our contemporaries."[15] Of course, there were objections and naysaying, most vituperatively from defenders of Black Nationalism and of the American Communist party, ideologies and organizations which took a beating in the novel. But, ironically, even the voices raised against *Invisible Man* were evidence that this extraordinary work possessed the staying power of a fire in a peat bog. It was a novel whose flame would smolder intensely and deeply, long after reviews, positive and negative, burned off the surface of literary consciousness.

Nevertheless, in 1955, after the hullabaloo of publicity from reviews, the bestseller list, and the National Book Award had worn off, Ellison offhandedly wondered if *Invisible Man* would be around in twenty years. "Don't you think it will be?" queried the editors of the *Paris Review*. "I doubt it," he replied. "It's not an important novel. I failed of eloquence," he added, failing to anticipate a contrary judgment by generations of readers. "If [the novel] does last, it will be simply because there are things going on in its depth that are of more permanent interest than on its surface" (*Essays*, 217). Again, musing on "the lower frequencies" of his art a decade or so after *Invisible Man* was named the "most distinguished single work" published in the last twenty years in a 1965 *Book Week* poll of almost two hundred eminent authors, editors, and critics, Ellison told John Hersey that "you just write for your own time, while trying to write in terms of the density of experience, *knowing perfectly well that life repeats itself. Even in this rapidly changing United States it repeats itself.*" Aware of the vicissitudes of literary longevity, Ellison paid homage to the mystery of art and the subterranean factor of luck: "If you're lucky, of course, if you splice into one of the deeper currents of life, then you have a chance of having your work last a little bit longer" (*Essays*, 806; my italics).

ELLISON'S own life—1914–1994—spanned most of the twentieth century. As a writer, he was blessed with an elastic sense of time. Always alert to the changes and shifting complexities of his own epoch, he kept one eye on the nineteenth century through the prism of the Civil War, while, fascinated by the accelerating impact of technology on human personality, he anticipated the twenty-first century with the other. "Novels achieve timelessness through time" (*Essays*, 111), he wrote, while acknowledging the distinction between the historian and the novelist. As Ellison saw it, the historian and the historical method operate "within the frame of chronology and time,"[16] but, for the novelist, the process

of consciousness is primary. Nevertheless, the making of self and
fiction is linked to the making of history or, at least, to the
development of historical consciousness. Both processes are continuous, and so it is that in *Invisible Man* Ellison aims for a temporal frequency expressive of the continuing present.

Form and time work contrapuntally in *Invisible Man*. Formally,
the prologue comes before the narrative. Chronologically, it
comes after. And in terms of consciousness the narrative proper
follows the prologue because, *as he writes*, Invisible Man's sense of
himself and his story deepens and changes. The conclusion or
epilogue follows the prologue and the narrative in the sense of
carrying forward both chronology and Invisible Man's consciousness in the verbal action of the present moment. Even if there
were no prologue or epilogue, the novel would open alluding
not to what has happened, but to what continues to happen. "It
goes a long way back, some twenty years," is the first sentence
of chapter 1, and Ellison concludes the paragraph with Invisible
Man's declaration "That I am nobody but myself. But first I had
to discover that I am an invisible man!" (15).

Invisible Man is, above all, a novel about the process of consciousness, about how the narrator's passage to selfhood is a passage through and beyond the versions of self prescribed by others.
As the writer he becomes, Invisible Man is able to see himself
from three angles; as he was, as his present self sees that former
self, and, finally, as the person he is in the present brooding on
the story he has just written. He rarely judges. Instead, he ob-
serves and reflects, recognizing that selfhood, like nationhood, is
a continuing process, and that identity is kept open and alert by
a fluid, tolerant, rigorous sensibility.

For Ellison, the relationship between history and imagination
is necessarily complex, and it is no surprise that there are some
principles scrupulously at work in *Invisible Man*. The prologue
makes chronology wholly a matter of consciousness, and it is not
until the beginning of the narrative that Ellison begins to clarify
the principle of his allusive-elusive, explicit-implicit approach to
historical time and chronology. When, for example, in chapter 1
Invisible Man speaks of "it" going back "some twenty years," he

signals that *this* is his time, and that it depends upon frequencies of consciousness. In the next breath he speaks of having been in the cards "about eighty-five years ago" (15)—a not so veiled reference to the end of the Civil War and the beginning of Reconstruction. Clearly, his intent is to link consciousness to a definite historical chronology, yet the reference is indefinite and inexplicit; the reader is left to particularize the context.

In the very first chapter when Invisible Man's grandfather claims to have been "a traitor all my born days, a spy in the enemy's country ever since I give up my gun back in the Reconstruction" (16), Ellison challenges his narrator (and the rest of us) to decode history. And that's not all. Thomas Jefferson, Abraham Lincoln, Frederick Douglass, Booker T. Washington, Marcus Garvey, the Civil War, Emancipation, Reconstruction, World War I, the Negro exodus from the rural South to the urban North, the Great Depression, the conformity of the postwar period: all are shifting, yet-to-be-comprehended images on Invisible Man's historical radar screen. Yet during his twenty-some years' experience in the narrative, he refers only obliquely to matters of history. Concerning the twenty years in question, presumably from *about* 1930 to *about* 1950, history is veiled and metaphoric. It's as if Ellison holds Invisible Man (and *Invisible Man*) accountable to the idea that history (matters of chronology and historicity) infiltrates narrative consciousness, and goads imagination to take responsibility for the word (and the world) in time present.

There is also a prescient dimension to Ellison's metaphoric use of time and history. "Literary truth amounts to prophecy," Albert Murray remembers him observing during the late 1940s and "[t]elling is not only a matter of retelling but also of foretelling."[17] Incubating in the surreal cauldron of *Invisible Man* are fictional children prophetic of history's trajectory in decades to come. The narrator's experience and reflections anticipate many accelerating changes in American life: the *Brown v. Board of Education* integration decision of 1954; the Civil Rights Movement of the 1950s and 1960s; the subsequent, turbulent, divisive emergence of Black Power; the fierce opposition to conformity of self and culture that came to pass in the sixties, an opposition which sometimes led to counterconformities; the transformation of the "woman question" into the far-reaching yet sometimes confusing Women's Rights Movement; ambiguous attempts to create a multiracial, multicultural Rainbow coalition in the 1980s; even hallucinatory descents into untrodden ways of consciousness under the spell of drugs; and, not least, extreme, contingent, postmodern conceptions of identity played out in the fractious arena of identity politics.

ON THE MATTER of form, too, Ellison broke new ground with *Invisible Man.* "Every serious novel," he would later contend in "Society, Morality and the Novel" (1957), "is, beyond its immediate thematic preoccupations, a discussion of the craft" (*Essays,* 695), and he brought to the writing of *Invisible Man* a theory and practice best described as the pragmatism of an American "thinker-tinker." In "Brave Words for a Startling Occasion," his 1953 speech accepting the National Book Award, Ellison acknowledged the "crisis in the American novel," and reflected that "though I was only vaguely aware of it, it was this growing crisis which shaped the writing of *Invisible Man.*" Referring to the "tight, well-made Jamesian novel" and the " 'hard-boiled' novel," two traditions dominant during the years he was composing *Invisible Man,* Ellison declared that neither fit his material, his sensibility, or his attitude toward American experience. The Jamesian novel would not do because for him "the diversity of American life with its extreme fluidity and openness seemed too vital and alive to be caught for more than the briefest instant" by a tradition "too concerned with 'good taste' and stable areas" of culture. Likewise, the "forms of the 'hard-boiled' novel" (presumably a reference to the Hemingway school and perhaps also to Richard Wright and other "proletarian" novelists), "with its dedication to physical violence, social cynicism and understatement" left little room for Ellisonian improvisation or riffs on the continuing theme of identity and change within society and individual personality. Neither did the latter tradition's "hard-boiled stance and its monosyllabic utterance," though "one of the shining achievements of twentieth-century American writing," heed the "rich

babel of idiomatic expression around me, a language full of imagery and gesture and rhetorical canniness . . . an alive language
swirling with over three hundred years of American living, a
mixture of the folk, the biblical, the scientific and the political"
(*Essays*, 151, 152).

On native grounds of form and language Ellison and his
protagonist-narrator, Invisible Man, confirm Henry Louis Gates's
proposition that "the fundamental structuring principle of Negro
art—improvisation—was also the essence of American democracy."[18] The novel's power to compel others to see *their* reality
through the prism of African-American experience follows from
Ellison's fidelity to "[a] whole unrecorded history" (471) whose
variable, vernacular richness equaled the range of spoken idioms
Shakespeare heard in the streets and inns of Elizabethan England.
Gates had it right when he called *Invisible Man* "an encyclopedia
of black culture," and declared that Ellison had delved "deeper
than anyone before him, into the fullest range of African-
American culture; music, art, folklore, storytelling traditions, signifying humor."[19] As has often been noted, Ellison brings symphonic form and the vernacular breaks, syncopation, and swing
of jazz and the tragicomic, lyrical tones of the blues to bear on
literary tradition. And he does so through the African-American
pattern of call-and-response, summoning every reader to respond
to Invisible Man's predicament. Always respecting the variety of
American traditions, even in Jim Crow days when "separate but
equal" and segregation were still the law of the land, Ellison
insisted that "we are yet one. On its profoundest level American
experience is of a whole" (*Essays*, 154).

Through his metaphor of invisibility Ellison created another
embodiment of what he called "*the* American theme" of identity
(*Essays*, 219), and made it uniquely his own. In an extraordinary
imaginative leap he hit upon a single word for the condition of
African Americans, Americans, and, for that matter, the human
individual in the twentieth century, and beyond. Invisibility "occurs because of a peculiar disposition of the eyes of those with
whom I come in contact. A matter of the construction of their
inner eyes" (3). It is a contingent condition, reductive of human

personality, yet, in an Ellisonian reversal, invisibility also invites those unseen or falsely seen to shape their own versions of identity and experience. African Americans, for instance, learned to use invisibility as an opening to put on a mask of subservience behind which they slipped the racial yoke and turned the joke back on white folks. As developed by Ellison, invisibility, though brilliantly expressive of racial blindness and bigotry, extends far beyond the dimension of race. As Albert Murray wrote in *The Omni-Americans*, Ellison's novel tells "a prototypical story about being not only a twentieth-century American but also a twentieth-century man, the Negro's obvious predicament symbolizing everybody's essential predicament."[20]

Which of us is truly visible to those who see us? And which of us truly sees ourselves, let alone knows who we are, especially as Americans? In Ellison's view "the nature of our society is such that we are prevented from knowing who we are." And *Invisible Man* is "a novel about innocence and human error, a struggle through illusion to reality" (*Essays*, 219). At the climax of the novel Invisible Man's embrace of "the beautiful absurdity of [his] American identity [and ours]" (559) leads him to affirm both the pursuit of freedom and what Ellison called the individual's "personal moral responsibility for democracy" (*Essays*, 151).

IN THE novel's last words Invisible Man asserts the indivisibility and interconnectedness of American experience. As a corollary, he acknowledges the frightening condition of the human heart, perhaps with special reference to the evasion of identity Ellison felt characteristic of the American experience. His call to readers fuses three of the novel's central points of reference: self, race, and nation. "And it is this which frightens me," Ellison's young African-American spokesman asserts before concluding with a profound rhetorical question which is also an ironic taunt: "Who knows but that, on the lower frequencies, I speak for you?" (581). His simultaneously beckoning and distancing, ironic and intimate words generalize the predicament of invisibility and identity from the novel's specific setting in the African-American experience. Of course universality follows only from the most exacting, utmost particularity. Without the rich, vivid, various explicitness of the black American experience, including the protest, which, despite assertions to the contrary by Irving Howe and other critics, Ellison consciously put into *Invisible Man*, the novel would have lacked universal appeal.

To the democratic vernacular tradition of Melville and Twain, whose *Moby-Dick* and *Huckleberry Finn* he considered "our two great nineteenth-century novels," Ellison brings the trajectory of a boomerang. After a "series of reversals" of which the "epilogue is the most final reversal of all," "the hero discovers what he had not discovered throughout the book: you have to make your own decisions; you have to think for yourself" (*Essays*, 223, 220, 221). The novel's episodes—it could have been titled *The Adventures of Invisible Man*—prepare for Invisible Man's emergence. Here, Ellison enacts his perspective, slowly arrived at, that "freedom was not only the recognition of necessity, it was the recognition of possibility" (499). For circumstances do not force Invisible Man to emerge; rather, he "comes up from underground because the act of writing and thinking necessitated it" (*Essays*, 220). It is "the mind, the *mind*" that spurs Invisible Man to reenter the world in which he had "been hurt to the point of abysmal pain, hurt to the point of invisibility" (579–80).

Riffing and signifying on Joyce, Ellison called *Invisible Man* "the portrait of the artist as a rabble-rouser" (*Essays*, 220). Like jazzmen engaged in musical "antagonistic co-operation" (*Essays*, 188), Ellison and his narrator lead the reader through a picaresque American labyrinth which, although rooted in time, manages to escape the limiting clutches of history, and, through timeliness, becomes timeless. And his narrator forges his passage from failed orator to desperate writer, "torturing myself to put it down" (579), by fidelity to an uproarious medley of American characters and incidents: a self-yielding, purging, transforming descent into layers of the past during which an old slave woman tells him prophetically that freedom "ain't nothing but knowing how to say what I got up in my head" (11); the battle royal with its symbolic enactment of racial rituals and taboos more powerful than any law; Jim Trueblood's outrageous, ambivalent yet manly tale of incest and the blues; the riotous confusion, chaos, and wisdom of the Golden Day where the vet dispenses a bitter, unheeded wisdom; blind Reverend Homer Barbee's minister-trickster's mix of history and myth in his Founder's Day sermon; college president Bledsoe's ruthless politics of self-interest and racial accommodation; Invisible Man's journey north and his astonished, unsettling witness of black and white passengers pressing against each other's flesh on a crowded subway; his encounters with folk characters like Peter Wheatstraw who combines traits of the devil's son-in-law with those of Saint Peter; old Lucius Brockway, a black man who carries the white man's burden in the boiler room of Liberty Paints; the yam vendor, whose luscious wares inspire Invisible Man's lovely pun, "I yam what I am" (266); the free papers of eighty-seven-year-old Primus Provo tossed in the street like chitterlings during his and his wife's eviction; Mary Rambo, everybody's mama, whose lesson—"I'm in New York, but New York ain't in me" (255)—goes long unlearned by Invisible Man; the Brotherhood's machinations and manipulations—"You were not hired to think" (469), Brother Jack declares at a moment of truth; Ras the Exhorter turned Ras the Destroyer's riotous ride, more suggestive of the Lone Ranger than of any African chief; Invisible Man's unlikely flight to freedom down a manhole to an underground lair, which, during his hibernation, he wires for sight and sound; and, finally, below ground, his brooding on the American "principle" as prologue to his emergence, like Jack the Bear in spring, into the "loud, clamoring, semi-visible world" (574).

In Ellison's vernacular labyrinth, in place of the classical Minotaur we encounter unforgettable walk-on characters like Mr. Norton, Brother Jack, Brothers Tobitt (Twobit) and Wrestrum (Restroom); Brother Tarp, whose leg iron tells the story of his courageous and cunning escape from the chain gang; the white woman in red who insists on "confusing the class struggle with the ass struggle" (418); Sybil: "You Were Raped by Santa Claus Surprise"; Dupre and Scofield, two black men, at last "capable of their own action" (548), who burn down their tenement; and old "Bad Air" (581), bad ass, black and blue, funky butt himself, Louis Armstrong.

Threading through the narrative's maze are the novel's principals: Invisible Man's grandfather with his deathbed acknowledgment and reversal of the infamous grandfather clause of black disenfranchisement; Tod Clifton, whose "head of Persian lamb's wool had never known a straightener" (366), and his despairing, ironic minstrel-borne "plunge outside history" (377); Ras the Exhorter's off-kilter but powerful and troubling Afrocentric rants; and, who could forget him, the Reverend B. P. Rinehart, the master of a "vast seething, hot world of fluidity" (498). ("[T]he P. is for 'Proteus', the B. for 'Bliss' " [*Essays*, 110], Ellison wrote slyly in 1957 just after naming one of the principals in his novel in progress, Bliss.) Issuing from the deep waters of imagination, Ellison's characters and episodes put fictional meat on the bones of his conviction that there are countless articulate but invisible men and women in the complex American underground who profess "a certain necessary faith in human possibility before the next unknown" (*Essays*, 764).

THROUGHOUT *Invisible Man* Ellison's quest is for eloquence. So is his narrator's. As a writer, Ellison becomes a citizen in the territory of the spoken word while his orator-narrator masters the craft of the written word. Because of the unfinished business of identity and American democracy, the act of eloquence is not simple. At times the pursuit of eloquence calls Invisible Man to think while he is acting and, at others, to act while he is thinking. Eloquence is bound up with persuasion, and, therefore, Invisible Man's eloquence turns on his ability to improvise in genuine response to a situation and an actual audience. In Ellison's view, previous generations of African Americans have been less inhibited working in the oral tradition and in jazz than with the written word. In a *tour de force* near the end of his 1981 introduction to *Invisible Man*, he identifies the improvisational forms and forces urging him to experiment with the novel:

> Having worked in barbershops where that form of oral art
> flourished, I knew that I could draw upon the rich culture of
> the folk tale as well as that of the novel, and that being un-
> certain of my skill I would have to improvise upon my ma-
> terials in the manner of a jazz musician putting a musical
> theme through a wild starburst of metamorphosis. (xxii–xxiii)

Who in America is not "uncertain of his skill"? And, as a test of
creative poise and energy, is not improvisation a potential act of
eloquence? Ellison's reliance on improvisation reinforces his (and
Invisible Man's) theme of identity, and the urgent appearance of
an invisible voice in protean form calls for techniques of performance. As a novelist whose sense of improvisational eloquence is
informed by jazz as well as speech, Ellison looks to the jam session
as inspiration for his collaboration with Invisible Man.

Ellison's writing on jazz provides a provocative clue to his intentions and highlights the significance of performance in his
novel. "In improvised jazz," he said in 1977, as if to describe *Invisible
Man*, "performance and creation can consist of a single complex
act."[21] And in a piece on Charlie Christian, Ellison calls jazz a
form of combat: "true jazz is an art of individual assertion *within
and against* the group" (*Essays*, 267; my italics). A jazz group achieves
its full effect only if the musicians test each other's skills and
through improvisation explore the full range of each member's
untapped potentialities:

> Each true jazz moment (as distinct from the uninspired com-
> mercial performance) springs from a contest in which each
> artist challenges all the rest; each solo flight, or improvisation,
> represents (like the successive canvases of a painter) a definition
> of his identity as individual, as member of the collectivity and
> as a link in the chain of tradition. (*Essays*, 267)

Intriguingly, throughout *Invisible Man*, the oral set pieces are per-
formed by a succession of characters who act like soloists sitting
in on a jam session. Likewise, Invisible Man's own "taunting, dis-

embodied voice" (xiv) challenges Ellison to try his skill to the uttermost. So, too, Ellison prods Invisible Man to tell of his efforts to be eloquent simultaneously in and against the grain of his different audiences, black and white, southern and northern— Americans all, optimistic or cynical, confused, knowing, or ignorant about the workings of individual and institutional power.

Through his experience as an orator and rabble-rouser, Invisible Man gradually discovers the combination of luck, will, and skill ("shit, grit, and mother-wit" [176]) and the coincidence of self and other required in order for "performance and creation" to merge in a "single, complex act." He is so thoroughly a performer that he defines and tests his identity on those occasions when he becomes a public voice. In his speeches Invisible Man's voice evolves into an instrument more and more keyed to the necessities, limits, and possibilities of call-and-response. To persuade others and move them to action, he relies mostly on techniques of improvisation. Sometimes after the jolt of reversal he learns that his words have consequences dramatically and drastically opposed to his intentions. Several times his speeches lead to unintended actions. For a long time he underestimates the dynamic mutual awareness required between performer and audience for an improvisation to become eloquent. Only gradually— too late for a career as an orator, in time for his new vocation as a writer—does he learn to challenge his audience's skills as well as his own.

Despite his failure to be eloquent with the spoken word, Invisible Man ends up committed to self-reliance as an optimist as well as an ironist. In the novel's paradox, he learns how and why the power of speech can be the power of action only when his potential eloquence falls on closed, Black Nationalist ears during the chaos of a race riot. In time he comes to see eloquence in much the same way as Ellison's literary ancestor and namesake, Ralph Waldo Emerson, understood it. "There is no orator who is not a hero," Emerson declared. "He is challenged and must answer all comers," and his words evoke Invisible Man's struggle for identity through improvisational oratory. But the comparison also breaks down because Invisible Man has been too obsessed with advancing to "the very top" (380) to embody Emerson's heroic conception of eloquence. "The orator's speech," wrote Emerson in the 1840s, when he and others relied on the power of the word to persuade Americans to live out their democratic ideals and free the slaves, "is not to be distinguished from action. *It is the electricity of action.*"[22] Nonetheless, Invisible Man attempts to make Emerson's metaphor work for him. He sends words out like so many charges intended to flow through his audience in a current of action. He misjudges the explosiveness of language and fails as an orator. But later, underground, solitary, and silent, he taps into a literal power line and drains off enough electricity from Monopolated Light and Power to provide light and heat while he generates the energy and symbolic action of his autobiography.

He tells us so in a voice at once brooding and insulting, peremptory and inquiring, in a prologue that is a self-conscious portrait of the artist as a frustrated, failed rabble-rouser. "Whoso would be a man, must be a nonconformist," Emerson wrote in "Self-Reliance."[23] In his prologue Invisible Man does not seek conversation; he can't—not yet. Truly responsive voices might talk back to him, question his motives, undermine his vulnerable, evolving self. Between the prologue and the epilogue, during the twenty-five chapters which tell the story of Invisible Man's life in the world, he fails of eloquence and political leadership because he is so out of touch, so much an isolated, solitary traveler, so much in the grip of illusion (his own and others'), and because he does not yet understand that he and his words are variables in the American equation of power and possibility. Only in the epilogue, having made ironic peace with his identity and his voice, is he ready for response, for conversation, ready to risk verbal acts of intimacy—ready, in short, for eloquence.

Nevertheless, even in his life as a failed orator, eloquence has a range of Emersonian meanings for Invisible Man. He sets out to be a leader whose speech is action, and not just symbolic action. Later, when he discovers the tricks of false eloquence and the requirements of genuine eloquence, he descends, and, during the interim it takes to write his memoirs, ascends to the symbolic action possible through literary form. His transformation from "an orator, a rabble-rouser," who succeeds or fails, lives or dies through eloquence, to a writer learning his craft in underground hibernation involves a reversal of form and identity. As an orator, at first freelance and later an employee of the Brotherhood committee, Invisible Man misses the subtle connections between speech and action, performer and audience. In the epilogue, however, he approaches the question of language and action as a writer able to affirm the very contradictions he resists during his quest for heroic eloquence. Becoming a writer, he transforms the power of the spoken word into the ironic, self-conscious, symbolic, potential action of his improvisational autobiography and Ralph Ellison's novel.

In the epilogue the act of writing is informing and anticipatory because it requires so much self-revelation. For this reason, Invisible Man's narrative of invisibility is an act of profound visibility. And the visibility of his words on the page hastens his decision to reenter the world. Moreover, he does not exaggerate the pleasures of the written word. "So why do I write," he asks, "torturing myself to put it down?" Because writing's disciplined contest with self moves his will closer to action. "Without the possibility of action, all knowledge comes to one labeled 'file and forget,' and I can neither file nor forget." Whereas throughout his time as an orator, he used acts of speech to restrain his audience's urge to action, now the act of writing commits him to action. The first consequence of his new vocation is a resolve "to at least *tell* a few people about it" (579)—about his journey to experience and knowledge, about the possibility and necessity of action. Like Emerson's *writing* on eloquence—like Douglass, Lincoln, and Twain, Emerson was a preeminent public speaker who infused the written with the spoken word—Invisible Man's epilogue calls his potential participatory audience to action.

At first, as was the case with his speeches, his initial intention differs from the effect of his words. "Here I've set out to throw my anger into the world's face, but now that I've tried to put it all down the old fascination with playing a role returns, and I'm drawn upward again" (579). But his written words turn him back to social action just as his spoken words so propelled his audiences. The act of writing sharpens his awareness of diversity and complexity, limitation and possibility, and at last leads him to accept the burden of love. "In order to get some of it down I *have* to love," he writes, ". . . so I approach it [life] through division. . . . I denounce and I defend and I hate and I love" (580). At the level of conjunction and relationship, *and* replaces *but* as the rhythm and meaning of his language signal reengagement with the world. Then, in his (and Ellison's) stunning boomerang of a last question—not as an orator or speaker, but as a writer— Invisible Man makes his most powerful and effective appeal for our participation. As readers, individuals more than members of any group, we are called to answer whether, and in what particulars, he does speak for us. And if he does, we are not let off the hook. "For when it comes to conscience," Ellison wrote while composing *Invisible Man*, "we know that in this world each of us, black and white alike, must become the keeper of his own" (*Essays*, 309).

ALTHOUGH Ellison never doubted the inviolability of his rights and responsibilities as an American, his outsider's minority status lent him an extra degree of perceptual and aesthetic freedom. As he would later tell (and no doubt embellish) the story of *Invisible Man*'s creation in his 1981 introduction, Invisible Man intruded on him in the doorway of a barn in Vermont during the summer of 1945 while he was "on sick leave from service in the merchant marine" (vii) and at work on a novel whose plot centered around the struggles of a downed Negro airman placed in charge of lower-ranking white American prisoners of war by a perverse Nazi commandant. "[T]hen," Ellison recounts:

> one afternoon, when my mind was still bent on its nutty wanderings, my fingers took over and typed what was to become the very first sentence of the present novel, "I am an invisible man"—an assertion so outrageous and unrelated to anything I was trying to write that I snatched it from the machine and was about to destroy it. But then, rereading it, I became intrigued. (*Essays*, 350)

Yet, looking to identify the intruding speaker, Ellison found "nothing more substantial than a taunting, disembodied voice" (xiv).

Like Dostoevski's narrator in *Notes from the Underground*, Invisible Man spoke up uninvited and unannounced. And although Ellison quickly sensed "that the voice of invisibility issued from deep within our complex American underground," he held back, "still inclined to close my ears and get on with my interrupted novel." But the voice spoke with such an insistent, syncopated, jazz rhythm that it lured Ellison to imagine "what kind of individual would speak in such accents." Consequently, for Ellison the problem of voice became the problem of character and form. To write a novel, he needed to *see* as well as hear this disturbingly familiar voice. And for Invisible Man to exhibit his skill in performance, Ellison needed to create an identity for the "taunting, disembodied voice." "I decided," he writes, "that it would be one who had been forged in the underground of American experience and yet managed to emerge less angry than ironic" (xviii).

Soon Ellison's inner eye saw as well as heard the spokesman for invisibility. He imagined him as "young, powerless (reflecting the difficulties of Negro leaders of the period) and ambitious for a role of leadership; a role at which he was doomed to fail" (xix) because he is so slow to grasp what Ellison elsewhere calls "the ambiguity of Negro leadership" in the United States (*Essays*, 76). Retrospectively, Ellison distinguished his task of composition from Invisible Man's act of performance. "*I* began to structure the movement of my plot, while *he* began to merge with my more specialized concerns with fictional form and with certain problems arising out of the pluralistic literary tradition from which I spring" (xix). And in his 1981 introduction Ellison was explicit about the new ground he wanted to break with the unsought, unwanted, unexpurgated voice of Invisible Man. Meditating on the state of the novel in the 1940s, he wondered "why most protagonists of Afro-American fiction (not to mention the black characters in fiction written by whites) were without intellectual depth" (xix). In any case, for Ellison the solution involved the literary idea and practice of democratic eloquence. "One of the ever present challenges facing the American novelist," he wrote, "was that of endowing his inarticulate characters, scenes and social processes with eloquence. For it is by such attempts that he fulfills his social responsibility as an American artist" (xix–xx). From his very first "taunting, disembodied" utterance, Invisible Man challenged Ellison to write in an urgent vernacular voice and in a form simultaneously novelistic and autobiographical— "*my* novel," as Ellison put it, "*his* memoir" (*Essays*, 537).

For Ralph Ellison, the struggle with form was always somehow bound up with America and the pursuit of the vernacular. Fascinated by the country, he affirmed its principles and possibilities in complicated, mysterious, tender, satiric, vulnerable, and multifaceted ways. Always, he refused to leave definition of the nation to others, especially those who tended to misunderstand or underestimate the richness, complexity, and possibility inherent in its vernacular culture and democratic ideals. In response to a characterization of him as a patriot writing *pro patria* as well as *pro domo*, Ellison responded in terms reminiscent of his riff on "the principle" in the epilogue to *Invisible Man*. "It ain't the theory which bothers me, it's the practice: My problem is to affirm while resisting."[24] That is exactly the complex patriot's creed Invisible Man embraces when, speculating on the meaning of his grandfather's riddle, he denounces the American founders' and framers' violations and compromises of freedom and equality, and in so doing propounds as riveting and profound a series of questions as have ever been posed about the American experiment. Weaving back and forth between all Americans and what Ellison would years later name as "that vanished tribe into which I was born: The American Negroes,"[25] Invisible Man asks whether "*we* had to take the responsibility for all of it, for the men as well as the principle, because *we* were the heirs who must use the principle because no other fitted our needs?" (574; my italics).

Paying homage to his grandfather, "an old slave" who "accepted his humanity just as he accepted the principle" (580), Invisible Man leapfrogs from his grandfather's words to extend the frame of reference to include African-American experience and the American reality since his grandfather's time:

Was it that we of all, we, most of all, had to affirm the principle, the plan in whose name we had been brutalized and sacrificed—not because we would always be weak nor because we were afraid or opportunistic, but because we were older than they, in the sense of what it took to live in the world with others and because they had exhausted in us, some—not much, but some—of the human greed and smallness, yes, and the fear and superstition that had kept them running. (574)

In an act of rhetorical transcendence, words that begin as a question modulate into a subtle, unequivocal affirmation of the moral ground occupied since slavery by American Negroes. It is verbal high ground soon to become a redemptive, national battlefield through the mix of love and politics expressed by the Reverend Martin Luther King, Jr., and his brothers and sisters in the nonviolent, passive resistance of the Civil Rights Movement.

Indeed, as an African-American moral historian of the imagination, perhaps Ellison influenced the direction of the American novel in somewhat the same way that the Civil Rights Movement of the 1950s and 1960s altered the character of American society—affirming while resisting. Even more intriguing, to paraphrase Invisible Man's last lingering question, who knows but that Ellison's articulate, artistic, and intellectual passion informed the struggles of the fifties and sixties? Who knows but that *Invisible Man* was a symbolic verbal catalyst for some of the energy and achievement of the Civil Rights Movement and, in our time, for the continuing pursuit of the riddle of American identity? Back in 1952, who would have imagined that in little more than a decade the president of the United States would utter the words, "And we shall overcome," as Ellison's friend, Lyndon Johnson, was to do before a joint session of Congress in 1965?

Certainly, few values were more unfashionable among American intellectuals during the writing of *Invisible Man* in the late 1940s and early 1950s than patriotism. For expressions of that attitude and tone, Ellison looked to the nineteenth century and discovered a sense of national complexity and responsibility, an experimental attitude appropriate to the metamorphoses taking place in *Invisible Man*. There, he declared, "the moral imperatives of American life that are implicit in the Declaration of Independence, the Constitution and the Bill of Rights were a part of both the individual consciousness and the conscience of those writers who created what we consider our classic novels—Hawthorne, Melville, James, and Twain." Yet Ellison could not simply return to the aesthetic terms of the nineteenth-century novel because, for him, "more than any other literary form, the novel is obsessed with the impact of change upon personality"—and with the impact of social change upon literary form. Nor could he merely innovate because for him form for form's sake renounces the novelist's responsibility to society. "[T]he novel," he insisted throughout the 1950s and beyond, "is bound up with the notion of nationhood" (*Essays*, 702, 698, 696).

When Ellison contends that "the interests of art and democracy converge," and when he connects "the development of conscious, articulate citizens" to "the creation of conscious, articulate characters" (xx), he makes indivisible the evolving twin experiments of democracy and the novel. In his view the novelist's individual imagination responds to the flux of American life. According to Ellison's conceit, Invisible Man already existed as a very real, if unimagined and as yet unrealized, version of the "conscious, articulate citizen." He did not so much invent him as create "the uncreated features of his face" (354) from the grain of his voice. Similar voices, yet to be identified and given palpable form in American fiction, excite Ellison's faith in the possibility of expressing that special American fluidity of class, culture, and personality. These variations on a volatile, seething, largely unheard, and ignored eloquence spur Invisible Man's call for collaboration with his American kinfolk at the narrative's end.

And there's another reversal involved in Ellison's form. When Invisible Man writes *you*, he refers to Ellison, as well as to potential and actual readers; after all, Ellison was his narrator's initial audience in the green shade of Vermont. In some sense narrator and writer each set the other free. Like the reader, Ellison the writer is enjoined to respond to Invisible Man's call, and his author's act of response builds on an earlier idea about the protean nature of fiction. Back in 1946, when *Invisible Man* was little more than a glint in his eye, Ellison had argued for the novel's potential as an artistic form and social action catalytic to the continuing experiment of American democracy. "Once introduced into society," he wrote, "the work of art begins to pulsate with those meanings, emotions, ideas brought to it by its audience, and over which the artist has but limited control" (*Essays*, 94). In his meditation masquerading as an introduction three decades after his composing the novel, Ellison strengthened his novelist's bill of rights with an amendment: before and after his act of composition, the writer is also audience to his work, and has the same rights and responsibilities as the rest of us—equally and individually, in the name of eloquence and action, in the name of democratic citizenship.

ELLISON'S ELEGANT, often eloquent meditations on *Invisible Man* in the decades since publication by no means tell the whole story of the novel's evolution. As the book came to seem a colossus astride the temple of post–World War II American fiction, and critics of all persuasions grappled with its subtly modulated defiance of labels and categories, Ellison did not hesitate to suggest that his intentions were well thought out, complex, and ambitious. Clearly, this was the case. At the same time his sometimes oracular comments created something of a myth—a tall tale too—out of the making of the novel as if he had been responding to the call of a mysterious, invisible American muse. But although classics tend to become fixed and frozen with the passage of time, a classic novel was not always classic, let alone finished. In the case of *Invisible Man*, it would be a mistake to think that the novel came into coherent existence in Ellison's mind at the moment in July 1945 when his fingers typed its magical first sentence.

The novel's long, slow gestation is a palpable fact. And, thanks to Mrs. Ellison's determination to follow her husband's wishes, it is now possible to discern how Ellison's early conception of his eponymous character and novel changed and developed during seven years of composition. Nonetheless, I must confess that Ellison's commentaries on his novel *after* its publication, though enormously rich and perceptive, threw me a little off the scent of young Br'er Ellison back in his sanctuary of the brier patch. I do not mean to suggest that Ellison led me off the track. If I had perked up my hound dog's ears, I would have caught the caveat in his myth-making introduction. "It would be misleading," he wrote, "to leave the impression that all of the process of writing was so solemn. For in fact there was a great deal of fun along the way" (xxii).

Ellison was right.

He was right about having had fun at the same time that his "sole preoccupation was with transforming a seemingly intractable body of material into a work of art."[26] Before going through his papers, I never would have guessed that they would provide enough clues for someone to write a biography tracking the making of *Invisible Man*. (How could I or any Ellison scholar have known, for example, that a 1944 Guggenheim application—unsuccessful by the way—would turn up the information that in 1937 young Ralph Ellison worked briefly for the A. C. Horn Paint Company as a laboratory technician? "KEEP AMERICA PURE WITH LIBERTY PAINTS," indeed!)

Ellison's "Working Notes," typescripts, and letters from 1945 to 1951 make *visible* his creation of the now-classic *Invisible Man*. Of these documents, the "Working Notes," undated but probably composed between 1946 and 1948, show tellingly how the "fledgling novelist's" (xv) early intentions evolved into quite a different sense of protagonist and plot during his protracted act of composition. Part I of the "Working Notes" consists of Ellison's initial deliberations on the nature and causes of invisibility. In the beginning he rooted his metaphor in what he named "two basic facts of American life." He noted the tension between that "racial conditioning which often makes the white American interpret cultural, physical, or psychological differences as signs of racial inferiority," and what he called "the great formlessness of Negro life wherein all values are in flux." "Except for its upper levels," he continued, "where it tends to merge with the American whole, Negro life is a world psychologically apart." He went on to speculate that "out of this conflict personalities of extreme complexity emerge" (*Essays*, 343)—perhaps an early recognition of Invisible Man's recurring, reflexive ambivalence.

At times in the penultimate draft Ellison's language is less complex, its lyricism less powerfully realized than in the finished novel. For example, what Ellison, with an appreciative nod to Kenneth Burke, would later delight in calling a satiric allusion to the "grandfather clause"[27] from Invisible Man's post–battle royal nightmare—"Keep This Nigger-Boy Running"—is here the less charged, less subtle "Keep this nigger running." In terms of the novel's eventual plot, Ellison's "Notes" closely anticipate Invisible Man's picaresque quest after a "false [American] dream" in the southern chapters of the finished novel. But in its projection of his enforced journey north and his adventures in New York up until the end of the book, Ellison's outline diverges dramatically from what he was to revise, refine, and publish in April 1952. As plotted and written in the early drafts, some of the northern episodes occasionally tend to be rough, flat, not yet maturely crafted. Likewise, the northern story of Invisible Man sketched out in part II of the "Working Notes" is more pedestrian and banal, less fully imagined than the modern urban labyrinth Ellison had invented for his character by the end of his labors.[28]

A few examples: instead of plotting Invisible Man's electro-shock therapy as a consequence of his violent encounter with Lucius Brockway at Liberty Paints, in the "Working Notes" Ellison plans to have the narrator develop stomach trouble due to "the inadequacy of the heavy Southern foods which he has continued to eat." After the trauma of his hospital experience, Invisible Man "selects a diet more in keeping with the tensions of the city." Boarding with a family of black newcomers to the North rather than the unforgettable Mary Rambo, Ellison's early incarnation of Invisible Man enters, like his successor, into rabble-rousing left-wing politics. However, he joins the "left wingers," not from hope or belief or ambition "but because they ask him during his moment of deepest despair." Unlike the character's eventual exasperation over white women who confuse the "class struggle with the ass struggle," Ellison's initial version of Invisible Man responds to his exclusion from the Brotherhood's inner councils "by making as many conquests with the women as he can." Discovered by one married woman's husband, he feels humiliated when, "in the interests of politics," the man ignores the adultery. According to Ellison, Invisible Man "would have regarded a divorce proceeding as evidence of his visibility" ("Working Notes," 4, 5, 6, 7).

Far from seeing his character as someone who is "incapable of a love affair," the perspective he would sharply defend in a 1955 interview with the *Paris Review,* in the "Working Notes" and early drafts Ellison invents a character named Louise whom he intends as "a woman of great charm" and "the one person in the organization whom [Invisible Man] can believe accepts him as a human being." Smitten by her as a woman, Invisible Man also imagines Louise as "a symbol of democracy, freedom and fertility." Compare Sybil in the finished novel whom, in a crass, comic exchange of value, he regards as a source of information. Finally, although Ellison chose early on to depict a race riot and Invisible Man's subsequent descent into a coal cellar, according to the "Working Notes" he did not intend to conclude the narrative with Invisible Man in hibernation about to come above ground. Rather, his original plan was to end *Invisible Man* with the narrator's emergence as a minister who, like the Reverend B. P. Rinehart in the completed novel, uses "technological gadgets as a means of exploiting the congregation—recording machines, P.A. systems, electric guitars, swing orchestras are all introduced" into a storefront Negro church ("Working Notes," 7, 9). Most telling of all, neither in the "Working Notes" nor in the full, unrevised typescript are there indications of the discrete prologue and epilogue with which Ellison was so brilliantly to frame Invisible Man's memoir and his novel.

In a June 1951 letter to Albert Murray, Ellison tells of cutting some 200 pages from the manuscript. This is not all he did. During this revision, he shaped an explicit prologue and epilogue out of the still somewhat disorganized raw material with which he had opened and closed the 781-page previous draft. Before he and his editor, Albert Erskine, began to "read aloud" the 612-page final typescript as catalyst for the final edit, the novel had all but become the masterpiece we know as *Invisible Man.* Yet even in these last stages of revision, Ellison is charmingly sly about his work. "Erskine's having a time deciding what kind of novel it is, and I can't help him," he writes Murray. "For me," he adds, "it's just a big fat ole Negro lie, meant to be told during cotton-picking time over a water bucket full of corn, with a dipper passing back and forth at a good fast clip so that no one, not even the narrator himself, will realize how utterly preposterous the lie actually is." With a skeptical nod anticipating reviewers and critics, he adds: "I just hope someone points out that aspect of it."[29] (To the end of his life Ellison had an abiding frustration with many critics' tendency to take the novel with such high seriousness that they missed the humor everywhere informing *Invisible Man*'s tragicomic vision. As far back as 1955, put off by humorless misreadings implicit in some of the questions posed by the editors of the *Paris Review*, he asked in some exasperation: "Look, didn't you find the book at all *funny*?" [*Essays*, 221].)

IN THE END because Ralph Waldo Ellison's notes and manuscripts are open to scholars and the public in his library of choice, the Library of Congress, readers will be able to marvel at, puzzle over, and try to account for the genius of improvisation and revision that enabled him to take the leap from a good and promising novel to the great one he published as *Invisible Man*. To take the most obvious, and perhaps the most telling example, consider the novel's famous last paragraphs:

> "Ah," I can hear you say, "so it was all a build-up to bore us with his buggy jiving. He only wanted us to listen to him rave!" *But only partially true:* Being invisible and without substance, a disembodied voice *as it were*, what else *could* I do? What else but try to tell you what *was really happening* when your eyes were looking through? *And it is this which frightens me:*
> Who knows but that, *on the lower frequencies*, I speak for you?
> (581; passages in italics added in Ellison's final typescript)

Between the penultimate and the final draft Ellison replaces *can* with *could* and *went on* with *happening*. He adds Invisible Man's powerful confessional words: "And it is this which frightens me[.]" Finally, he restores *on the lower frequencies*, the haunting phrase of the novel's last line, earlier typed in, then crossed out in his hand. Where, we might ask, would Ellison's character, his novel, and his readers be without the conditional verb, a little rhetorical engine that *could*, propelling author, narrator, and readers alike toward the uncertainties, the dangers, and the possibilities of the future? Where would we be without Ellison's move to the improvisational word "happening"? and without Invisible Man's offhand, ironic acknowledgment that the likes of him speaking for his readers is frightening confirmation of the "beautiful absurdity" of American identity?

And, my God, where would we be without "the lower frequencies" on which all the tones and tunes of American personality are heard stubbornly fighting through the static in the culture? Who knows that Ralph Ellison and his Invisible Man speak for us? Who knows indeed? Perhaps it is best to leave things up in the air and let the question reverberate. Maybe it's enough to say that Ralph Waldo Ellison realized his dream of a novel "fashioned as a raft of hope, perception and entertainment that might help keep us afloat as we [try] to negotiate the snags and whirlpools that mark our nation's vacillating course toward and away from the democratic ideal" (xx–xxi). And who knows but that, as Walt Whitman hoped would be the case for "poets, orators, singers, musicians to come,"[30] we, in our strivings to realize "the principle," may not only answer Ellison but justify him?

Notes

1. Ellison in conversation with the author, February 19, 1994, and on earlier occasions.

2. Ralph Ellison, *The Collected Essays of Ralph Ellison*, ed. John F. Callahan (New York: Random House, 1995), 195–96, 197, 208. Subsequent quotations from the *Collected Essays* will be cited in the text in parentheses as *Essays*.

3. Ralph Ellison, *Invisible Man* (New York: Random House, 1952), 10.

Subsequent quotations from *Invisible Man* will be to the second Vintage international edition, 1995, and will be cited in the text in parentheses.

4. Ellison to Morteza Sprague, May 19, 1994, Ellison Papers, Library of Congress, Container 68.

5. Ellison quoted by Jervis Anderson in "Profiles: Going to the Territory," *New Yorker,* November 22, 1976, 94.

6. Ralph Ellison, *Flying Home and Other Stories,* ed. John F. Callahan (New York: Random House, 1996), 17.

7. Ellison quoted by Anderson in "Profiles," 70.

8. Ellison's inscription in the author's copy of *Going to the Territory.*

9. Ellison letter of October 17, 1937, addressed to "Dear Folks," Ellison Papers, Library of Congress, Container 15.

10. Ellison to Richard Wright, October 27, 1937, Ellison Papers, Library of Congress, Container 76.

11. T. S. Eliot, "The Waste Land," *The Waste Land and Other Poems* (New York: Harcourt Brace Jovanovich, 1934), 37.

12. Ellison letter to Albert Murray, February 4, 1952, in *Trading Twelves: The Selected Letters of Ralph Ellison and Albert Murray,* ed. John F. Callahan and Albert Murray (New York: Random House, 2000), 31.

13. Fanny Ellison to Langston Hughes, April 2, 1952, Ellison Papers, Library of Congress, Container 51.

14. Saul Bellow in *Commentary* (June 1952), Richard Chase in *Kenyon Review* (Autumn 1952), Irving Howe in *Nation* (10 May 1952), R. W. B. Lewis in *Hudson Review* (Spring 1953), Alain Locke in *Phylon* (March 1953), Wright Morris in the *New York Times Book Review* (13 April 1952), Orville Prescott in the *New York Times* (16 April 1952), Delmore Schwartz in *Partisan Review* (May–June 1952), and Anthony West in the *New Yorker* (31 May 1952), among others.

15. Saul Bellow, *Commentary* 13, no. 6 (June 1952): 608.

16. Ralph Ellison, "The Uses of History in Fiction," *Conversations with Ralph Ellison,* ed. Maryemma Graham and Amritjit Singh (Oxford: University Press of Mississippi, 1995), 153.

17. Ellison quoted by Albert Murray, preface to *Trading Twelves,* xxi.

18. Henry Louis Gates, Jr., "The Last Sublime Riffs of a Literary Jazzman," *Time,* June 28, 1999, 66.

19. Gates quoted by Malcolm Jones in "Visible Once Again," *Newsweek,* May 24, 1999, 69.

20. Albert Murray, *The Omni-Americans* (New York: Da Capo Press, 1970), 167.

21. Ellison quoted in "The Essential Ellison," in *Conversations with Ralph Ellison*, 344.

22. Ralph Waldo Emerson, *The Journals and Miscellaneous Notebooks of Ralph Waldo Emerson*, vol. IX, 1843–1847, ed. Ralph H. Orth and Alfred Ferguson (Cambridge, Mass.: Belknap Press, 1971), 425–26; my italics.

23. Emerson, *The Selected Writings of Ralph Waldo Emerson*, ed. Brooks Atkinson (New York: Random House, 1992), 134.

24. Ellison letter to the author, August 12, 1983, Ellison Papers, Library of Congress, Container 40.

25. Ellison's dedication to *Juneteenth*, ed. John F. Callahan (New York: Random House, 1999), vii.

26. Ellison's statement to the National Book Award Foundation, 1959.

27. Kenneth Burke, "Ralph Ellison's Trueblooded *Bildungsroman*," in *Speaking for You: The Vision of Ralph Ellison*, ed. Kimberly W. Benston (Washington, D.C.: Howard University Press, 1987), 351.

28. Part II of Ellison's "Working Notes for Invisible Man" is found in the Ellison Papers, Library of Congress, Container 147. Subsequent references to part II of the "Working Notes" will be cited in the text in parentheses as "Working Notes."

29. Ellison letter to Murray, June 6, 1951, in *Trading Twelves*, 21.

30. Walt Whitman, "Poets to Come," *The Portable Walt Whitman*, ed. Mark Van Doren (New York: Penguin Books, 1977), 182.

Part III

♦　♦　♦

EPILOGUE

On Initiation Rites and Power

A Lecture at West Point

RALPH ELLISON

◆　◆　◆

I HARDLY KNOW WHERE to start. It should be with an apology, I suppose, because as I recall how annoyed I was that I had been assigned certain novels as a student, I find it extremely ironic that now my own is being passed along to you, and that I'm responsible.

I suppose the best way to get into this is to just be autobiographical, since you are concerned with my novel, because the novel isn't autobiographical in an immediate sense, and it'll be necessary to enlarge upon what Colonel Capps had to say about my background in order to spell out to you just why, and in what way, it is *not* autobiographical. I was, as he said, a music major at Tuskegee, but I was also one who read a lot, who lived in books as well as in the sound of music. At Tuskegee I found myself reading *The Waste Land*, and for the first time I was caught up in a piece of poetry which moved me but which I couldn't reduce to a logical system. I didn't know quite why it was working on me, but being close to the jazz experience—that is, the culture of jazz—I had a sense that some of the same sensibility was being expressed in poetry.

Now, the jazz musician, the jazz soloist, is anything if not eclectic. He knows his rhythms; he knows the tradition of his form, so to speak, and he can draw upon an endless pattern of sounds which he recombines on the spur of the moment into a meaningful musical experience, if he's successful. I had a sense that all of these references of Eliot's, all of this snatching of phrases from the German, French, Sanskrit, and so on, were attuned to that type of American cultural expressiveness which one got in jazz and which one still gets in good jazz. But between feeling intuitively that this was what was going on and being able to confirm it, there was quite a gap. Fortunately Mr. Eliot appended to the original edition of *The Waste Land* a long body of footnotes, and I began to get the books out of the library and read them. That really was a beginning of my literary education, and actually it was the beginning of my transformation (or shall we say, metamorphosis) from a would-be composer into some sort of novelist.

The thing about reading these footnotes, and about reading criticism generally, was that they made me as conscious of the elements and traditions which went into the creation of literature as I had long been taught to be conscious of the various elements which went into musical styles and traditions. One had to be conscious; there was no question about this. And for me there was another powerful motive for being conscious, and that was because I came out of my particular southwestern background (as an Oklahoma native), with parents who were from Georgia and South Carolina, and my racial background, which naturally at that moment seemed to separate me from the conscious intentions of American literature. Because in far too many instances, I seemed to appear, or my *people* seemed to appear, only in the less meaningful writing. I felt that I would have to make some sort of closer identification with the tradition of American literature, if only by way of finding out why I was *not* there—or better, by way of finding how I could use that very powerful literary tradition by way of making literature my own, and by way of using literature as a means of clarifying the peculiar and particular experience out of which I came.

Well, to jump ahead. During the war, I was a sea cook in the Merchant Marine. During the winter of 1944, I had received a fellowship from the Rosenwald Foundation in order to write a novel. It was about $1,500, as I recall, and I had an interesting story to tell. Some of my friends were in the Air Force. That is, friends from college, friends from Tuskegee, had become pilots, combat pilots, and so on, and during that moment of the war, they were very active. But preceding that activity, there had been a lot of political agitation on the part of Negro Americans because we were not being allowed to fight, and those young men, those friends of mine, those pilots, were being withheld from duty, and that concerned me very much. So I thought that my first novel would have such a plot as this (you can see that I was very naïve at the time), and I set my story in Nazi Germany in a prisoner-of-war camp. (This is where it becomes complicated.) The ranking officer of the camp was to have been a black pilot who had beneath him in rank a whole slew of white pilots. The devil of the piece was to have been a Machiavellian Nazi prison-camp official who spent his time pitting the black American against the white Americans. I was trying to write this, by the way, as our ship traveled in convoys of some eighty ships and flattops, and so on, taking supplies over during what was actually the battle of the Bulge. Well, we got into Le Havre during the night, and it was so "hot" around there that that novel went up in sweat, and it's very good that it did.

However, one good effect of that experience was that I not only forgot the novel, but I experienced such tension under these conditions of combat that when I got back to stateside the physicians told me that I should take a rest. I took that rest by going up to Waitsfield, Vermont, where a friend had an old farmhouse on which a few years before I'd helped make some repairs. While there, I tried to write, not knowing quite what I would write but quite aware that my original idea would not work. One afternoon I wrote some words while sitting in an old barn looking out on the mountain, and these words were "I am an invisible man." I didn't know quite what they meant, and I didn't know where the idea came from, but the moment I started to abandon them, I thought: "Well, maybe I should try to discover exactly what it was that lay behind the statement. What type of man would make that type of statement, would conceive of himself in such terms? What lay behind him?" After that, it was a process of trying to make a meaningful story out of what seemed to be a rather wild notion.

Now, having said that, let me say something else. By this time I was very much aware of the elements which went into fiction. I wanted to tell a story. I felt that there was a great deal about the nature of American experience which was not understood by most Americans. I felt also that the diversity of the total experience rendered much of it mysterious. And I felt that because so much of it which appeared unrelated was actually most intimately intertwined, it needed exploring. In fact, I believed that unless we continually explored the network of complex relationships which bind us together, we would continue being the victims of various inadequate conceptions of ourselves, both as individuals and as citizens of a nation of diverse peoples.

For after all, American diversity is not simply a matter of race, region, or religion. It is a product of the complex intermixing of all these categories. For even our racial experience is diverse within itself, and rendered more complex by the special relationships existing between my own group and the various regions in which Negro Americans find their existence—and by reason of the varied relationships shared by blacks and whites of various social backgrounds. These, in turn, are shaped by the politics, social history, and climatic conditions existing within the country's various political and geographical regions. Nor is this all, for there is also the abiding conditions of mystery generated by the diversity of cultural and political experience within the Negro American group itself. For despite the overall unity of black experience in the United States, the experience of southern blacks differs in certain important aspects, both cultural and political, from that of northern blacks; that of southwestern blacks differs from that of *southeastern* blacks, while the experience of those who grew up in Nevada, California, and Washington state differs in many ways from all of these, if only for having developed during a later period of historical time. Such factors make for important variations in experience, and make necessary the exercise of conscious thought even on the part of those black Americans who would "know the Negro." So that was one part of it.

The other part of it was the fact that I was reading certain books. I was reading Lord Raglan's *The Hero*, which has to do with tradition, myth, and drama. As you will recall, Lord Raglan was concerned with the manner in which myth became involved with the histories of living persons, became incorporated into their personal legends. I seem to recall that he noted about twenty-two aspects of character and experience that were attributed to most heroes, and he discovered that historical figures—figures from religion, military heroes, and so on—all tended to embody clusterings of these same mythological aspects, and this whether they were figures of fact or fantasy. Thus it would seem that the human imagination finds it necessary to take exemplary people—charismatic personalities, cultural heroes—and enlarge upon them. The myth-making tendency of the human imagination enlarges such figures by adding to their specific histories and characters accomplishments and characteristics attributed to heroes in the past. So that it isn't unusual in the mythology of mankind to find figures said to have been conceived (that's the proper term, any way you see it) through virgins. Nor is it unusual to find leaders who were exposed to death as infants only to have their lives saved by humble people, and who then through various accidents attending the mysterious process of life, and through their own heroic assertions in the drama of social intercourse, became great leaders. According to various accounts, a number of them married their mothers and killed their fathers, but if that still happens today, we no longer talk about it.

Anyway, I was concerned with such findings of Lord Raglan's as a literary matter, but at the same time I was concerned with the nature of leadership, and thus with the nature of the hero, precisely because during the historical moment when I was working out the concept of *Invisible Man* my people were involved in a terrific quarrel with the federal government over our not being allowed to participate in the war as combat personnel in the armed forces on an equal basis, and because we were not even being allowed to work in the war industries on an equal basis with other Americans. This quarrel led to my concern with the nature of Negro leadership, from a different and nonliterary direction. I was very much involved with the question of just why our Negro leadership was never able to enforce its will. Just what was there about the structure of American society that prevented Negroes from throwing up effective leaders? Thus it was no accident that the young man in my book turned out to be hungry and thirsty to prove to himself that he could be an effective leader.

On the other hand, as I began working seriously on the novel, I had to become aware of something else. I had to learn that in such a large and diverse country, with such a complex social structure, a writer was called upon to conceive some sort of model which would represent that great diversity, to account for all these people and for the various types of social manners found within various levels of the social hierarchy, a structure of symbolic actions which could depict the various relationships between groups and classes of people. He was called upon to conceive some way of getting that complexity into his work in the form of symbolic action and metaphor. In other words, I discovered, for myself at least, that it was necessary to work out some imaginative integration of the total American experience and discover through the work of the imagination some way of moving a young black boy from a particular area and level of the society as close as he could be "realistically" moved to sources of political power. This was not only necessary in order to structure a meaningful story, but also necessary if I were to relate myself to certain important and abiding themes which were present—or which I *thought* were present—in the best of American literature.

So now I was working in the exalted form of the novel, or trying to work in that literary form, and as I read back in American literature and tried very seriously to identify myself with the concerns of the classical American novelists, it began to seem to

me that American fiction had played a special role in the development of the American nation. It had had to play that role, had
had to concern itself with certain uniquely American tasks even
in those instances in which it was not read (or not widely read,
and I think here of *Moby-Dick*). This was for a number of reasons.
One, as a literary form the novel has been primarily concerned
with charting changes within society and with changes in personality as affected by society. Two, the novel developed during
a period which marked the breakup of traditional societies, of
kingship, and so on, and by the 1850s, the great masters of the
nineteenth century had fashioned it into a most sensitive and
brilliant form for revealing new possibilities of human freedom,
for depicting the effects of new technologies upon personality,
and for charting the effects wrought by new horizons of expectation upon the total society.

Of course this type of change (and its consequences) has been
an enduring part of the American experience, and it has always
concerned our great American novelists. But even if we concern
ourselves with those American writers who were *not* novelists, we
see that the makers of American literature were also concerned
with spelling out that which was peculiarly *American* about the
American experience—this, because we did not start here. We
started in Europe. We made a formulation here of what we were
and who we were, and what we expected to be, and we wrote it
down in the documents of the Bill of Rights, the Constitution,
the Declaration of Independence. I mean that we put ourselves
on the books as to what we were and would become, and we
were stuck with it. And we were stuck with it partially through
a process of deification which came through the spilling of blood
and through the sacrifices which were endured by those people
who set up this great institution here on this particular point of
the Hudson River.

By the 1830s, or the late 1820s, several things were being demanded. One, that we have a literature which would be specifically American, which would tell us who we were and how we
varied, and how we had grown, and where we were going—and
most importantly, how the ideals for which we had sacrificed so

many young men were being made manifest within the society. There's no point in spelling this out too much. I think the very walls around here speak to you about such matters. But for novelists, for poets, for men of literature, something else obtains. You find that American artists are stuck with two major problems which come upon them through the very tradition itself, through the very history of this society. One is the necessity of being conscious of how one section of the country differs from the others, of how one section of the society differs from the others. And, two, we have upon our shoulders the burden of conscientiousness. I think in your motto you say "duty," a sense of duty, a sense of responsibility, for the health of the society. You might not like the society; invariably we Americans (as Henry James pointed out, and as others have pointed out) have an ongoing quarrel with our lives, with the condition that we live in. At our best moments we have a quarrel with how we treat or fail to treat and extend the better part, the better aspects, the better values, the good things of the society, to all levels of the society.

So I found, as I worked with my little book—trying to build my fiction, trying to structure my "lie" in such a way as would reveal a certain amount of truth—that I, too, had to be aware of how we were faring and where we were going. I realized, fighting for a certain orientation (as a Negro writer who was taking on the burden of the American literary tradition), that I would have to master, or at least make myself familiar with, the major motives of American literature, *even when written by people who philosophically would reject me as a member of the American community.* How would I do that without being, in my own eyes, something of a slave, something less than a man?

It occurred to me that what some of my "teachers" were calling "white literature" was not really *white* at all. Because as I began to grasp the background of the American experience in literature, I began to realize that even before we were a nation, people of African background had been influencing the nature of the American language, that amalgam of English English, of French and German and Dutch and American Indian dialects, and so on. All of this, long before we were a nation, had already begun to form;

American culture began to evolve before we were a nation. And some of the people contributing to it were my own people. This was very necessary for my sense of morale and for my sense of the complexity of the society, or at least of the *culture* of the society, because there's no doubt that we were slaves; both of my grandparents on both sides were slaves. (It hasn't been that long ago.) Nevertheless, part of the music of the language, part of the folklore which informed our conscious American literature, came through the interaction of the slave and the white man, and particularly so in the South. Mr. Faulkner, who has lectured here, had no doubt about that, and some of our most meaningful insights into the experience of the South have come through his understanding of that complex relationship. And because he did understand, he has been responsible for some of the real glories of our literature.

But here again I had to find out where *I* stood. In reading, I came across Whitman, who was writing very early (I think 1848 or so), finding in the American Negro dialect—the dialect of the slaves, as he put it—the possibility of an American grand opera, the possibility of a new music in speech. Of course this possibility was there. As I looked around the South, and as I looked around New York, and as I noticed the white crewmen on my ships at sea, I began to say, "Well, now, something here that you are saying, a certain rhythm in your speech, I first heard in my particular community. A certain way that you swing your shoulders, or your legs when you walk (especially southern boys), you've gotten a lot of that from us." Maybe we got it from them, too. The point, of course, was to be relieved of the burden of interpreting all of life and its works in racial terms. Therefore, for me personally it was a matter of saying, "I am going to learn how to write a novel; I will not ignore the racial dimensions at all, but I will try to put them into a human perspective."

So my little book starts out by taking a young man who has an infinite capacity for making mistakes (and being a fool, I think), and who—in his *passion* for leadership, in his *passion* to prove himself within the limitations of a segregated society— blunders from one point to another until he finally realizes that

Americans society cannot define the role of the individual, or at least not that of the *responsible* individual. For it is our fate as Americans to achieve that sense of self-consciousness through our own efforts.

The story itself, after all this pretentious-sounding talk, was a rather simple story: about how a young man grew up, and about the conditions which it was necessary for him to confront as he grew up. Because our society was divided, at that time, into one region which was primarily agricultural, and another which was primarily industrial (or more dominated by technological considerations than by the seasons), the narrator of the story goes through a number of rites of passage, rites of initiation. And as I tried to tell my story, I began looking at the meaning of certain rituals. No one had ever told me that the battle royal was a rite, but I came to see that it was. It was a rite which could be used to project certain racial divisions into the society and reinforce the idea of white racial superiority. On the other hand, as a literary person trying to make up stories out of recognizable experience, and as one who was reading a lot about myth and the function of myth and ritual in literature, it was necessary that I see the battle royal situation as something more than a group of white men having sadistic fun with a group of Negro boys. Indeed, I would have to see it for what it was beyond the question of the racial identities of the actors involved: a ritual through which important social values were projected and reinforced.

To use it artistically, I would have to step away from it a bit so that I could see it even more objectively and identify it as one of those rites of initiation called "fool's errands." When I played hooky for the first time and went to water the elephants of the Ringling Brothers Circus in Oklahoma City, I was sent on such an errand. The circus workers told me to go to a certain man and bring back the "tent wrench." Well, after I had exhausted myself traveling around the circus grounds I learned that there was no such thing as a "tent wrench." But I also discovered that this practical joke was not necessarily a racial device, because I observed it being used on other people as well. In hotels new workers ("squares") are also sent on such errands. In fact, many of the rites of passage, those rituals of growing up, found in our society are in the form of such comic, practical-joking affairs which we ignore in the belief that they possess no deeper significance. Yet it is precisely in their being regarded as unimportant that they take on importance. For in them we ritualize and dramatize attitudes which contradict and often embarrass the sacred values which we proclaim through our solemn ceremonies and rituals of nationhood.

Because while great institutions glamorize themselves through rituals, Americans tend to require supplementary rites that are more modest, more down-to-earth, and often it is these which serve to give dramatic form to our warmest emotions.

But in our democratic society, which is relatively unstructured as societies go (and unstructured precisely because we had to play it by ear as we got it going), such patterns are not widely recognized for what they are, or at least they are not codified, and thus are not institutionalized. Primitive societies are much more efficient and consistent; they are much more concerned with guiding the young through each stage of their social development, while we leave much of this to chance, perhaps as part of the responsibility of freedom. Today we are having great trouble with young people of educated, sheltered, and financially well-heeled backgrounds who despite their social advantages have not been taught that they shouldn't play with heroin. I suppose that in a tightly structured and well-run society we would develop a special rite of initiation for dealing with the availability of drugs. Or at least we would teach such individuals how to take heroin without destroying themselves. Now that, of course, is a joke, meant to demonstrate that it is indeed possible to make comedy of such serious matters.

But not only have we failed to provide rites of passage adequate to the wide variety and broad freedom of experience available to the young, we also have failed to find ways of keeping up with much of what happens in our society. Therefore one of the things I wanted to do was to provide the reader with—or discover for myself—some sense of how *ideas* moved from one level of society to another. This was important for me to understand because, after all, when I was at Tuskegee, I couldn't go to a theater without being discriminated against, and in Birmingham, I couldn't move around the streets without worrying about Bull Conner (oh yes, Bull Conner was there even then). Yet under such conditions of social deprivation, I was reading T. S. Eliot. I was concerned with the nature of power; I was trying to find a way of relating myself to the major concerns of our society.

So I felt that if we had a real sociology of ideas in this country, we would have a means of judging the impact of ideas as they came to rest within the diverse groups which make up American society. We would have a way of predicting, of saying, "Well, now, out there in such and such a section there are persons whose background, experience, and temperament have made them receptive to certain notions, concepts, and ideas. Therefore we can expect one or two such people to go about making something out of them, or at least making a try." But our failure to deal with the mystery of our diversity makes such generalized predictions impossible. Relying upon race, class, and religion as guides, we underestimate the impact of ideas and the power of lifestyles and fashion to upset custom and tradition. Some of our intellectuals even forget that Negroes are not just influenced by ideas that are within the public domain, and that such is the nature of freedom in our democracy that even shoeshine boys may criticize the lifestyles and tastes of great entrepreneurs, which shoeshine boys are given to doing, and that they can also go to the library and read books which entrepreneurs *should* be reading but usually don't. So that our failure to grasp the mysterious possibilities generated by our unity within diversity and our freedom within unfreedom can lead to great confusion. It also leads to the loss of potential talent, just as our failure to recognize the social implications of cultural developments taking place on the lower levels of the social hierarchy can lead to social confrontations which can rock society to its very summit.

But however we choose to look at it, there exist pressures which compel the individual American (and the individual black American) to respond to the intellectual, emotional, political currents and pressures which affect the entire society—just as the stock market or fads in clothing or automobiles affect the lives of sharecroppers, whether or not the sharecropper knows that the stock market exists. Thus I tried as best I could to weave a tale which would at least be cognizant of these many interconnecting possibilities of relationships.

About the story, there is little I can say, unless you ask me questions. Because I haven't read it in a good while and I don't think I'll ever read it again in its entirety. It was too difficult for me to get rid of, and not because I didn't write fast and wasn't inventive. But there was something else. There was a sense of isolation, a feeling that for all my concern to make it so, it couldn't possibly have much value to others. I thought that I would be lucky if I sold between five hundred and a thousand copies. I was very much concerned with the link between the scenes and the actions—that is, the problem of continuity—because I realized even then that it was not enough for me simply to be angry, or simply to present horrendous events or ironic events. I would have to do what every novelist does: tell my tale and make it believable, at least for as long as it engaged the attention of the reader. I could not violate the reader's sense of reality, his sense of the way things were done, at least on the surface. My task would be to give him the surface and then try to take him into the internalities, take him below the level of racial structuring and down into those areas where we are simply men and women, human beings living on this blue orb, and not always living so well. This is what I tried to do.

The rest became a confrontation with technical problems: How do you "tell" it, how do you put it together? How do you foreshadow events, how do you handle irony? How do you fabricate that artifact which we call a novel? How, in other words, do you tell a story that will not embarrass the great literature which has gone before you? How do you join the club? How do you justify the assertion of arrogance that is necessary to a man who would take a society which everyone "knows" and abstract certain of its elements in an effort to reduce it to a symbolic form which will simultaneously involve the reader's sense of life while giving expression to his, the writer's, own most deeply held values? I refer to the arrogance of the artist, and a very necessary arrogance it is. For I think it is one reason why the novel is important. I think its presence aids the novelist in attacking the enormity of his task, which is that of reducing a society, through the agency of mere words, to manageable proportions—to proportions which will reflect *one* man's vision, *one* man's sense of the human condition, and in such volatile and eloquent ways that each rhythm, each nuance of character and mood, indeed each punctuation mark, becomes expressive of *his* sense of life and, by extension, that of the reader.

Related to this is a discovery which I think most American writers must make before they are through: it is that each writer has a triple responsibility: to himself, to his immediate group, and to his region. He must convey each of these aspects of his own experience as he knows them. And he must convey them not only in such a manner that members of his own particular group can become aware of what has been happening in the flux and flow, the thunder and lightning of daily living, but in such a way that individuals belonging to groups and regions of the society other than his own can have his report on what was happening in his particular area of the society, to his particular type of people, and at that particular point in time. All this so that readers may become more conscious of themselves and more aware of the complex unity and diversity not only of Americans but of all human life. Here the movement is from the specifically imagined individuals to the group, to the nation, and, it is hoped, to the universal.

This becomes a function of creating and broadening our consciousness of American character, of creating and recreating the American experience. It is a serious function because it is our good-and-bad fortune that we Americans exist at our best only when we are conscious of who we are and where we are going. In this process our traditions and national ideals move and function like a firm ground bass, like the deep tones of your marvelous organ there in the chapel, repeating themselves continually while new melodies and obbligatos sound high above. In literature this is the process by which the values, ideals, assumptions, and memories of unique individuals and groups reach out across the divisions wrought by our national diversity and touch us all. It is one of the important social functions of literature because our traditions and values must be constantly revivified; again and again they must be given further extension.

Having said all that, I'll now say this, and then I'm finished. My first principal in grade school was a Professor Whittaker. He was a man of erect military bearing, although he must have been fairly old when I knew him. He had white hair, clear, piercing blue eyes, and a goatee. Professor Whittaker was a West Point man. Somehow he did not graduate; he must have been here during the Reconstruction. Nevertheless he was a marvelous man who managed to get something of West Point into those little Negro grade and high schools in which he taught when I was growing up. I suppose I mention him because I never thought I would ever come to West Point. But I also mention him by way of suggesting that even here there are extensions and dimensions of which we are not aware and of which we *should* be aware. Because in these United States the crucial question is not one of having a perfect society, or even of having at any given moment a viable society. Rather, it is to keep struggling, to keep trying to reduce to consciousness all of the complex experience which ceaselessly unfolds within this great nation. Certainly that was all I was trying to do with my book, and if I managed even a little of that, then I think the effort worthwhile.

I'm pleased to have been here, and if you have questions, I would be very pleased to answer them, or to try.

Mr. Ellison, I have a question about the whole point of the novel, the purpose of the novel: whether you considered it to be just about the Negro relationship with the white man, or, as your last statement indicates, perhaps to everyone. Part of the class thought it was merely the Negro-white man relationship, and then that perhaps toward the end as an afterthought you sort of put in the everyone idea, because it didn't seem to tie in. And the other part of the class thought you tried to show the relationship between all minority groups and majority groups.

Yes, thank you. Well, I conceived of the novel as an account, on the specific level, of a young Negro American's experience. But I hoped at the same time to write so well that anyone who shared everything except his racial identity could identify with it, because there was never any question in my mind that Negroes were human, and thus being human, their experience became metaphors for the experiences of other people. I thought, further, that if literature has any general function within any society and throughout the world, it must serve at its best as a study in comparative humanity. The role of the writer, from that point of view, is to structure fiction which will allow a universal identification, while at the same time not violating the specificity of the particular experience and the particular character.

Mr. Ellison, concerning your novel, I'd like to know exactly to what extent some of the scenes in it happened to you.

Well, let's put it this way, they all happened to me—in my head. Now, remember that you're dealing with the imagination and not with sociology. For instance, one summer when I was still in high school, I was looking for a job (and it gets to be 105 to 110 in the shade in Oklahoma City; it used to, anyway). I met a friend and he said, "If you go up to Broadway between Ninth and Tenth, there's a car lot there, and the man wants someone to help him around the car lot." He said, "I couldn't take it because I got another job, but you better hurry up there." So I turned on the fan, as they say, and by the time I arrived, I was pretty moist. There was this white man sitting out under a tree; and I said, "Sir, I understand you need someone to work here"; and he said, "Yes, sit over here on this box." (He had a crate with a cushion on it.) He said, "Sit over here and tell me about yourself." He began to ask me about my grades, about my parents, and so on, and I began to feel that I was getting the job. Then, at the moment when I was most certain that the job was mine, I felt a charge of electricity in my tail, and I went up into the air and I came down.

The whole thing, again, was a ritual of initiation—a practical joke—wherein a Ford coil, a coil from the old Model T Ford, had been hooked up to a battery. That was the whole point. Of course there was no job, but what my imagination has made of that is the scene in the battle royal where the boys struggle for money on the rug. Am I giving away secrets, do you believe that? But that's how the imagination worked and conjured up the scene.

Sir, your novel has been called "episodic," with the theme of white domination over the Negro with the express purpose of keeping the Negro in his primitive state; however, in your lecture here I've gotten a different idea, that it was merely a thematic representation of the American Negro and his drive to excel. The question I have is, was it your purpose to show this white domination over the Negro and of keeping the Negro in his primitive state, or was it merely to show in an episodic manner this drive to excel?

Certainly I didn't start . . . Do you want to repeat that? The answer is *No*.

Mr. Ellison, would you consider yourself a pioneer in writing about the Negro relationship to white groups; if not, who else besides Eliot influenced your writing?

Well, in the first place, I don't think that it's a function of writing to tell the reader what it feels like to be a Negro, as critics say over and over again about plays and novels and poems by black writers. I think the function of literature, all literature that's worthy of the name, is to remind us of our common humanity and the cost of that humanity. This is the abiding theme of great literature, and all serious writers find themselves drawn to spelling it out in all its detail and multiplicity. As for people who influenced me, the first two novels that I read when I arrived in New York were given to me by Langston Hughes (whom I had just met), who wanted me to deliver them to a friend of his, but he told me that I could keep them long enough to read them. Those two novels were André Malraux's *Man's Fate* and *The Days of Wrath*. I have certainly been influenced by Dostoevski. The first words of *Invisible Man*, the rhythm of the prologue, go right back to *Notes from Underground*. I have been influenced by Malraux, by Melville, by Faulkner, by almost all of the good ones.

Sir, in your story it seems as if the narrator was struggling with disillusionment, and then toward the end of the story, when you cut it off, you don't explain simply whether he found himself or not. Was it your intention to start the narrator off being disillusioned and follow him throughout this complete cycle to where he did find himself, or were we simply supposed to draw our own conclusion?

Well, as I recall the book . . . the narrator managed to avoid a basic confrontation through most of the story, and when he finally makes that confrontation, he's freed. Part of his problem was not that of being dominated by white society. Part of his problem was a refusal to demand that people see him for what he wanted to be. Always he was accommodating. If you notice, he was being told who he was, he was given several names throughout the novel, and always he accepted them 'til the very last. As to the last part of your question, I would say that yes, he comes out of the ground, and this can be seen when you realize that although *Invisible Man* is *my* novel, it is really *his* memoir. I'm a little prejudiced here, because I do feel that books represent socially useful acts—so we can say that. I left it at this point because I assumed that by finally taking the initial step of trying to sum up the meaning of his experience, he had moved to another stage of his development.

Mr. Ellison, the Brotherhood has the characteristics of a socialistic society; I was wondering what this had to do with the Communist tradition that in such an organization the depressed can find a way out of their condition.

Here again is a fabrication, just as the machines in the paint factory are fabrications. They never existed. They're images there for certain literary reasons. I did not want to describe an existing socialist or communist or Marxist political group, primarily because it would have allowed the reader to escape confronting certain political patterns, patterns which still exist and of which our two major political parties are guilty in their relationships to

Negro Americans. But what I wanted to do at the same time was to touch upon certain techniques of struggle, of political struggle, certain concepts of equality and political possibility which were very much present in our society. I think we have absorbed them into the larger parties in many ways.

I also wanted to draw upon the tinge of subversion which some of these parties tend to represent. So the Brotherhood was this, but at the same time, in the life of the narrator it was one more obstacle that he had to confront in order to arrive at some viable assessment of his own possibilities as a political leader. Remember, Tod Clifton is killed, and there's a funeral, an improvisation, an improvised funeral, that he (the narrator) leads, which polarizes feelings around what the narrator thought would have been to the Brotherhood's best interest. But they were no longer interested because they were not concerned basically with Negro freedom, but with effecting their own ends. It was very important for this young man, this would-be leader, to understand that all political parties are basically concerned with power and with maintaining power, not with humanitarian issues in the raw and abstract state.

Mr. Ellison, could you tell us the significance of the scene near the end of Invisible Man *when the narrator falls down the open manhole? Two white men are chasing him, and after he falls in the manhole he tells them, "I still have you in this brief case."*

Well, I'll try. What I wanted him to be saying was that these men who were hurling racial epithets down at him were not aware that *their* fate was in this bag that he carried—this bag that he had hauled around with his various identifications, his diploma, with Clifton's doll, with Tarp's slavery-chain link, and so on—and that this contained a very important part of their history and of their lives. I was also trying to say that you will have to become aware of the connection between what is in this bag (which is his fate, that is, the fate of the Negro narrator) and the racist whites who look upon him mainly as a buffoon and a victim.

Sir, there seem to be a few comparisons between your novel and Native Son *in that both protagonists seem to be fighting a losing cause through the entire novel, and the fact that they both have ties with the Communist party and confront white women. Was this by coincidence or were you influenced by Mr. Wright as you wrote the novel?*

I knew Mr. Wright from about the second day he arrived in New York in 1937; I guess it was June. I wrote my first book review for him, a published book review, and I wrote my first short story for a magazine which he was in New York to edit. It was a Harlem-based magazine, a literary magazine, and not a communist organ. But he accepted my story, and then the magazine failed. But by 1940 I was not showing Mr. Wright any of my writing because by that time I understood that our sensibilities were quite different, and what I was hoping to achieve in fiction was something quite different from what he wanted to achieve.

As to what you call communism and the white women, I would say that anyone writing from the Negro American point of view with any sort of thoroughness would certainly have had to write about the potential meaning and effects of the relationship between black women and white men and black men and white women, because this became an essence, and a great part of the society was controlled by the taboos built around the fear of the white woman and the black man getting together. Great political power and, to some extent, great military ardor were brewed from this socio-sexual polarization. Hence any novelist who is going to write from the Negro background would certainly have to deal with these particular aspects of our society. They're unpleasant, and yet it is in the unpleasant, in that which is charged with emotion, with fears, with irrationality, that we find great potential for transforming attitudes. So I tried to face them with a certain forthrightness, to treat them ironically, because they are really destructive in a kind of comic and absurd way— except when we consider the old rite of lynching. But you'll notice that I did not drag in that particular aspect of the sociology of interracial relationships.

Sir, was it your intention to include any protest in the novel?

Protest in the novel?

Yes, sir, would you call it a protest novel?

I would think that implicitly the novel protests. It protests the agonies of growing up. It protests the problem of trying to find a way into a complex, intricately structured society in a way which would allow this particular man to behave in a manly way, and which would allow him to seize some instrumentalities of political power. That is where the protest is on one level. On another level, the protest lies in my trying to make a story out of these elements without falling into the clichés which have marked and marred most fiction about American Negroes—that is, to write literature instead of political protest. Beyond this, I would say simply that in the very act of trying to create something, there is implicit a protest against the way things are, a protest against man's vulnerability before the larger forces of society and the universe. We make fiction out of that kind of protest, which is similar to the kind of protest that is involved in your mastering your bodies; your mastering the physical, intellectual, military, and legal disciplines which you are here for. All of this is a protest, a human protest against that which *is*, against the raw and unformed way that we come into the world. I don't think you have to demand any more protest than that. I think, on the other hand, if the novelist tells the truth, if he writes eloquently and depicts believable human beings and believable human situations, then he has done more than simply protest. I think that his task is to present the human, to make it eloquent, and to provide some sense of transcendence over the given—that is, to make his protest meaningful, significant, and eloquent of human value.

Selected Bibliography

Books

Baker, Houston A., Jr. *Blues, Ideology, and Afro-American Literature: A Vernacular Theory.* Chicago, Ill.: University of Chicago Press, 1984.

————. *The Journey Back: Issues in Black Literature and Criticism.* Chicago, Ill.: University of Chicago Press, 1980.

————. *Singers at Daybreak.* Washington, D.C.: Howard University Press, 1974.

Baumbach, Jonathan. *The Landscape of Nightmare: Studies in the Contemporary American Novel.* New York: New York University Press, 1965.

Bone, Robert. *The Negro Novel in America.* New Haven, Conn.: Yale University Press, 1965.

Bryant, Jerry. *The Open Decision: The Contemporary American Novel and Its Intellectual Background.* New York: Free Press, 1969.

Busby, Mark. *Ralph Ellison.* Boston: Twayne, 1991.

Butler, Robert. "The City as Psychological Frontier in Ralph Ellison's *Invisible Man* and Charles Johnson's *Faith and the Good Thing*" in *The City in African-American Literature,* edited by Yoshinobu Hakutani and

Robert Butler. Teaneck, N.J.: Fairleigh Dickinson University Press, 1995.

Byerman, Keith. *Fingering the Jagged Grain: Tradition and Form in Recent Black Fiction.* Athens: University of Georgia Press, 1985.

Callahan, John F. *In the African-American Grain: Call-and-Response in Twentieth Century Black Fiction.* Urbana: University of Illinois Press, 2001.

Cooke, Michael G. *Afro-American Literature in the Twentieth-Century: The Achievement of Literacy.* New Haven, Conn.: Yale University Press, 1984.

Dietze, Rudolf F. *Ralph Ellison: The Genesis of an Artist.* Nuremberg: Verlag Hans Carl, 1982.

Dixon, Melvin. *Ride Out the Wilderness.* Urbana: University of Illinois Press, 1987.

Eichelberger, Julia. *Prophets of Recognition.* Baton Rouge: Louisiana State University Press, 1999.

Gates, Henry Louis, Jr. *Figures in Black: Words, Signs, and the Racial Self.* New York: Oxford University Press, 1989.

———. *The Signifying Monkey: A Theory of African-American literary Criticism.* New York: Oxford University Press, 1988.

Gray, Valerie Bonita. Invisible Man's *Literary Heritage:* Benito Cereno and Moby Dick. Amsterdam: Editions Rodopi, 1978.

Harper, Michael S., and Robert B. Stepto, eds. *Chant of Saints: A Gathering of Afro-American Literature, Art, and Scholarship.* Urbana: University of Illinois Press, 1979.

Hassan, Ihab. *Radical Innocence: Studies in the Contemporary American Novel.* Princeton, N.J.: Princeton University Press, 1961.

Jackson, Lawrence. *Ralph Ellison: Emergence of Genius.* New York: Wiley, 2002.

Klein, Marcus. *After Alienation.* Cleveland, Ohio: World, 1965.

Klotman, Phyllis Rauch. *Another Man Gone: The Black Runner in Contemporary Afro-American Fiction.* Port Washington, N.Y.: Kennikat Press, 1977.

List, Robert N. *Dedalus in Harlem: The Joyce-Ellison Connection.* Washington, D.C.: University Press of America, 1982.

Margolies, Edward. *Native Sons: A Critical Study of Twentieth-Century Negro American Authors.* Philadelphia: Lippincott, 1968.

McSweeney, Kerry. Invisible Man: *A Student's Companion to the Novel.* Boston: Twayne, 1988.

Murray, Albert. *The Omni-Americans.* New York: Outerbridge and Dienstfrey, 1970.

Nadel, Alan. *Invisible Criticism: Ralph Ellison and the American Canon.* Iowa City: University of Iowa Press, 1988.

O'Meally, Robert G. *The Craft of Ralph Ellison.* Cambridge, Mass.: Harvard University Press, 1980.

Petesch, Donald A. *A Spy in the Enemy's Country.* Iowa City: University of Iowa Press, 1989.

Porter, Horace A. *Jazz Country: Ralph Ellison in America.* Iowa City: University of Iowa Press, 2001.

Rogers, Lawrence R. *Canaan Bound: The African-American Great Migration Novel.* Urbana: University of Illinois Press, 1997.

Rosenblatt, Roger. *Black Fiction.* Cambridge, Mass.: Harvard University Press, 1974.

Scruggs, Charles. *Sweet Home: Invisible Cities in the Afro-American Novel.* Baltimore, Md.: Johns Hopkins University Press, 1993.

Smith Valelrie. *Self-Discovery and Authority in Afro-American Literature.* Cambridge, Mass.: Harvard University Press, 1987.

Stepto, Robert B. *From behind the Veil: A Study of Afro-American Narrative.* Urbana: University of Illinois Press, 1979.

Sundquist, Eric I. *Cultural Contexts for* Invisible Man. Boston: St. Martin's, 1995.

Tanner, Tony. *City of Words.* New York: Harper and Row, 1971.

Warren, Kenneth W. *So Black and Blue: Ralph Ellison and the Occasioin of Criticism.* Chicago: University of Chicago Press, 2003.

Watts, Jerry Gafio. *Heroism and the Black Intellectual: Ralph Ellison, Politics, and Afro-American Intellectual Life.* Chapel Hill: University of North Carolina Press, 1994.

Collections of Essays

Benston, Kimberly W., ed. *Speaking for You: The Vision of Ralph Ellison.* Washington, D.C.: Howard University Press, 1987.

Bloom, Harold, ed. *Ralph Ellison.* New York: Chelsea House, 1986.

Gottesman, Ronald, ed. *The Merrill Studies in* Invisible Man. Columbus, Ohio: Merrill, 1971.

Hersey, John, ed. *Ralph Ellison: A Collection of Critical Essays.* Englewood Cliffs, N.J.: Prentice Hall, 1970.

Morel, Lucas, ed. *Ralph Ellison and the Raft of Hope.* Lexington: University Press of Kentucky, 2004.

O'Meally, Robert G., ed. *New Essays on* Invisible Man. New York: Cambridge University Press, 1988.

Parr, Susan Resneck, and Pancho Savery, eds. *Approaches to Teaching Ellison's* Invisible Man. New York: MLA, 1989.

Reilly, John M., ed. *Twentieth Century Interpretations of* Invisible Man. Englewood Cliffs, N.J.: Prentice Hall, 1970.

Tracy, Steven, ed. *A Historical Guide to Ralph Ellison.* New York: Oxford University Press, 2004.

Trimmer, Joseph, ed. *A Casebook on Ralph Ellison's* Invisible Man. New York: Crowell, 1972.

Special Issues of Journals

Carleton Miscellany 18 (1980).

CLA Journal 13 (March 1970).

Delta (Montpellier, France) 18 (1984).

Oklahoma City University Law Review 26 (Fall 2001).

Articles and Book Chapters

Abrams, Robert E. "The Ambiguities of Dreaming in Ellison's *Invisible Man*." *American Literature* 49, no. 4 (Jan. 1978): 592–603.

Anderson, Jervis. "Going to the Territory." *New Yorker* 22 (Nov. 22, 1976): 55–108.

Baker, Houston. "To Move without Moving: An Analysis of Creativity and Commerce in Ralph Ellison's Trueblood Episode." *PMLA* 98, no. 5 (Oct. 1983): 828–45.

Benston, Kimberly. "Ellison, Baraka, and the Faces of Tradition." *Boundary* 2, no. 6 (Winter 1978): 333–54.

Blake, Susan L. "Ritual and Rationalization: Black Folklore in the Works of Ralph Ellison." *PMLA* 94, no. 2 (1979): 121–36.

Bone, Robert. "Ralph Ellison and the Uses of the Imagination." In *Anger and Beyond,* edited by Herbert Hill, 86–111. New York: Harper and Row, 1966.

Bucco, Martin. "Ellison's Invisible West." *Western American Literature* 10 (1975): 237–38.

Butler, Robert. "Dante's *Inferno* and Ellison's *Invisible Man*: A Study in Literary Continuity." *CLA Journal* 28, no. 1 (Sept. 1984): 54–77.

———. "Down from Slavery: Invisible Man's Descent into the City and the Discovery of Self." *American Studies* 29, no. 2 (Fall 1988): 57–67.

―――. "Patterns of Movement in Ellison's Invisible Man." *American Studies* 31, no. 1 (Spring 1980): 5–21.

―――. "The Plunge into Pure Duration: Bergsonian Visions of Time in Ellison's Invisible Man." *CLA Journal* 33, no.3 (Mar. 1990), 260–279.

Callahan, John F. "The Historical Frequencies of Ralph Waldo Ellison, *Chant of Saints,* edited by Michael S. Harper and Robert B. Stepto, 33–52 (Urbana: University of Illinois Press, 1979).

―――. "Democracy and the Pursuit of Narrative." *Carleton Miscellany* 18, no. 3 (Winter 1980): 51–69.

―――. "Riffing and Paradigm-Building: The Anomaly of Tradition and Innovation in *Invisible Man* and *The Structure of Scientific Revolutions.*" *Callaloo* 10, no. 2 (Winter 1987): 91–102.

―――. "Frequencies of Eloquence: The Performance of Composition of *Invisible Man.*" In *New Essays on Invisible Man,* edited by Robert O'Meally, 54–94 (New York: Cambridge University Press, 1988).

Chisholm, Lawrence. "Signifying Everything." *Yale Review.* 54, no. 3 (Spring 1965): 450–54.

Christian, Barbara. "Ralph Ellison: Critical Study." In *Black Expression,* edited by Addison Gayle, Jr., 353–65 (New York: Weybright and Tally, 1969).

Clipper, Lawrence J. "Folklore and Mythic Elements in *Invisible Man.*" *CLA Journal* 13 (Mar. 1979): 239–54.

Cohn, Deborah. "To See or Not to See: Invisibility, Clairvoyance, and Re-visions of History in *Invisible Man* and *La casa de les espiritus.*" *Comparative Literature Studies* 33, no. 4 (1996): 372–95.

Collier, Eugenia. "The Nightmare Truth of an Invisible Man." *Black World* 20 (Dec. 1970): 12–19.

Deutsch, Leonard. "Ralph Waldo Ellison and Ralph Waldo Emerson: A Shared Moral Vision." *CLA Journal* 16 (1972): 160–73.

Dietze, Rudolf F. "Ralph Ellison and the Literary Tradition." In *History and Tradition in African-American Culture.* Edited by Gunter H. Lenz, 18–29. Frankfurt: Campus Verlag, 1984.

Dixon, Melvin. "O Mary Rambo, Don't You Weep." *Carleton Miscellany* 78 (Winter 1980): 98–104.

Dupre, F. W. "On *Invisible Man.*" *Book Week* (*Washington Post*) 26 (Sept. 1965): 4.

Fass, Barbara. "Rejection of Paternalism: Hawthorne's 'My Kinsman, Major Molineux' and Ellison's *Invisible Man.*" *CLA Journal* 14 (1971): 317–23.

Frank, Joseph. "Ralph Ellison and a Literary 'Ancestor': Dostoevski." *New Criterion* 2 (Sept. 1983): 140–52.

Goede, William. "On Lower Frequencies: The Buried Men in Wright and Ellison." *Modern Fiction Studies* 15 (1969): 483–501.

Gordon, Gerald T. "Rhetorical Strategies in Ralph Ellison's *Invisible Man.*" *Rocky Mountain Review* 41 (1987): 199–209.

Harding, James M. "Adorno, Ellison, and the Critique of Jazz." *Cultural Critique* 31 (Fall 1995): 129–58.

Harris, Trudier. "Ellison's Peter Wheatstraw: His Basis in Folk Tradition." *Mississippi Folklore Register* 6 (1975): 117–26.

Horowitz, Floyd. "The Enigma of Ellison's Intellectual Man." *CLA Journal* (Dec. 1963): 126–32.

———. "Ralph Ellison's Modern Version of Brer Bear and Brer Rabbit in *Invisible Man.*" *Midcontinent American Studies Journal* 4 (1963): 21–27.

Howe, Irving. "Black Boys and Native Sons." In *A World More Attractive*, 98–122 (New York: Horizon, 1963).

Hyman, Stanley Edgar. "Ralph Ellison in Our Time." *New Leader* 47, no. 22 (Oct. 26, 1964): 21–22.

Kaiser, Ernest. "A Critical Look at Ellison's Fiction and at Social and Literary Criticism by and about the Author." *Black World* 20, no. 2 (Dec. 1970): 53–59, 81–97.

Kent, George. "Ralph Ellison and the Afro-American Folk and Cultural Tradition." *CLA Journal* 13, no. 3 (Mar. 1970): 265–76.

Kostelanetz, Richard. "The Politics of Ellison's Booker: *Invisible Man* as Symbolic History." *Chicago Review* 19, no. 2 (1967): 5–26.

Lee, Kun-Jong. "Ellison's *Invisible Man*: Emersonianism Revisited." *PMLA* 107, no. 2 (Mar. 1992): 331–44.

———. "Racial Variations on American Themes." *African-American Review* 30, no. 3 (Fall 1996): 421–44.

Lewis, R. W. B. "The Ceremonial Imagination of Ralph Ellison." *Carleton Miscellany* 18, no. 3 (Winter 1980): 34–38.

Lieberman, Marcia R. "Moral Innocents: Ellison's *Invisible Man* and *Candide.*" *CLA Journal* 15 (Sept. 1971): 64–79.

Lyne, William. "The Signifying Modernist: Ralph Ellison and the Limits of the Double Consciousness." *PMLA* 107, no. 2 (Mar. 1992): 319–30.

Marvin, Thomas F. "Children of Legba: Musicians at the Crossroads in Ellison's *Invisible Man.*" *American Literature* 68, no. 3 (Sept. 1996): 587–608.

McPherson, James Alan. "Indivisible Man." *Atlantic.* 226, no. 6 (Dec. 1970): 45–60.

Mengeling, Marvin. "Walt Whitman and Ellison: Older Symbols in a Modern Mainstream." *Walt Whitman Review* 12 (Sept. 1966): 67–70.

Ostendorf, Berndt. "Ralph Waldo Ellison: Anthropology, Modernism, and Jazz." In *New Essays on Invisible Man*, edited by Robert O'Meally, 95–122 (New York: Cambridge University Press, 1988).

Parrish, Timothy. "Ralph Ellison, Kenneth Burke, and the Form of Democracy." *Arizona Quarterly* 51, no. 3 (Autumn 1995): 117–48.

Pinckney, Darryl. "The Drama of Ralph Ellison." *New York Review of Books* 44 *no.* 8 (May 15, 1997): 52–60.

Reed, Brian. "The Iron and the Flesh: History as Machine in Ellison's *Invisible Man.*" *CLA Journal* 37, no. 3 (Mar. 1994): 261–73.

Reilly, John M. "The Testament of Ralph Ellison." In *Speaking for You: The Vision of Ralph Ellison,* edited by Kimberly W. Benston, 49–62. Washington, D.C.: Howard University Press, 1987.

Richardson, Brian. "White on Black: Iconography, Race, and Reflexicity in Ellison's *Invisible Man.*" *Southern Humanities Review* 30, no. 2 (Spring 1996): 139–50.

Rovit, Earl H. "Ralph Ellison and the American Comic Tradition." *Wisconsin Studies in Contemporary Literature* 1 (1960): 34–42.

Sale, Roger. "The Career of Ralph Ellison." *Hudson Review* 18 (Spring 1965): 124–28.

Sanders, Archie. "Odysseus in Black: An Analysis of the Structure of *Invisible Man.*" *CLA Journal* 13 (Mar. 1970): 217–28.

Schafer, William J. "Ralph Ellison and the Birth of the Anti-Hero." *Critique: Studies in Modern Fiction* 10 (1968): 81–93.

Schaub, Thomas. "Ellison's Masks and the Novel of Reality." In *New Essays on Invisible Man,* edited by Robert O'Meally, 123–56 (New York: Cambridge University Press, 1988).

Schultz, Elizabeth A. "The Illumination of Darkness: Affinities between *Moby Dick* and *Invisible Man.*" *CLA Journal* 32 (Dec. 1988): 170–200.

Scruggs, Charles. "Ralph Ellison's Use of *The Aeneid* in *Invisible Man.*" *CLA Journal* 17 (Mar. 1974): 368–78.

Sisney, Mary F. "The Power and Horror of Whiteness: Wright and Ellison Respond to Poe." *CLA Journal* 29 (Sept. 1985): 82–90.

Skerrett, Joseph T., Jr., "The Wright Interpretation: Ralph Ellison and the Anxiety of Influence." *Massachusetts Review* 21 (1980): 196–212.

Stepto, Robert. "Literacy and Hibernation: Ralph Ellison's *Invisible Man.*" *Carleton Miscellany* 18, no. 3 (Winter 1980): 112–41.

Tuttleton, James W. "The Achievement of Ralph Ellison." *New Criterion* 14, no. 4 (Dec. 1995): 5–10.

Vautheir, Simone. "Not Quite on the Beat: An Academic Interpretation of the Narrative Stance in Ralph Ellison's *Invisible Man.*" *Delta* 18 (Apr. 1984): 69–88.

Vogler, Thomas. "Somebody's Protest Novel." *Iowa Review* 1 (Spring 1970): 64–82.

Walling, William. " 'Art' and 'Protest': Ralph Ellison's *Invisible Man* Twenty Years After." *Phylon* 34 (June 1973): 120–34.

Walsh, Mary Ellen Williams. "*Invisible Man*: Ralph Ellison's Wasteland." *CLA Journal* 28 (1984): 150–58.

Wilner, Elenor R. "The Invisible Black Thread: Identity and Nonentity in *Invisible Man.*" *CLA Journal* 13 (1970): 242–57.

Wright, John. "Dedicated Dreamer, Consecrated Acts: Shadowing Ellison." *Carleton Miscellany* 18, no. 3 (Winter 1980): 142–99.